Oracle Embedded Programming and Application Development

Oracle Embedded Programming and Application Development

Lakshman Bulusu

CRC Press
Taylor & Francis Group
Boca Raton London New York

CRC Press is an imprint of the
Taylor & Francis Group, an **informa** business

AN AUERBACH BOOK

CRC Press
Taylor & Francis Group
6000 Broken Sound Parkway NW, Suite 300
Boca Raton, FL 33487-2742

First issued in paperback 2017

ISBN-13: 978-1-4398-1644-8 (hbk)
ISBN-13: 978-1-138-11523-1 (pbk)

Library of Congress Cataloging-in-Publication Data

Lakshman, Bulusu.
    Oracle embedded programming and application development / Lakshman Bulusu.
      p. cm.
    Includes index.
    ISBN 978-1-4398-1644-8 (hardcover : alk. paper)
    1. Oracle (Computer file) 2. Computer software--Development. 3. Embedded computer systems--Programming. 4. Programming languages (Electronic computers) I. Title.

QA76.76.D47L343 2011
005.26--dc22
                                                          2010023851

Visit the Taylor & Francis Web site at
http://www.taylorandfrancis.com

and the CRC Press Web site at
http://www.crcpress.com

Dedication

This book is dedicated to the loving memory of my father Prof. B.S.K.R. Somayajulu whose untiring efforts and unprecedented passion, encouragement, and advice have enabled me to "understand where I stand" (to quote his own words), in each and every step in the journey of my life to-date and will be a beacon light shining in each step of my life onward.

Contents

Foreword

As an IT professional living in the real world, I am always struggling to get the various application layers to work well with each other, providing the required functionality without errors or performance issues. I am sure I am not the only one struggling with this conundrum – whether you are a developer, DBA, Architect or support person, all of us in the IT industry face such challenges every day.

This is where an experienced professional like Lakshman Bulusu steps in to help us all with this book. With almost two decades of experience in software management, design, and development using Oracle and related technologies backing him up, Lakshman has distilled this knowledge of embedded programming and application development using Oracle into the various chapters. Taking an Oracle-centric approach, Lakshman skillfully guides you through the maze of various popular programming languages and environments including .NET, C/C++, Perl, PHP, Java and even SQL and PL/SQL – not only showing you how they interact with Oracle but also which language is the best fit for a given situation. In my early days as a programmer many, many moons ago, I was enamored with specific features of a language or technique and allowed this to override the fact that my choice may not be the ideal one for that application. Lakshman is very well aware of this common issue, and makes a strong case to allow application architecture requirements moderate the argument about which feature set and which language is best for that application. The book is also replete with application development and code design frameworks and best practices in these various languages that will help you move in the right direction.

A separate chapter is devoted to best practices for constructing architecture and code design methodologies using these languages, and how they can be used for a generalized and standardized approach to application development. Lakshman also knows that troubleshooting applications does not depend on luck or arcane skills that only few gurus posses—it depends on understanding, observation, and interpretation of logs from the application itself. In Chapter 8, he deals exclusively with frameworks that can be used for common requirements such as auditing, error logging, performance tuning and debugging. Implementing this very practical and useful set of frameworks will greatly assist everyone in the stack—from the programmer and the DBA down to the support person who has to debug the issue in production.

I can say much more, but I will stop here and allow you to dive in head first into this book!

Best regards,
John Kanagaraj
Executive Editor, IOUG SELECT Journal

Acknowledgements

I want to thank my uncle Prof. B.L. Deekshatulu and his family, whose left no stone unturned to help me in caring and sharing, as well as going those extra miles needed, in unison with my parents and siblings, to help me stand where I am today in this too-slippery complex world of webs, whims, and wishful-waters!

I thank my 'lovely and insightful' wife Anuradha and my two 'lovely and bright' kids, Pranati and Pranav, whose presence is more than just being 'in sight', but one that welcomes sunny days and shining nights, making every day my day in a bright way.

I also want to thank Ms. Sheila Cepero of Oracle Publishing, Oracle Corporation, USA, for not only recognizing my Oracle talent but also rewarding me with a recommendation to Mr. Theron Shreve (DerryField Publishing Services) that was both high-assuring and true-to-the-letter honest. My special kudos to you, Ms. Ceparo for I will always remember and respect this goodwill gesture of yours that opened the gates to another new world of publishing.

I take great pleasure in thanking Mr. John Wyzalek, Senior Acquisitions Editor of CRC Press, all the associated members of the Editorial and Publishing team at CRC Press, and Mr. Theron Shreve, for their coordinated effort and co-operation in the journey of my book from manuscript editing to seeing it in print.

And how can I forget all the readers of my earlier books whose practice-oriented suggestion and feedback was a boom-zoom-bloom serving of tips, techniques, and intelligent guidelines? This helped me in enhancing the content of the same and re-factoring them to fit into the current one, wherever applicable.

About the Author

Lakshman Bulusu brings 17+ years of experience & expertise in the management, supervision, mentoring, review, design & development of Oracle Database, DW/BI, & application-solutions for clients across U.S, Europe and Asia. He is well versed in the primary Oracle technologies through Oracle11g using SQL & PL/SQL; Oracle-related embedded programming for Web applications that are PL/SQL, .NET, Java, Open source(Perl, PHP/AJAX), and C/C++-based; He has engineered the design of Application Development Frameworks using Oracle PL/SQL tailored towards full Software Life-Cycle Development, right from design to coding to testing to debugging to performance to BI, used by Fortune 500 companies. In addition he has provided the Design, Development, and Optimization of a Common Data Quality Framework using SQL Server 2008 & T-SQL, for Summarization, Comparison, and Discrepancy Isolation across disparate multi-vendor large-scale databases. Recently, he was instituted as a FOCUS EXPERT in April 2010 for high-quality contributions to the Focus community. He has authored 6 books on Oracle, 2 books on English Poetry, & many technical articles in various Journals/Magazines in the US and UK.

Introduction

THE SINGLE-GOAL-OF-TRUTH IS "RESULTS ARE ALL THAT MATTER". (NO PUN INTENDED!)

Programming is program coding and a program is code—all code and nothing but code.

Oops! Did I state it correctly, or not just correctly but also accurately? The answer to this lies in the rollercoaster ride that programming has been through from its inception to its current state.

Programming as it stands today extends far beyond blazing-fast computations and subcomputations to accommodate so-termed applications, application platforms, and solutions. The fundamentals behind the foundations of programming, from synthesizing computations to synthesizing code to hiding code details (referenced via such famous terminology as *algorithms, subroutines, divide-and-conquer*, etc.) and those behind its usability (or the results of executing programs for the best possible accuracy, simplicity, and efficiency) still hold as the crux of programming. However, programming as such as evolved from a coding-only paradigm (code-running-as-a-program) to one that is solution-oriented (code-running-as-an-application-solution-platform). In this process, the incorporated high-level (or, rather, next-level) feature set has also evolved from code to code design to code patterns and code design patterns, which is more tailored towards solution design than just pure code. And this emergence in programming encompasses multiple dimensions in terms of procedural-to-declarative code modularization, object-oriented programming (OOP), practices such as *code inheritance* and code encapsulation (which has re-conceptualized the programming paradigm by enabling code to be viewed in terms of analogous objects in the real world), code reuse, code archiving, best-possible, best-in-time, best-fit, and so on. This breadth has resulted in the design of new and proven code structures and more, such as code templates, code libraries (statically and dynamically linkable), software layers that comprise code-design architectures in addition to code, hot-pluggable code (during development as well as at run-time (object code libraries)), *code dynamism* (which includes code that's not fully interpretable until execution time as well as *code-generating code*); managed code and unmanaged code; organized code (this includes not only the technical aspect but also the documentation aspect—*code that's well-documented is code that has greater maintainable lifetime value*); extensible-code; reverse-engineering and re-engineering code (this applies especially to code-as-a-solution-platform); code deployment using a multitude of implementations, some specific to a language and some generic across multiple languages; and finally *independent code* that's portable cross-hardware, cross-OS, and cross-tier (interactivity and integration across multiple tiers or layers of the solution architecture); for example:

Database Layer → Middle Layer → Application Layer

- Middle Layer: application servers, application boosters, application accelerators, Web servers, etc.
- Application Layer: unified presentation layer for end-user access, transparent caches, translucent caches (as in mobile access points), disconnected data sources, etc.

This is an exponentially evolving curve—consider the possibilities of code suited for an application solution platform that can be used as SaaS (software as a service) and regulatory code (Governance, Risk, and Compliance (GRC) guidelines, including access and identity management compliance), far beyond its use as just an (executable) software program.

Because programming has so many facets, an architectural layer must be designed and implemented well before the actual coding can begin. The design and coding process is in turn governed by an established set of rules and methodologies, from coding design standards to coding standards, and from code ethics to software ethics, and solution architecture best practices. Close on their heels are the administration tasks, in terms of managing the designed and coded solution that begin with testing to achieve a tried, tested, and true grade level.

After the code is ready to be implemented, there's another new task, that of *configuring the code.*

And then there is the issue of security, which introduces a whole new dimension:

- Authenticity and authorization (who should use what and in what manner in terms of delegation of duties and localization of access control)
- Application output and data protection (within and beyond the enterprise, including externalized deployments, those that are remotely accessed, and so forth)
- Securing code and code authenticity, in terms of protecting the misuse of code using mechanisms like signing code (digitally) as well as code verification and validation procedures (which ensure that code and/or application/solution software is genuine and not one that has been intruded, before the code/software is used, installed, or deployed).
- Adhering to regulatory compliance standards for GRC and auditing practices

Although much has changed in programming and program-coding, the core principle of programming can still be understood in terms of its primary goal: *usability*. The "why, what, and who" of programming is still conspicuously constant.

Let's re-examine these facets using an actions-results perspective:

Actions
- Passive code to active code to proactive code to pre-emptive code
- Code-driven data (data output governed by the way the code runs on it) to data-driven code/policy-driven code (using data as the user wants it) to changing the way the code can auto-adapt/dynamically output results (again, as the user wants it)
- Code outputting data to code enabling decision support/business insight
- Code-driven user-interaction to user-interaction-driven code (which enables dynamic user-interactivity and responsiveness) instead of code driving user actions; code adapting itself "live" according to user actions

Results
- Accuracy
- Simplicity
- Efficiency, including performance and reliability, with the time factor calculated based on optimal time-to-deliver, time-to-deploy, time-to-value, time-to-market, and the emerging imperative of

time-to-insight (related to deriving actionable business intelligence from data)
- Maintainability
  And all of this must be achieved at the lowest possible cost!

THE SINGLE-GOAL-OF-TRUTH IS "RESULTS ARE ALL THAT MATTER". (NO PUN INTENDED!)

What This Book Covers

This book is the first book of its kind focused on the best practices in cross-technology–based Oracle embedded programming, not only in terms of "what" and "how" but also "why" and "when." It emphasizes the best ways that embedded programming practices can be used but delves deeper, explaining why and when these practices are considered best practices, thus enhancing their usability in application-development and code-design methodology, in addition to producing quality and optimally performing code in real-world scenarios. It details the best practices and expert techniques involved, as well as application development frameworks using 3GL and 4GL high-level language code as embedded code segments across .NET, Java, and open source technologies, in conjunction with SQL and/or PL/SQL and the Oracle RDBMS through version 11gR2.

Cover to cover, this book takes the reader beyond the relevant professional and reference texts or online tutorials and guides available. It details these tried, tested, and true best practices in Oracle-related embedded programming, including design and code-development techniques, for varied applications bases—not only in terms of the technologies and methodologies used, but also in terms of how well the designed, developed, and deployed solution conforms to the emerging and next-gen trends. We start with applications that are PL/SQL-only (using HTML, XML),.NET-based (using C, C++, C#, J#), and Java-based (using SQLJ, JDBC, Java Stored Procedures, and Java Libraries), and continue with those that are PHP-based (using PHP Web pages), Perl-based, and C or C++ based (outside the .NET environment, using external procedures). We also discuss the conformance and usage of Web 2.0–based RIA functionality, regulatory compliance practices involving auditing (of both data and application) and security (including access and identity compliance, transparent data encryption for data protection, near-zero data loss, data archiving, and special security protocols for security in wireless deployments—WEP

(Web Encryption Protocol) versus WPA/WPA2 (WiFi Protected Access), etc.). We also focus on end-to-end application solution consolidation, using grid-based, virtualization-based, and/or cloud-based (data and application) integration and interoperability technologies, *n*-tier deployment-specific features, and next-level solution mobility (anywhere, anytime, by anyone, on-the-go, and on-the-fly usability) that is on par with on-premise solution usability.

The book also concentrates on the more important pragmatic aspects, describing the techniques and practices that facilitate more efficient integration and interaction with the Oracle database through version 11g, thus giving concession to the nitty-gritty concepts of better compiling and executing using the programming language involved.

Who is This Book For?

This book is targeted towards two categories of audience: those who use Oracle professionally, and those who are teaching or learning about Oracle. The book assumes a working knowledge of SQL and PL/SQL, and the embedded programming language(s) involved.

Oracle professionals—those who develop Oracle-based Web-enabled applications in PL/SQL, Java, C, C++, .NET, Perl, and PHP—constitute the primary group that would benefit from this book. Oracle application developers, technical solution architects, implementers, technical leads performing peer code reviews, and subject matter experts (SMEs) working on code design and improvements aspects, as well as consultants in the role of Oracle Database-Application Integration Specialists, will benefit from the book's description of techniques for constructing architecture and code design methodologies for live application development projects that can be *generalized and standardized* as application development and code design frameworks.

Additionally, this book is also geared towards students, learners, mentors, and faculty in the academic field who are devoted to a course in application development practices that involve Oracle and the related embedded language(s). These academic users will find the book handy in obtaining problem-solution key takeaways, best practices techniques and scenarios-in terms of both theory and practical programming aspects.

Why a Separate Book?

This book essentially deals with Oracle-based programming using embedded languages (C, C++, Java, Perl, PHP, Ajax, Groovy, HTML, and XML), in addition to SQL and PL/SQL, and its various aspects, from code design to an end-to-end solution in terms of best practices for architecture, methodologies, and standardized coding that will enable a solution to remain in place for not only the life cycle of the technology involved, but also the life cycle of business for which the solution is being used.

It is a fact that a host of information is available in books and online to augment the knowledge base of both information technology (IT) and non-IT personnel. This information includes Web sites, blogs, frequently asked question (FAQ) compilations, technical- and business-oriented articles in journals and magazines, quick-start guides, tips and techniques, developers' guides, expert techniques, and so on. This information has been provided by authors who have varying levels of expertise: professionals, programmers, experts, peers, gurus, avatars, and so on. The information has been tried, tested, and found to be true.

So why should there be another book? The reasons fall under two categories:

Pervasiveness

- The business requirements of the solution are not only many, but also multidimensional in terms of what is required, who needs what, and in what way.
- The solution delivered spans disparate technologies, methodologies, architectures, and deployment environments.
- The usability of the solution in terms of the end-users ranges from help desk support for business (non-technical) users to those in corporate management— just about anyone who is authorized to use it.

Solution Life Cycle

- The solution is to remain in place for the life cycle of the technology involved.

To demonstrate the usability aspect of pervasiveness, here's a list of some real-world scenarios that exemplify it:

- From executive management to IT professionals, many business users need to look at high-value reports containing critical business data, which is usually summarized (aggregated across huge datasets). This is a dire necessity in situations when the corporate IT team are not in the office, yet are connected via wireless, asking the reason for a loss that they feel is potentially huge, reported to them seconds ago on the BlackBerry. Who knew a day would arrive when both of them would be on par in regard to proactive analysis of the data in this report!

- Some users demand semantic data/report outputs. In other words, they want to see output such as "This numeric value is negative due to..." as they point and move the cursor on a seven-digit value (parenthesized and in red) in the report. This is akin to a higher level of contextual auto-hint, tooltip, or bubble help that's somewhat dynamic in nature.
- Who knows—tomorrow, some business users' requirement specifications might include the same dynamic tooltip help to be auto-audible as they point and move the cursor, or they might request a visually converted explanation in a click-boom-zoom fashion.
- Last but not least, the so-called business intelligence and enterprise performance management landscape has necessitated a "totally virtual business enterprise" to make the business better, faster, easier, and cheaper, and at the same time one that has optimal outreach in all possible dimensions and scenarios (best-case to worst-case). Who doesn't want more for less?

Putting these principles in practice to enable implementation of an Oracle-based embedded solution requires *all* of the following:

- Reliable and robust design
- Real programming in real time
- Live troubleshooting in real time
- Invisible transparency—The only thing the user can see is what he or she has access to; the rest is "under the hood" and the user can be assured that all's well that works well!
- Centralized, secure, and shareable

This, in turn, returns a high-yield solution that:

- Enables in-time implementation
- Is up and running in near-real time, and running (available) all the time

- Has near-zero downtime and uptime. As regards uptime, this means that it should be possible for the solution to be upgraded/ migrated/upscaled/started/deployed in the minimum time possible and as easily as possible—e.g., by pushing a button or making a single click.
- Improves scalability in terms of scaling-out and scaling-up
- Is industry-compliant (standards-based and regulatory compliance)
- Is simple to use (deploy, customize, and manage (including self-manageability))
- Is unique and universal—*Unique* in terms of business functionality and ability to leverage in-place architectures (both business processes and IT infrastructure); *universal* in terms of being shareable and globally accessible, interoperable, hot-pluggable, embeddable, extensible, and self-adaptable (i.e., without IT intervention)
- Is pervasive across both the vertical user ladder and the horizontal user line (i.e., is used globally by just about anyone, from help desk support to business (non-technical) users to those in corporate management)

The reason for this book is simple: the book, in its entirety, aims to put these principles into practice in the best possible manner to result in a "best-fit" solution, encompassing all possible Oracle-based embedded programming solution scenarios—just that and nothing but that. This book details the what, when, when not, why, and how of delivering a best-fit solution in terms of the business/customer perspective, the technology perspective and the important (but less-focused-on) programmer/developer/technical-solution architect/implementer perspective.

NOTE: Information text appears throughout the document with double-lines above and below as shown here.

Chapter 1

Embedded Programming—An Oracle-Centric Approach

In this Chapter

- Embedded programming from the Oracle perspective: the primary indicators and the solution life cycle
- What's in and what's not: Programming languages, platforms, and solution options available for an Oracle-based solution
- The foundations: architecture, technologies, and methodologies for integration and interaction with Oracle
- Oracle database-specific code versus non-Oracle 3GL and 4GL code in conjunction with SQL and PL/SQL: key differentiators

This chapter details the foundations of embedding and using non-Oracle-based programming languages/applications, such as Java, C/C++, C#/J#, PHP/Ajax, Groovy, or HTML/XML, in those that are SQL/PL/SQL–based to architect, build, deploy, and customize an Oracle11g-based end-to-end solution. Starting by identifying the key indicators necessary for the solution orientation, the chapter goes on to explain the end-to-end life cycle, categorized across three major dimensions: the business landscape, the technology landscape, and the programmer-to-implementer landscape. Then it describes the programming languages, platforms, and solution options supported for an Oracle11g-based solution, in terms of what's in and what's not. The third section outlines what's involved in building the targeted solution so that it meets business needs and deploying it at a customer site (or using it otherwise). The chapter then discusses key points regarding what, how, and when to use the available options so that the resulting solution is a best fit for the business needs, and gives the better-business-benefit (B-B-B) takeaway. Finally, the chapter highlights the key differentiators between SQL and PL/SQL code versus embedded programming language code (e.g., Java-based, .NET-based, PHP/Ajax-based, or

1

Perl-based) from a code design, coding, code design patterns, compilation, execution, and efficiency standpoint.

1.1 Embedded Programming from an Oracle Perspective: The Primary Indicators and the Solution Life Cycle

Let's revisit the last paragraph of the Introduction: *to put these principles into practice in the best possible manner to result in a "best-fit" solution, encompassing all possible Oracle-based embedded programming solution scenarios—just that and nothing but that. This book details the what, when, when not, why, and how of delivering a best-fit solution in terms of the business/customer perspective, the technology perspective and the important (but less-focused-on) programmer/developer/technical-solution architect/implementer perspective.*

Any application solution is focused on a combination of the business landscape, the solution technology landscape and the user landscape. There is no one-size-fits-all single out-of-the-box solution that encompasses the three major landscapes in terms of business and user requirements and the technologies, architectures, and programming languages involved. The same is true for an Oracle-based embedded programming solution. This is because the business needs (functionality and user experience combined), the business value (performance and lifecycle), and the technologies and methodologies used are like snowflakes—no two are alike. However, a solution that is a *best fit* is the ideal implementation answer that intersects the three landscapes.

The following list highlights the primary indicators that drive the embedded programming solution and the big picture of its end-to-end life cycle, using Oracle11g as the primary database:

- Alignment of IT and business processes for the life cycle of the business to supplement, support, or extend the business side of the solution
- Flexibility and adaptability to new and emerging technologies (at least at the design level, in terms of solution architecture model, business process model, and IT process model), in case the life cycle of the technology involved in the IT solution is short compared to the life cycle of the business; this might involve extension of the existing technical architecture by adding/changing new technical modules and/or submodules to arrive at the same business results (scope, time, cost, and quality)

- Seamless architecture under the hood that allows for extensibility, adaptability (the ability to seamlessly incorporate business/IT changes by caching the customer experience or technology innovation), and integration—three areas critical to any architectural design from a solution life cycle perspective.
- Consistency; reusability; ease of coding, deployment, and use; effectiveness; and efficiency
- Openness in terms of usability and acceptance by the customer— native look and feel combined with seamless, rich user interface (UI) rendering
- Scalability (both for scaling out and scaling up), durability, high availability, security, portability
- Common integration platform for application development tools and applications (create/generate)
- Unified framework in terms of UI, proactive and pre-emptive testing and debugging, source code versioning, and source code configuration management

Figures 1.1, 1.2, and 1.3 give a snapshot of the solution life cycle involved from an Oracle11g perspective. It might not depict the road ahead for a best solution, but certainly gives the plan for a best-fit solution, which is always a "win-win" compared to the "best" solution, in terms of business landscape, technology landscape, and the programmer-to-implementer landscape.

1.2   What's In and What's Not: Programming Languages, Platforms, and Solution Options Available for an Oracle-Based Solution

This section details the various embedded programming scenarios from an availability perspective in terms of programming languages that can be used for embedding SQL/PL/SQL code or vice versa, as well as the platforms and/or solution options for design, development, and deployment of an Oracle-based solution. The subsections within these sections cover the use of .NET-based languages, Java/J2EE-based languages, and PHP/Ajax-based languages and highlight what's in and what's not for an Oracle11g-based embedded programming solution.

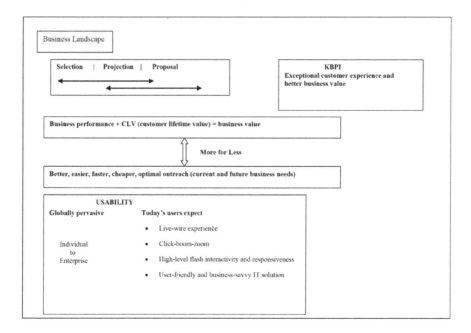

Figure 1.1   Typical solution life cycle from a business landscape.

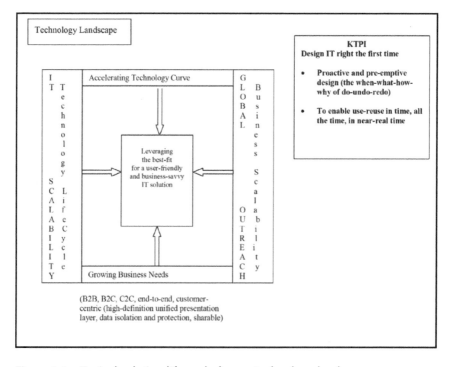

Figure 1.2   Typical solution life cycle from a technology landscape.

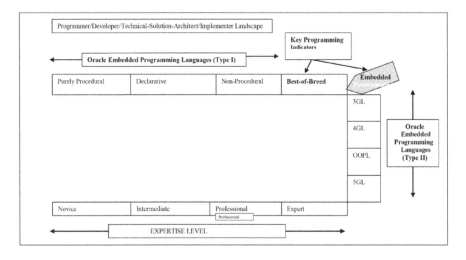

Figure 1.3   Typical solution life cycle from a programmer-to-implementer landscape..

1.2.1   Using .NET-Based Languages

- The recommended language for .NET-based embedded language solution is C#. In addition, there is J# (which simulates a Java language base for .NET like C# does for C/C++).

  Oracle Data Provider for .NET is a native-managed data provider that enables Oracle to leverage the Oracle11g-specific database and high-performance features such as Real Application Clusters (RACs), Automatic Storage Management (ASM), in-memory database cache (IMDB cache), real application testing, database vault, virtual private database (VPD), Oracle spatial option, SQL analytics, and user-defined types (UDTs), ensuring optimal use of the central processing unit (CPU) and memory, high performance and throughput, and high availability. These are implemented using:
  - OPD.NET load balancing
  - Fast connection fail over
  - File system–like performance
  - De-duplication, compression, and encryption of unstructured data (LOBS, Binary XML, etc.) using SecureFiles to enable storage space reduction and improve security and performance
  - ODP.NET statement caching (minimizes reparsing)
  - Metadata caching

- Client-side result-set cache (auto-refreshable result-set cache on the client side that is consistent with the database)
- Dynamic data fetch size control via correlation to the fetched data row size for optimal data retrieval
- Support for PL/SQL procedures and result sets (.NET calling PL/SQL) using REF CURSOR to optimize query data retrieval from Oracle to the .NET application
- Database resident connection pooling (DRCP) and enhanced Oracle-based security using proxy authentication (to allow multiple unique users to share the same connection pool user connection—for scalability)
- Application context tracking via ODP.NET client identifiers

- Oracle DB extensions for .NET accommodate for complex .NET logic that also mandates intensive data access from Oracle. These extensions are written as stored procedures and functions in C# or as another .NET-managed language stored procedures and are deployed inside the database or otherwise. They are callable from SQL, PL/SQL, other .NET code, or a Java stored procedure. They are written using MS Visual Studio 2010, 2008, 2005, or 2003 and deployed using Oracle Developer Tools for Visual Studio.
- Oracle Provider for ASP.NET is an Oracle driver enabling Microsoft ASP.NET languages to access an Oracle database—useful for ASP.NET Web applications running Oracle on the database Tier.
- Oracle Developer Tools for Visual Studio is a.NET-on-Oracle integrated development environment (IDE) that enables develop and deploy .NET-embedded applications that are Oracle11g-based. It provides:
  - Automatic-code generation for create, retrieve, update, and delete (CRUD) operations, for Web-based embedded applications (ASP.NET or rich Internet applications, or RIA) using Oracle, and UDT custom class code generation capabilities
  - Deployment and testing of .NET stored procedures
  - Integrated PL/SQL debugging

1.2.2   Using Java-Based Languages (Java Libraries, Java via JDBC, Java via SQLJ, Java via Java Stored Procedures)

Because Java is a Tier 1 legacy object-oriented programming language, with unprecedented open source use, portability, scalability, and high-performance;

robust application server methodologies (J2EE, servlets, JMS, multithreading, interoperability, etc.); and rich client capabilities (JSP, JSF, etc.), it is also a major embedded language of choice for database-based rich Web application (RWA) development, deployment, and migration; The combination of Oracle11g and Java provide a best-fit end-to-end solution that not only scales across the enterprise for high-volume transaction-based processing across the DB and application levels, but also has a legacy footprint and at the same time extreme flexibility in terms of the functionality stated above. Support for Java in Oracle11g from an embedded programming solution perspective can be listed as follows:

- Support for EJB 3.0/ Java Persistence API (JPA) and Java Server Faces:
  - Querying JPA entities using Native SQL and JPQL
  - Using Java for enhanced Web services
  - Exposing SOA services via rich UI
  - Universal resource locator (URL) controls (e.g., URL data controls in ADF)
  - Next-gen user interfaces (presenting contextual information seamlessly)
  - Database Web Services, using SOA to web-enable Oracle DB functionality (using Oracle JPublisher).
- Automating Java performance tuning
  - JDBC and SQLJ for Java in the database
  - Securing Java applications from code to execution
  - Improved data integrity and encryption in JDBC
  - Thin, strong and OS authentication
  - Improved JDBC performance and scalability (row prefetch in first roundtrip)
  - URL support for loadjava
  - Programmatically turning JDBC logging on/off using JMX in JDBC via MBean
  - Programmatic (with proper authentication and authorization) startup and shutdown of Oracle DB from JDBC-Java code
- Oracle ADF (application development framework), which simplifies development of Java EE-based Web-services-enabled/enabling (SOA) applications using component-based reusable objects that can be broadly classified as:

- *Presentation*: Rich UI—using ADF Faces and Oracle Web-Center (Web 2.0 for the Enterprise), the framework renders desktop-based RCA (rich client applications—ADF Swing that's on par with Office applications) as well as those that are browser-based (ADF Faces that's on par with JSP or JSF). ADF Faces uses reusable rich client components that leverage the best-of-breed from Ajax, Flash, JavaScript, and DOM, as well as including additional functionality such as data visualization, partial page rendering, advanced data streaming, templating, reusable flows, etc.

- *Application/Business Logic:* This is exposed as business services using Web services (SOA-based using the Oracle SOA Suite for integration and agility) and ADF business components (ADFbc—reusable, SQL-based components that manage DB access and logic, separating the data view from application/ business logic view) on par with persistent business objects (Enterprise Java Beans (EJB)/JPA entities and Java classes) and Web services. The primary goals are to provide for object rela-tional mapping (ORM), to manage CRUD operations, to implement business rules for validation and application logic, and to be standards-based and reusable.

- *DB (Data Services)*: Oracle11g-based ADF model/binding components that leverage relational data, XML data, legacy data, and external data. These binding components declara-tively bind UI to business services, perform ORM, and manage persistence (ORM and DML/DQL) and caching, automatic event and state management, and memory scope via a control-ler-based strategy called ADF Taskflow that's declarative in nature (similar to Struts or JSP workflow). In addition, ADF Taskflow enables declarative definition of Web pages, too.

On the pure Java side, there's support for Java EE5 (EJB, JPA) in conjunction with SOA, Web 2.0 (RIA), Ajax/PHP, JavaScript, BPEL, SOAP, RMI, WSDL, RMI, JNDI, JDBC, O/R, HTML, XML, and DOM.

- Development/Deployment Platforms: Oracle JDeveloper, Oracle JPublisher, Oracle WebCenter (which offers Web 2.0 services as content repositories, tags, wiki pages, etc.), Oracle SOA Suite (for AI and agility).

1.2.3   Using PHP-Based Languages (PHP-only, PHP and Ajax, PHP Web Pages)

PHP is an advanced scripting language that enables development of rich Web user interfaces in conjunction with Web 2.0 technologies like Flash, Ajax, Adobe Air, and so on. The combination of PHP and Ajax aligns perfectly with the scripting flexibility provided by PHP and the high-definition, interactive controls based presentation functionality provided by Ajax. Oracle11g supports out-of-database PHP/Ajax application development as well as a pre-integrated Oracle-PHP stack called Zend Core. The key features in place are as follows:

- The PHP OCI8 extension (supports PHP6) fully leverages Oracle11g functionality for optimal performance.
- The PDO (PHP data object) extension for database-independent PHP coding can be useful in scenarios where the same PHP code is to be deployed in heterogeneous DB environments, and the abstraction libraries (ADOdb) are useful for high-performance external C-language embedding. PEAR Db and PEAR MDb are like ODBC, but for PHP. The Oracle driver for PDO is called PDO_OCI. PDO configured for Oracle uses the OCI8 Extension internally.
- Database resident connection pooling;SQL and result-set optimizations, and a rich UI presentation using Ajax and PHP.
- Zend Core is a prepackaged and optimized Oracle-PHP(OCI8) extension.
- Oracle APEX (APplication EXpress) is an integrated development environment (IDE) and application (generation) platform that supports RIA development based on fact that the application-solution is generated inside the Oracle DB, thus providing seamless execution with SQL/PL/SQL code.

Architecture Top N
- Extensibility (technical aspects using plug-ins/add-ins—.NET built, Java-built, etc., dynamic plug-ins, schema-based extensions, choosing existing code for others to extend/configure).
- IDE platform and RIA platform in one: Oracle APEX, Oracle JDeveloper, ODT.NET IDE and RIA platform to create/generate RIA applications—seamless, with native look-and-feel.

- Hot plug-and-play capability is achieved through the Oracle Enterprise Grid (consisting of the Application Grid and the Database Grid) and/or virtualization at all levels:
  - Hardware, including storage (ASM) and network, OS, application (end-to-end, desktop, or at the end-point level which means at the end-user device level that is typically wireless)
  - Database, using RAC/Clustering, database services that enable dynamic load-balancing of multiple DB connections (from the application) to be in-directed or redirected across one or more DB instances
  - Data provisioning (storing and using a dataset as a Web Service—in other words, as a Data Service; storing and using data integration workflows and jobs as a Web Service, i.e., as a Data Integration Service)

  The key to an optimal solution architecture when using the Grid is the ability to design and configure the Oracle Grid architecture to best fit the solution for optimal efficiency (performance and reliability—that is, not breakable), scalability, high availability, and "live" user experience. This can be done by choosing a Services-based, dynamic provisioning–enabled design that also delivers dynamic deployment capabilities—independent of the physical infrastructure, the Oracle database, the applications, and the end-user interaction and responsiveness. The only thing visible is what the user sees (or has access to).

- Integration:
  - Application integration: Oracle AIA, Oracle Coherence (an in-memory distributed grid for optimized performance ; a special implementation of the Enterprise Grid termed Application Grid, typically useful for high-performance distributed transaction processing)
  - Data integration: ODI, cloud and cluster-based deployments for high-performance and secure data integration using Oracle in the Cloud, etc.

- Managing the data side of the solution: The goal is to improve performance, prevent data loss and leakage, and mitigate risk. The key indicators are data growth (pre-grow the DB size to n times the current data size to pre-empt DB failure due to running out of space), real-time archiving (archiving online as the data is being accessed/created), content, and unstructured data—storing, retrieving and mashing documents, encoded binary files, and other unstructured data in multiple fashions.

- Managing the application side of the solution: overall system performance and response, rich user experience, end-to-end security and compliance, high-availability, and scalability in terms of data volume, user volume, and application functionality (adding new modules on the fly).

1.2.4   The Foundations: Architecture, Technologies, and Methodologies for Integration and Interaction with Oracle

In simple terms, the foundation consists of determining what's involved and designing, developing, delivering, and rendering the solution accordingly, using "what's in" and augmenting for "what's not in." This approach puts the embedded programming solution in line with "what's required" (by the user) to the best possible extent. Here are the details:

- Implicit database-level and tuning features, including online database backup and recovery: Oracle Data Pump, Oracle Data Guard, and Oracle Streams
- Flashback and point-in-time recovery (as-is and as-of), including deploying the IMDB (in-memory database) cache inline within the DB or at the application level
- Scalability at the resource/application/solution level (scaling out through application partitioning, RAC)
- Data scalability (in terms of VLDB query performance) achieved through database partitioning (11g-specific Interval, System, and Reference partitioning) and dynamic partition pruning, columnar data compression, as well as auto-tuning capabilities at the database and SQL levels
- Application solution reliability—flexibility to test on a snapshot of the "live" environment using Real Application Testing (stress testing, regression testing, performance testing)—Oracle Enterprise Performance Management (EPM)
- Code refactoring capabilities—improving/optimizing code design independent of the actual code (e.g., automatic inlining of procedural code stored and executed inside the Oracle11g database; subquery refactoring; high-performance-centric embedded language functionality using the native ODP.NET Data Provider, which can leverage the best-of-breed in terms of database-centric performance

and application-centric optimization, both of which are needed for the overall solution performance; dynamic result-set interoperability between the DB and the application (with embedded programming languages like C#, Java, C/C++, PHP, Perl, etc.) using REF CURSORs, connection pooling, and client-side result cache. For applications that use SQL and PL/SQL only (with HTML, XML via PSP, or Web Toolkit), the REF CURSOR is to-and-from transformable to the API-based DBMS_SQL, giving greater flexibility and the ability to choose the best of both or the best using both for optimal performance in terms of parsing, execution, and/or delivering the result-set data to the application.

- Rich Internet application (RIA) solutions, using various embedded programming technologies: Oracle and PL/SQL; Oracle and Java/J2EE; Oracle and PHP/Ajax; Oracle and .NET (ODP.NET, ODT for .NET, C/C++/C#); Oracle and Perl
  - Robust and high-performance features for the particular embedded language in each combination
  - Flexible, simple, and fast development using rich IDE like Oracle APEX, Oracle JDeveloper, Oracle Developer Tools for .NET (that includes MS Visual Studio 2010/2008/2005)
  - "Rich" refers to using the latest and next-gen Web technologies (also termed Web 2.0) to deliver and render a better, enhanced user experience. The key differentiator of RIA from simple Web browser–based applications is the enhanced capabilities of the former, such as high-definition GUI, dynamic "look-and-feel", and real-time user interaction and response. It's something similar to an airplane dashboard—from static controls to touchscreen to Flash-based controls—to the extent that the browsed-based Web page seems like a Flash page as you see, totally and in real-time.

Key Indicator: The goal is to take the GUI to a higher dimension so the end-user experience is at a higher level in terms of ease of use, actionable "live" productivity, and efficiency—making the end user an expert in using the application solution more and more. This calls for a richer functionality, as stated above, to be in-built into the GUI. The latest Web 2.0 comes with at least four different technologies: Ajax, Flash, Flex, and AIR. Oracle11g has two methodologies in place to deliver an RIA solution:

- *Using Oracle11g and PHP/Ajax directly in the database.* A declarative PL/SQL API calls Ajax (JavaScript, PHP, XML, etc.) code, which implements the desired rich UI functionality and renders it straight to the Web browser (no middle-Tier code/software is needed). It is along the nonprocedural lines of programming, except that the Ajax code is to be written *only* once and embedded in SQL/PL/SQL using the declarative API. That's it. Everything else is done by the database.
- *Using Oracle11g and the traditional embedded Web languages like Java or .NET-based (C#, C/C++), in conjunction with XML/ HTML.* This works fine too, and also achieves the same functionality using legacy technologies—except that it involves a middle-Tier layer that compromises some benefits of in-database processing, including application logic and UI presentation.

Key Indicator: Using other RIA technologies like Flash, Flex, AIR, etc. to achieve the RI effect has a downside, in that they cannot always be used to generate and render the entire application, especially those tailored for the enterprise. The difference is apparent when we compare rendering a Web-based promotion campaign site to delivering a unified presentation layer for a global enterprise-wide solution that has more to it than just the front end.

RIA benefits the enterprise, developers, and users. Enhancing UI by consolidating Web-based technologies can save costs, provide openness in terms of being (public) Internet-based, and gain customer acceptance for reuseable and sharable Web services and data services capability.

- *Secure data protection* is one of the most critical and key aspects of an application solution. Transparent data encryption is handled at the column level (10gR2), table-level (11gR1), and at the table space level (11gR2); customer-specific data isolation is handled by using "private cloud" deployments (Oracle Database in the Cloud, Enterprise Grid, Oracle Database Appliances such as HP-Oracle Database Machine (Exadata v1) for DW/OLAP-only, and the Sun-Oracle Database Machine (Exadata v2) for OLTP and OLAP
- *Flexible, on-the-fly integration and interoperability of applications and data* using Oracle Application Integration Architecture (AIA)

along with Enterprise Oracle Data Integrator (ODI) and Enterprise Oracle Warehouse Builder (OWB), taking into consideration what's lacking and identifying ways to get the missing part done using supplemental/alternative technologies/methodologies.

- *Better business agility*, in terms of under-the-hood synchronization of business and IT processes involved.

- *Oracle11g DB-level optimization* for the application at the end-user level—secure data access via FGAC that is group-policy-based and role-based, Data Loss Prevention and Data Protection using SIAM (Security Information Access Management)-compliant policies—single-sign-on, Oracle Database Vault, bidirectional database activity monitoring, Insider Threats and Intrusion prevention via OASIS eXtensible Access Control Markup Language (XACML), Security Assertion Markup Language (SAML) for XML threats, etc.; secure content management via auto-generation of output files with their corresponding extension suffixed with the letter 's' for 'secure' (e.g., .PDFS for a .PDF document etc.) that enables actual application output files such as report,output, to be binary-encoded to prevent unauthorized out-of-the-application access, as can happen when files are e-mailed, etc.).

- *Real-time capabilities* for the application-solution (using application grid for incremental scaling of applications/dynamic provisioning); using Business Activity Monitoring (BAM), Complex Event Processing (CEP), and automation for continuous and real-time application activity monitoring (starting from business processes to data flow to work flow including end-user activity) and alerting the end-user in near real-time.

- *Real-time DI*, using ODI, OWB, or otherwise; real-time querying (as-is, as-of) and analysis (descriptive (as-is, as-of) and predictive (what-if)) for ad-hoc querying and reporting capabilities-using pipelined streamed execution that works on operational databases to get the data as-is in near real-time; Operational Business Intelligence with minimal Time-to-Insight; etc.

- *High-performance and real-time data capture* using CDC (asynchronous and synchronous), Oracle Data Pump, and next-gen technologies like leveraging SOA-based mechanisms based on Cloud and Cluster-based designs.

- *On-the-fly data compression* to linearly scale the data access that gives the added advantage of eliminating extra storage.

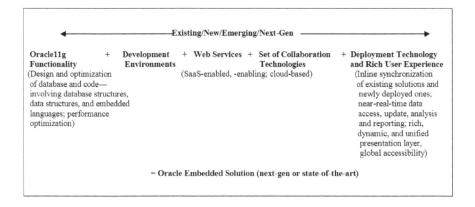

Figure 1.4   Typical view of an Oracle solution based on embedded programming languages..

Figure 1.4 contains an overview of an Oracle solution based on embedded programming languages.

Explore various embedded programming languages and how Oracle11g- supported functionality (existing/new/emerging/next-gen), in terms of technology, architectures, and methodologies, can be fit into this equation and leveraged to the best possible extent to deliver a real-world solution that in turn delivers better business value (across business/customer and IT dimensions).

1.3 Oracle Database-Specific Code versus Non-Oracle 3GL and 4GL code in Conjunction with SQL and PL/SQL: Key Differentiators

This section describes the key differentiators of Oracle database-specific code executed inside the database versus non-Oracle 3GL and 4GL code embedded with SQL and/or PL/SQL, from a code design, programming, execution, and management standpoint.

Rarely can an out-of-database application engine beat the Oracle database engine and the power of in-database processing, no matter the language used or the add-on engines in place.

All the differentiators detailed below revolve around leveraging the Oracle11g database and SQL, PL/SQL benefits in terms of compilation, execution, extent of coding, and architectural design involved, which are derived implicitly with the powerful and high-performance functionality of the Oracle11g database in terms of data integrity, data and application security, high availability, usability, efficiency, and interoperability.

- *Type of processing involved in the application solution*—database-intensive, computation-intensive or a union of both. This plays a key role in deciding the embedded programming language of choice.
- *Type of interaction with the Oracle database*—the ability to process and share data between the Oracle DB and the embedded application, and the ability to share data between applications.

1.3.1   Data Processing Differentiators

Handling Data-Flow Management

This depends on how the embedded programming language used manages the data flow to and from the Oracle DB in terms of 100 percent compatibility and accuracy as well as minimal data loss (qualitatively and quantitatively). Data structure management and data management, starting from data type compatibility, mismatch, and conversion (implicit and explicit) including native types, relative to the embedded language and Oracle) to data structure compatibility (that involves syncing data stored in a language-specific structure/object and an Oracle-specific structure/object)—both of these are essential for data input/output (I/O). This is especially critical when the data involved is unstructured, as each embedded language has its own limitations for handling unstructured data and hence it becomes complex for such data I/O. The best solution in this regard is to design an abstraction layer that is as close a match as possible to incompatibility involved—*study the data and coding data structures in place, and arrive at a code design that can be generalized as a code-design pattern.*

Handling the Way the Data is Processed

Also of importance is the way the data is processed—from small sets of rows to huge result sets. Oracle provides very efficient dataset retrieval and manipulation by utilizing array processing using static and dynamic SQL. The use of static and/or dynamic SQL/PL/SQL code in the embedded language is critical to the performance gains in regards to both compilation and execution. How the static and dynamic code (embedded or otherwise) is treated outside Oracle by the embedded language itself (and in the application) also has an impact on the execution.

1.3.2   Data Sharing Differentiators

Bidirectional Exchange of Result Sets

As regards sharing data between Oracle and the embedded programming application, the often-required user-oriented functionality is the bidirectional exchange of result sets between Oracle DB and the application. This is achieved by using procedural functions or sub-programs having SQL-based code for retrieval and/or update—and more often than not, the sub-programs being parameterized. The same issues of data management and data structure management as outlined above apply to the parameters as well. There are a number of ways to do this, keeping in mind that the Oracle DB is the final persistent store of the data being shared. The typical ones in an embedded programming solution environment are:

- *Using REF CURSORs to pass result sets to and from the DB.* This again depends on the functionality of the embedded language interface with Oracle. Some provide for one-way sharing only—from the DB to the application—while others allow two-way sharing.
- *Real-time streaming of the data from Oracle DB to the application.* This is often a requirement in applications that are analysis-intensive and involve only data retrieval—high-volume data in real-time speed. This is achieved by pipelined and parallel execution of the functions, enabling row-by-row "live" streaming of the data to the application. The data is available to the application as the function is executing but hasn't completely finished. This, too, depends on the inherent functionality of the embedded language interface involved.

This process of pipelining can be channelized as a pipeline chain to eliminate intermediate processes/data stores to obtain optimal performance gains. However, the usability of this special technique is solution-specific.

- *Result set caching*—Per-SQL query result set, per-function result set on the DB side; client-side result set caching of the same; and IMDB Cache on the application Tier.

- Database resident connection pooling and statement caching
- Using bind variables and parameterization in Dynamic SQL (Queries and DML), SQL Injection

Ability to Share Data Between Applications

This is a more generic scenario of the above, involving the same data being shared by multiple applications. Key issues are, in addition to those stated above:

- Result set sharing and caching
- Data in-direction and out-direction with minimal DB round-trips
- Connection pooling
- Code abstraction layer for synchronizing data flow and result set sharing between applications, based on different embedded language solutions
- Data and code isolation (centralization versus decentralization of code and data)
- Globalizing data and code; localizing data and privatizing code
- Internationalization at the application level independent of the embedded language used and the solution in place—using Unicode is only part of the tasks involved.

A code modularization framework can be designed and used as a template for an embedded solution that is cross-language, cross-functionality.

1.3.3   Code Manageability Differentiators

- *Managed versus unmanaged code*: This is a key differentiator in .NET-based embedded language solutions (C#). Knowing what's managed (or unmanaged), in what way, and how are the deciding criteria in terms of the suitability and design architecture of the embedded programming solution. Here's a cursory glance of the inside picture:
  - In-database managed
    - In-database code life cycle
      - In its entirety from compilation to execution
      - Interactivity with outer-layer application

- Integration with external application (i.e., one that's not in the application solution architecture)
- Out-of-database managed
  - How much of it is managed outside of Oracle? (fully or partially)
  - Interactivity with outer-layer application

1.3.4   Error Handling Differentiators

- *Error and exception handling*: This is one of the indispensable aspects of any software application/solution, not to mention an Oracle-based solution. When an embedded programming language that is outside the Oracle database language set (either native or specific to Oracle) is involved in the Oracle-based solution, *the exception handling has to be exceptional.* This involves:
  - Trapping the error—asynchronously, for real-time error alerting and autonomous error logging independent of the transaction/process that raised the error; and synchronously, for halting further processing in case of errors with a higher severity level
  - Tracking the source of the error
  - Handling the error (preemptively and otherwise)
  - Decoding the database-specific and language-specific error message, and encoding it into a user-friendly and business-savvy format (as and when necessary)
  - Customizing the error (in the case of application-specific errors related to validation and otherwise)
  - Propagating the error from the database to the end-user UI
  - Auditing the error (including its fix)
  - Troubleshooting (debugging and beyond), on the database side and on the application side; if everything is database-based (except the UI layer), it's easy to manage this aspect.

1.3.5   Other Key Differentiators

- *Rendering of the end-user interface*: The key differentiator here is in using the embedded programming language–based UI code inside the database, thereby tying the data and UI in a back-end-->front-end fashion. This is akin to a "virtual reality" scenario in which the middle Tier actually exists but is inline with the Oracle DB, as opposed to using the regular approach of separating the Web part (both the UI presentation logic as well as the corresponding application logic (code) involved) from the Oracle DB part. A simple example is using HTML in PL/SQL for the former scenario and using PL/SQL in HTML for the latter. A similar analogy applies to other embedded languages. There are pros and cons for each of the two methodologies, and the deciding criteria are based on the end solution desired. Referring to the earlier example, the former approach involves a plug-and-play of the embedded language code into a declarative Oracle-based API (which is primarily PL/SQL/SQL–based) and running the application without the need to install and configure middle-Tier software such as Web Application Server, UI-required language-specific SDK, drivers/providers, libraries, etc. (when using Java, .NET, etc.), as is essential in the latter approach.

■ *Response time*: As there is an application layer involved (and there has to be) on top of the database layer, not all of the application-related code can be inlined in the database whatsoever. This is a critical issue for time-sensitive applications in terms of response time and throughput. To get super-fast response times, the IMDB cache can be deployed in the application layer and used in conjunction with the Oracle database so that end-user data I/O can be done at the speed of RAM, thus eliminating excessive and expensive database round-trips. This is suitable for the millisecond and microsecond response times required for near-real-time data access and/or update, as compared to the second and subsecond response achieved by using only Oracle DB without the IMDB cache in the application layer.

■ Both static and dynamic caching in the application Tier , using persistent cache-once and cache-in-cache-out

■ On-the-fly cached data refresh from the DB to the application IMDB cache and vice versa (in situations when temporary caching of un-committed user data proves effective until the data is marked for *commit*, especially in online Web applications involving transactional data).

■ Provides high availability and fault-tolerance by leveraging the Oracle database-level clustering and Data Guard technologies.

■ Enables the processing of unstructured data using large objects (LOBS) by leveraging the Oracle DB LOB functionality. This

SELECTION AND SUITABILITY CRITERIA FOR A PRAGMATIC AND PRUDENT SOLUTION ARCHITECTURE

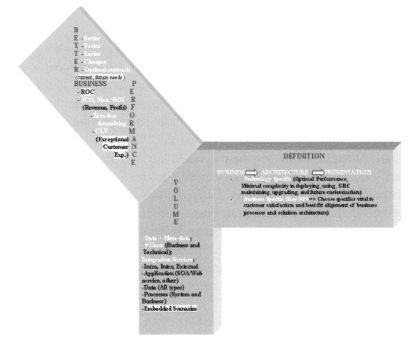

Figure 1.5   A best-fit Oracle embedded programming solution—the big picture..

is not possible if the IMDB cache is used as a stand-alone deployment (i.e., having no Oracle DB underneath).

- Can be used with most of the embedded language data access interfaces, such as JDBC, ODBC, OCI, and Proc*C (C/C++), and of course, SQL and PL/SQL.

- *Syncing, encoding, and decoding*: Oracle-specific and embedded language–specific, in a seamless manner.

- Integration with external applications (i.e., one that's not in the embedded application solution architecture): This is a topic in and of itself and involves permutations and/or combinations of all of the above stated criteria and much more. This topic is discussed in detail in Chapter 8 under "Application Development Frameworks."

Here's the big picture of primary deciding factors for a best-fit Oracle embedded programming solution, not only in terms of technical accuracy and efficiency, but also in terms of getting what you want, from a business/customer standpoint:

Summary

This chapter covered the fundamentals of an embedded programming solution using Oracle database. It started by identifying the Oracle-centric programming languages, platforms, and solution options available. It also dealt with the under-the-hood architecture, methodologies, and technologies that are in place, emerging, and next-gen for building such a solution/application. The details presented not only covered the "What's In" "When-How-Why" and "What's Not In" for these options, but also highlighted "What's Involved"—or in other words, what's needed for such a solution lifecycle. The chapter also discussed the key differentiators of Oracle-specific code versus embedded code, starting from interaction and integration with Oracle to end-user interactivity. The next chapter details the new functionality introduced in Oracle11g through a feature-set and solution-set perspective for an Oracle-based embedded programming application.

Chapter 2

Feature-Set and Solution-Set Enhancements

In This Chapter

■ New feature and functionality options in Oracle11g
■ New feature functionality options in Oracle10g

2.1   Introduction

This chapter discusses the top enhancements Oracle has introduced in versions Oracle 11g and 10g from an embedded language programming perspective, as well as those that are useful from the overall solution standpoint. These new features include better exception handling, code design improvements, performance-related improvements (database and code), and new declarative PL/SQL API. Whenever possible, code snippets are provided for implementing these concepts. The use of these features in application architecture and coding will optimize your Oracle-based embedded programming solution in terms of productivity and efficiency.

2.2   New Feature and Solution Options in Oracle11g

2.2.1   SQL/PL/SQL

Oracle 11g takes design and coding using SQL/PL/SQL to a higher level with new features that enhance its usability and performance. The best-in-class of the new options are outlined in this section.

New PLW-06009 Warning When a WHEN OTHERS Clause Does Not Have a RAISE or RAISE_APPLICATION_ERROR

If a PL/SQL stored subprogram has a WHEN OTHERS EXCEPTION section without a RAISE or RAISE_APPLICATION_ERROR, a compile-time warning is issued. This is very useful in trapping and tracking the source and propagation of Oracle server-based errors in the solution.

Listing 2.1   Code for New PLW-06009 Warning

```
ALTER SESSION SET PLSQL_WARNINGS = 'enable:all';
CREATE OR REPLACE PROCEDURE p_test
(ip_id NUMBER, ip_status VARCHAR2)
IS
BEGIN
UPDATE test_tab
SET status = ip_status
WHERE id = ip_id;
EXCEPTION WHEN OTHERS THEN
NULL;
END;
/
```

Here's the warning that's displayed:

```
PLW-06009: procedure "P_TEST" OTHERS handler does not
end in RAISE or RAISE_APPLICATION_ERROR
```

This feature is an addition to the existing list of compile-time warnings introduced in Oracle 10g. Before Oracle 11g, this feature was benchmarked as a PL/SQL error-handling standard that recommended coding an EXCEPTION WHEN OTHERS section with proper handling of the error, in every subprogram, no matter what, to prevent raising of unhandled exceptions (in the executable section).

New SQL Hint for INSERT statements

Oracle11gR2 allows an INSERT statement to bypass rows violating the DUP_VAL_ON_INDEX SQL exception during the INSERT operation by specifying the new IGNORE_ROW_ON_DUPKEY_INDEX hint for the INSERT statement. Here's an example of the same:

```
INSERT /*+ IGNORE_ROW_ON_DUPKEY_INDEX */
INTO tgt_tab
SELECT ... FROM src_tab ...;
```

Fine-Grained Dependency Tracking (FGD)

This feature reinvents the implicit invalidation and re-compilation of database-level objects in the dependency-chain subprogram hierarchy. Before Oracle11g, a single invalidation in a particular subprogram invalidated all the subprograms in the tree up to the level of the single subprogram. With FGD, only database objects that are relevant to the particular (single) subprogram being executed are invalidated, eliminating the cascade effect, which helps avoid excessive recompilations (think efficiency). Examples are when columns are added to underlying tables, or when the package specification has new cursors or procedures added. In these cases, the dependent objects are not invalidated or recompiled.

Dynamic SQL Enhancements

Dynamic SQL is optimized for faster execution and enhanced functionality. In terms of native dynamic SQL, string length is now unrestricted to accept Character Large Object (CLOB) input. EXECUTE IMMEDIATE and DBMS_SQL (DBMS_SQL.PARSE) can accept a CLOB () input. A more powerful enhancement in this respect is the interoperability of DBMS_SQL cursors and REF CURSORs. This means you can code a dynamic SQL SELECT statement using a DBMS_SQL cursor, parse it and execute it using DBMS_SQL, and then process the result set using native dynamic SQL using a REF CURSOR. This is extremely useful for embedded programming languages, as REF CURSOR is the most efficient structure for sharing data result sets between Oracle and the application.

Moreover, this interoperability can take advantage of bulk operations. The API transforms the DBMS_SQL to REF CURSOR, using the DBMS_SQL.TO_REF_CURSOR function. The reverse is also possible, using the API DBMS_SQL.TO_CURSOR_NUMBER. Finally, DBMS_SQL now supports user-defined types as well as dynamic bulk operations on these types.

PL/SQL Triggers Enhancements

The ability to specify the order of trigger execution and the new compound trigger that enables the use of sections in a single trigger for multiple trigger actions are useful in cases in which the application code needs to be supplemented for data integrity in a transparent manner. This need for transparent data integrity is felt more when the data input/output (I/O) is tied to an embedded language that is non-Oracle based. All this comes with performance benefits, too; compound triggers have a common state and preserve this state for the life of an entire DML operation; and DML triggers have been geared up to be 25 percent faster. Row-level triggers performing updates on tables other than the triggering table might benefit from this.

In Oracle 11g, the FOLLOWS clause can be used to specify trigger-firing order. Here's a simple syntactical example:

```
CREATE OR REPLACE TRIGGER trg_demo
AFTER INSERT ON demo_tab FOR EACH ROW
FOLLOWS trg_ai_demo1
BEGIN
/* Some logic */
END;
/
```

This creates a new (implicit) trigger-based dependency chain in terms of trigger execution order. However, Oracle11gR1 does not have the fine-grained dependency control of this type of trigger-based dependencies. This functionality has been added in Oracle11gR2, along with a new PRECEDES capability that accounts for trigger-upon-trigger dependency tracking.

Oracle 11g introduced the concept of a compound trigger. Instead of defining multiple triggers, each of a separate type, the compound trigger has sections for BEFORE/AFTER and STATEMENT/EACH ROW. This way, the state of the variables can be maintained. For example, any variables defined before the BEFORE STATEMENT section persist until the triggering statement finishes. Here's a sneak peek at how such a trigger might look:

```
CREATE OR REPLACE TRIGGER trig_demo_compound
FOR INSERT ON demo_tab
COMPOUND TRIGGER
g_val NUMBER;
BEFORE STATEMENT IS
BEGIN
/* Some logic */
END BEFORE STATEMENT;
AFTER EACH ROW IS
BEGIN
/* Some logic */
END AFTER EACH ROW;
AFTER STATEMENT IS
```

```
BEGIN
/* Some logic */
END AFTER STATEMENT;
END trig_demo_compound;
/
```

PL/SQL Intra-Unit Inlining (Efficiency)

Oracle 11g has incorporated intra-unit inlining of PL/SQL code, which allows for dynamic substitution of the actual code of a subroutine for a subroutine call when the subroutine is invoked. This means there is no control transfer to and from the main routine to the subroutine, thus eliminating the overheads of function calls. The object code is generated after the substitution. This capability brings PL/SQL that is 4GL-based in line with 3GL and conventional procedural programming languages that have similar macro functionality. This is also true for locally declared subprograms. This feature is an asset in execution efficiency in regard to interaction of the embedded code with Oracle DB.

Oracle determines whether a particular subprogram can be inlined or not, based on performance-centric criteria. There is no coding change involved, but the PLSQL_OPTMIZE_LEVEL has to be set to 3 for automatic inlining. The value of 3 is new in Oracle 11g. Intraunit inlining also works with PL/SQL_OPTIMIZE_LEVEL set to 2 (in fact, at least 2). However, in this case, a pragma has to be invoked programmatically just before the subprogram call to initiate the inlining process. Here's an example:

```
CREATE OR REPLACE PROCEDURE demo_child_proc
IS
BEGIN
/* Some logic here */
END demo_child_proc;
/
CREATE OR REPLACE PROCEDURE demo_parent_proc
IS
BEGIN
/* Some logic here */
/* Conditionally call demo_child_proc here */
IF (<condition>) THEN
PRAGMA INLINE(demo_child_proc, 'yes');
demo_child_proc;
```

```
END IF;
END demo_parent_proc;
/
```

This code instructs the compiler that demo_child_proc is a potential candidate for inlined compilation.

The word *potential* is relevant in this context because the compiler might reject the inlining task for internal reasons. This is true even with automatic inlining enabled. However, when both automatic inlining and the pragma are specified, the pragma takes precedence. Thus, when the second argument of the pragma has a value of "no," the inlining process is skipped.

SQL and PL/SQL Result Caching (Efficiency)

Using the RESULT_CACHE hint for SQL SELECT statements and RESULT_CACHE clause for the subsequent execution of PL/SQL functions after the initial (first) time, can improve the run-time performance many times faster-in situations when the data is more or less static. The /*+result_cache*/ SQL hint lets the result data be cached in the data block buffers and not in the intermediate data blocks, as was the case pre-Oracle 11g. This means that subsequent calls are super-fast. In terms of PL/SQL functions using result caching, it is beneficial to result-cache functions that include data-intensive SELECT statements or those that are called from SQL. And to add more value, the results are cached at the database instance level, and hence available to any/all sessions connected to that instance.

New Client-Side Result Cache (Efficiency)

This feature is very useful for embedded programming language–based applications running against the Oracle database. This applies to OCI (C/C++), C# (.NET environment), Java, PHP/Ajax, and XML/HTML, in conjunction with SQL/PL/SQL. This new functionality enables caching the database result set retrieved, on the application client Tier, ensuring auto-refresh of the same to maintain consistency of theunderlying data changes in the Oracle DB.

Enhanced Native Compilation

Oracle11g enables compilation of PL/SQL code without requiring a C compiler. Only a single initialization parameter controls the native compilation— PLSQL_CODE_TYPE. Before Oracle 11g, PL/SQL-stored subprograms and anonymous PL/SQL blocks could be natively compiled to a dynamic link library (DLL) format and executed faster. However, this process involved translating the PL/SQL code to C code, converting the C code to a native DLL using an external C compiler (which had to be resident in the same system where the application is running), and taking care of linking and loading.

Oracle 11g eliminates the need for the last two steps by directly generating native DLL compatible with the client system hardware and by internally performing the linking and loading functions. This in turn eliminates not only the third-party C compiler but also the file system directories that had to be maintained in earlier versions.

Miscellaneous Enhancements

- A single Date format can be set at the application-level when generating applications using Oracle APEX. This is very useful in embedded programming, especially in FLASH-based interactive applications that require date values localization by application to display a consistent date for all reports in the specific application. As a note, this applies to input date values too. (Oracle11gR2)
- PL/SQL data type SIMPLE_INTEGER has a native format, wraps instead of overflowing, and is faster than PLS_INTEGER.
- Fine-grained access control (FGAC) for UTL_SMTP, UTL_TCP, and UTL_HTTP enables security to be defined on ports and URLs using access control elements and access control lists.
- Improved native Java and PL/SQL compilers provide autocompilation in the native mode in certain cases.
- Regular expression enhancements have been made for SQL/PL/SQL.
- A *disabled* state is available for PL/SQL stored objects (in addition to *enabled* and *invalid* in dba_objects).

Implicit Database/SQL Tuning Feature Set

- Oracle11gR2 allows for in-memory parallel execution that contributes to improved performance and scalability in SQL-intensive operations. These are the new techniques introduced:
  - It enables in-memory parallel execution of queries by "intelligently" autocaching the necessary database objects in-memory (as opposed to the data blocks), thus drastically reducing or (in some cases eliminating) the physical I/O needed for the parallel

operation. Additionally, it enables determination of the degree of parallelism required on the fly, based on the size of the DB object(s) involved, the complexity of the SQL operation involved, and the physical resource availability.

- It provides a programmatic PL/SQL-based API for creating and automating parallel operations that otherwise necessitated manual coding and scheduling in the Oracle database. Using the new DBMS_PARALLEL_EXECUTE package, any DML operation (including MERGE) can now be parallelized and scheduled for auto-execution based on ROWID or PRIMARY KEY/SURROGATE UNIQUE KEY values. This is a performance enhancer in terms of response time, transaction state independence, and scalability. As a result, transform-like SQL operations on a VLDB table are now customizable as needed, without compromising the efficiency of the same. For example, tasks like splitting large tables based on ROWID/PK ranges, distributing new data rows across partitions based on context-specific business rules (using ROWID or PK ranges again), and so on can now be implemented and automated in one shot.

- New virtual columns and virtual column partitioning enable enhanced business performance because they are able to simulate the performance characteristics of their actual table column counterparts—a business column (which might be actually a combination of multiple attributes) translates logically and directly into a computed virtual column in the same table; an invisible index status enables a "preview" impact analysis of an added (new) index in "live" environments without affecting system/application performance.Oracle11gR2 supports reference partitioning with virtual columns as part of the primary or foreign key of the so partitioned table.

- Read-only tables isolate business-critical data from being modified pervasively.

- Automatic SQL Tuning is available, including statistics collection of related multiple columns and private statistics (which enables a "preview" analysis of the collected statistics before use by the query optimizer).

- Transparent tablespace encryption in 11g ensures tighter database (and hence data) security. This is very useful in encrypting the entire database at once pertaining to (a particular) application(s) and/or business domain(s) by allocating a single tablespace for (each of) the same. Oracle10gR2 introduced transparent table-level encryption that added a finer granularity to the Oracle data protection landscape.

2.2.2   New Functionalities That Benefit the Enterprise Grid

- Just-in-time database backup and recovery for high availability can now be accomplished using the new Network-Aware Duplication, which enables the creation of a duplicate database using the data files of the "live" database (no prior backups of the source database are needed); flashback archival with automatic historical data management; SQL Repair Advisor, and Data Repair Advisor (these two advisors provide detour capabilities for fixing failed SQL and data via SQL patches without having to change the existing SQL and lightweight data fixes).
- Oracle11gR2 introduces an Oracle Secure Backup Cloud Module that enables secure and easy-to-manage backup of the DB to Amazon Simple Storage Service (S3)—a Web Services–enabled storage solution that minimizes/eliminates the need for an on-premise solution in terms of cost and administration.
- Automatic database diagnostics monitoring of the Oracle RAC environment in the Database Grid layer of the Enterprise Grid is available.
- The new SQL performance analyzer enables identification of the impact of change and variance in the system on the performance of SQL, a key performance indicator in embedded programming scenarios
- Real-time standby database for query is available in addition to standby snapshot and logical standby databases. Along with the new fast-start failover improvements and Automatic Health Monitor, this adds pre-emptive, proactive, and reactive database recovery and monitoring.
- Automatic Storage Management (ASM) comes as a boon for the Enterprise Grid. It enables auto-virtualization of the physical storage layer of the Enterprise Grid. It also isolates the administrative privileges of the database administrator (DBA) from that of the storage administrator (SA) by adding a third DB role, sysasm (the first and second being sysdba and sysoper).

- Auto-enablement of auditing at the database (for some SQL statements only) and user-profile levels ensures regulatory security compliance with SOX and PCI. This also tracks the sign-in and sign-on information. Transaction-level auditing (e.g., for each SQL statement) can be enabled by setting the AUDIT_TRAIL initialization parameter to the value EXTENDED_DB. In addition, Oracle11gR2 ensures application security beyond the enterprise (i.e., in externalized deployments such as cloud) by enabling Federated Identity & Access Management policies enforcement that are SOA-based, Security Identity and Access Management (SIAM)-, Security Assertion Markup Language (SAML)-, and Extensible Access Control Markup Language (XACML)-compliant and XML-threat proof. This is made possible via Oracle11gR2 Identity Management and Content Management Solutions.
- Fine-grained network access from within the database for accessing resources outside of the database adds an enhanced layer of security to the overall solution architecture.
- With high-availability FAN (fast application notification), database event notifications (and their subsequent handling) are communicated to an -embedded application via callbacks and event handlers (e.g., ODP.NET callbacks and event handlers for a .NET-based embedded application). Also, Oracle11gR2 enables e-mail notification to users for any Oracle Scheduler–based job activity.
- The new Oracle Application Testing Suite for .NET-based embedded applications (and Web services) delivers a fully-integrated pre-deployment testing environment capable of load testing, functionality testing, and defect tracking, which can be used for improving quality, scalability, and high availability.

2.2.3 PHP/Ajax

- The new IDE and application platform using Zend Core for developing/generating PHP/Ajax-based Oracle11g database applications is fully integrated with Oracle database to leverage the power and performance potential of the latest 11g database functionality.
- Database resident connection pooling for greater scalability of PHP applications simulates the benefit obtained from using a multithreaded server for persistent-session sharing, in regard to connection pooling. This in effect creates a shared pool of connections resident in the database that can be used for both dedicated server

processes and shared server processes, having Oracle manage the auditing of the same (exposed via the DBA_CPOOL_INFO data dictionary view). All it takes to leverage this benefit is to add an additional option (SERVER=POOLED) to the connection string in the code for the PHP application and use its value for an additional parameter-argument in the corresponding OCI call:

```
OCISessionPoolCreate (…, …, const OraText *connStr,
…)
```

The OCI supports 8-byte native data type support, the 8-byte integer, for Pro*C and Pro*COBOL applications that perform bind/define operations using INSERT/FETCH statements. Also supported is the 8-byte native numeric host variable for Pro*C and Pro*COBOL INSERT and FETCH statements (via OCI).

2.2.4   Oracle, .NET and C#

- OPD.NET can now leverage Oracle's Advanced Queuing (AQ) operations via a programmatic API. The corresponding AQ resources are manageable by the ODT for Visual Studio.
- New in-built ODP.NET functionality to self-tune the embedded application by dynamically tuning the statement cache size, using baselines obtained through auto-sampling of runtime query execution. Another addition in this respect is the Visual Studio Oracle Performance Analyzer for analyzing change and variance impact, and tuning the embedded .NET application from Visual Studio (ODT for Visual Studio).
- All ODP.NET transactions that run against a single database are auto-localized, by default. These transactions are promoted to the distributed level only if a second database needs to be involved.
- Performance-optimized ODP.NET inherent data retrieval components enable faster data access at the application level.
- Declarative Oracle security is available for code access.
- SQL scripts can now be generated for the .NET application based on any Oracle schema object or group of objects; additionally, we now have the ability to compile any number of stored procedures or functions at the same time.

2.2.5 Java

- Oracle11g supports J2SE 1.5 functionality in its JVM. This functionality enables Java-based Oracle embedded applications to leverage the generic classes' definition functionality in the embedded Java code, a benefit similar to compiler hints in PL/SQL that alert Oracle to use performance-enabled features when appropriate to minimize CPU and memory overheads.
- Oracle11gR2-based embedded Java applications are Daylight Savings Time–compliant by way of simplified patching for applications using the TIMESTAMP WITH TIME ZONE data type. Also, JDBC support has been extended to allow for SecureFile Zero-copy LOB I/O and LOB pre-fetching. This feature is an accelerator for data-content unification because it allows Java-based access to structured, semi-structured, and unstructured data in a seamless, secure and high-performing manner.
- Just-in-time (JIT) compilation for Java methods in embedded code. This functionality auto-selects (ahead of compilation) Java methods for native compilation and then auto-compiles the same into native code to obtain compilation gains that are performance-centric. This is in a way analogous to the new native compilation feature for PL/SQL code, combined with the auto-recompilation of invalid PL/SQL program units during subsequent call invocations. JIT is enabled by default, and embedded Java code can not only benefit from automatic native compilation, but also from automatic recompilation of invalid Java methods and the automatic persistence of these methods across database calls, sessions and instances (the last benefit is similar to the one for achieving database cross-session persistence of PL/SQL packaged subprogram calls, by specifying PRAGMA SERIALIZABLE).
- Java JAR files can now be loaded and saved in the Oracle11g database as separate DB objects in addition to those created for each of the extracted .class files in the .jar file. Also, Oracle auto-links the new JAR DB object with its corresponding individual DB objects (created for each of the corresponding .class files). This offers an advantage on the database side similar to the one that JAR files give on the Java side.
- A new ojvmtc tool pre-resolves and auto-generates stubs for unresolved class references relative to a class path so that the final code is compilation-ready without having to manually resolve and/or

code each of them during the compilation process. In addition to saving development time and effort, this gives the added advantage of being able to load a class library that references classes in other libraries that are not required for the embedded program in context, but the contextual library cannot otherwise be loaded due to unresolved references.

2.2.6   XML

- On-the-fly changes to XML Schemas enable ensure near-zero downtime.
- New binary XML format in the database minimizes cost of hard-parsing.
- XMLCast enables data type-casting using XML. (Useful in embedded language code implementations involving XML data and an unified data/content format for access/storage/delivery).
- XMLIndex enables faster XML data retrieval by driving the indexing mechanism based on the internal structure of the XML data.
- New SQL-based XML operations using XMLDiff and XMLPatch enable functionality similar to compare and merge operations, but integrated with Oracle via SQL exposure to leverage the benefits of SQL-like structured data.

2.3   New Feature and Solution Options in Oracle10g

Oracle version 10g introduced a number of great features for the application developer. The best of these new features, in regards to a better and more efficient embedded language code for database interaction, are presented in this section.

2.3.1   Regular Expressions

Oracle 10g has introduced the ability to describe, query, and manipulate patterns of text in PL/SQL by means of regular expressions. UNIX style–based regular expressions for performing enhanced queries and string manipulations have been introduced in PL/SQL by means of predefined patterns and functions that are useable in SQL queries and PL/SQL assignment expressions. The patterns are bracket expressions, the escape character, alternation, sub-expressions, back references, and more. The functions are REGEXP_LIKE,   REGEXP_INSTR,   REGEXP_REPLACE,   and

REGEXP_SUBSTR. These are similar to the LIKE, INSTR, REPLACE, and SUBSTR functions pertaining to string manipulations. For example, REGEXP_LIKE enables the matching to be performed beyond the realm of "_" and "%". Here's an example:

```
DECLARE
v_src_str VARCHAR2(200) := '998 999 7096';
v_like_str VARCHAR2(10) := '[0-9]{3} [0-9]{3} [0-
9]{4}';
BEGIN
IF NOT REGEXP_LIKE(v_src_str, v_like_str) THEN
DBMS_OUTPUT.PUT_LINE('Invalid Phone Number');
END IF;
END;
/
```

Regular expression–based LIKE searches can be used using the REGEXP_LIKE in JDBC and other embedded language interfaces to speed up the contextual search processing needed for rich UI presentation layers.

2.3.2   DBMS_JAVA.SET_OUTPUT

This enables redirection of DBMS_OUTPUT.PUT_LINE output to the Java environment.

2.3.3   Tracking the Error Line Number

Oracle 10g PL/SQL offers an elegant way of knowing the actual line number in the execution of which an exception was raised. Before Oracle 10g, it was possible to know only the error number, the error message text, and the error stack in a PL/SQL program by calling the packaged function DBMS_UTILITY.FORMAT_ERROR_STACK. In Oracle 10g PL/SQL, you can obtain the actual line number by calling the packaged function DBMS_UTILITY.FORMAT_ERROR_BACKTRACE. This functionality is new in Oracle 10g and returns the error backtrace stack of the raised error, which includes the program owner, program name, and *actual line number where the error occurred, but without the actual error number.* If this function is called in the block in which the error was raised, it gives the line number in the execution of which the exception was first raised. Should the exception be raised again, this function gives the line number in which the last re-raise occurred.

The best way to use this feature is to call the FORMAT_ERROR_BACKTRACE function as an argument to DBMS_OUTPUT.PUT_LINE procedure from a WHEN OTHERS exception handler. To get more elaborate information about the error, it pays to call the FORMAT_ERROR_STACK function as an argument to DBMS_OUTPUT.PUT_LINE in the same WHEN OTHERS handler. This way, the subprogram owner, the subprogram name, the error number, the error message text, the actual line number, and the error stack can be obtained for any PL/SQL error. In case of a package, the subprogram name returned is the name of the package, not that of the individual packaged subprogram.

Combining the usage of FORMAT_ERROR_BACKTRACE, FORMAT_ERROR_STACK, and DBMS_OUTPUT.PUT_LINE with DBMS_JAVA.SET_OUTPUT results in a powerful error-tracker in Java-based environments.

Listing 2.2 shows an example of using this feature.

Listing 2.2   Listing 2.2 Use of DBMS_UTILITY.FORMAT_ERROR_BACKTRACE

```
CREATE OR REPLACE PROCEDURE p_insert(
p_process_id IN NUMBER,
p_job_id IN NUMBER,
p_pj_flag IN VARCHAR2)
BEGIN
INSERT INTO work_for_job VALUES(p_process_id,
'Process '||TO_CHAR(p_process_id), p_pj_flag);
COMMIT;
END;
/

CREATE OR REPLACE PROCEDURE p_delete
IS
BEGIN
```

```
DELETE work_for_job WHERE process_id = 102;
IF SQL%NOTFOUND THEN
RAISE_APPLICATION_ERROR(-20001, 'Process '
||'is not in job queue. Cannot delete.');
END IF;
COMMIT;
END;
/

CREATE OR REPLACE PROCEDURE p_dml (
p_flag IN VARCHAR2,
p_process_id IN NUMBER,
p_job_id IN NUMBER,
p_pj_flag IN VARCHAR2)
IS
BEGIN
IF (p_flag = 'I') THEN
p_insert(p_process_id, p_job_id, p_pj_flag);
ELSIF (p_flag = 'D') THEN
p_delete;
END IF;
EXCEPTION WHEN OTHERS THEN
dbms_output.put_line('Begin Error Stack');
dbms_output.put_line(
DBMS_UTILITY.FORMAT_ERROR_STACK);
dbms_output.put_line('End Error Stack');
dbms_output.put_line('Begin Error Backtrace');
dbms_output.put_line(
DBMS_UTILITY.FORMAT_ERROR_BACKTRACE);
dbms_output.put_line('End Error Backtrace');
END p_dml;
/
```

The code in Listing 2.3 illustrates a call to p_dml and the corresponding output.

Listing 2.3   Listing 2.3 Sample Output of
DBMS_UTILITY.FORMAT_ERROR_BACKTRACE

```
SQL> begin
2 p_dml('I',101,1,'PJ');
3 end;
4 /
Begin Error Stack
ORA-01722: invalid number
End Error Stack
Begin Error Backtrace
ORA-06512: at "PLSQL10G.P_INSERT", line 7
ORA-06512: at "PLSQL10G.P_DML", line
8
End Error Backtrace
PL/SQL procedure successfully completed.
```

Notice the error line number in the p_insert procedure. It indicates the line where the PL/SQL error occurred. The corresponding line number in p_dml indicates where p_insert was called.

2.3.4   Enhanced FORALL Statement for Handling DML Array Processing with Sparse Collections

By default, the collection used in a FORALL statement cannot have missing elements. Oracle 10g allows you to use sparse collections (that is, collections with many intermediate missing elements) with the FORALL statement in two ways:

1. *Using the INDICES OF clause* allows a collection with deleted intermediate elements to be a part of the FORALL statement. This is an efficient method to deal with sparse collections. Before Oracle 10g, too many intermediate deleted elements resulted in a performance overhead with the SAVE EXCEPTIONS clause.

2. *Using the VALUES OF clause* allows you to create a secondary collection, the element values of which are the indices of the primary collection. This is a handy alternative to copying

collections, as was the case with the traditional FORALL statement for handling deleted elements.

Also, exception handling with INDICES OF and VALUES OF is possible.

INDICES OF in FORALL

If you have a sparse collection and want to take advantage of bulk operations, you can code a FORALL statement using the INDICES OF and SAVE EXCEPTIONS clauses.

VALUES OF in FORALL

Here, you create a secondary collection whose element values are the indices of the primary collection. Then you use this value as the subscript in the original collection, which enables you to bulk process based on subsidiary collections that drive the DML being processed. This in turn eliminates the duplication or replication of the original collection elements to be included as part of the secondary collection, which is then used in the FORALL statement.

2.3.5   Conditional Compilation (Oracle 10GR2)

Conditional compilation allows you to conditionally select or include PL/SQL source code to be compiled and thus executed, for example, based on the version of the Oracle database. This is done by specifying certain conditions. The conditions are specified using preprocessor directives, inquiry directives, predefined compiler flags, PL/SQL expressions (with restrictions), initialization parameters, and predefined and user-defined package constants. One can draw an analogy of PL/SQL code incorporating conditional compilation with that of a UNIX shell script. A very good use of conditional compilation is to write code that is database multi-version specific, and then compile and execute it on different database versions. This way it enables the same code to run on multiple versions of the database. Also, activating debugging and tracing code conditionally is possible simply by recompiling.

The preprocessor directives, like UNIX shell environment variables, start with a $ sign followed by the identifier name. Examples are $IF, $ELSEIF, and $END. They are used as follows:

```
$IF condition1 $THEN
action1
$ELSEIF condition2 $THEN
action2
$END
```

The above pseudo-code is similar to the PL/SQL IF statement, but not syntactically. Inquiry directives start with $$ followed by a flag name and are mostly used to check the compilation environment. Here's an example:

```
$$warning_flag
```

A user-defined package specification with static constants can also be defined in place of predefined package constants. However, in this case, the package so defined should be exclusively used for conditional compilation. Also, the post-processed source code resulting from conditional compilation can be obtained using the predefined packaged procedure DBMS_PREPROCESSOR. PRINT_POST_PROCESSED_SOURCE.

2.3.6   Compile-Time Warnings

These warning messages are thrown out at compile time as a result of using improper or inefficient constructs. This feature enables code to be pre-tested in a development environment before deploying in production. Responding to the warnings given, the code can be improved before it runs live. These warnings start with the code PLW. You can enable and disable these warnings in three ways:

1.   At the database level, by setting the plsql_warnings initialization parameter.
2.   At the session level, using the ALTER SESSION SET plsql_warnings command.
3.   Using the DBMS_WARNING package.

The plsql_warnings parameter is to be set as follows:

```
[ENABLE | DISABLE | ERROR]:
[ALL|SEVERE|INFORMATIONAL|PERFORMANCE|warning_number
]
```

Here's the command to enable all the three types of warnings to be enabled at the session level:

```
ALTER SESSION SET PLSQL_WARNINGS = 'enable:all'
```

To enable or disable a particular warning, the five-digit warning number should be used instead of "all". The messages from PLW-5000 to 5999 are severe warnings, from 6000 to 6249 are informational warnings, and from 7000 to 7249 are performance-related warnings. The actual warning message can be obtained by from the data dictionary view DBA_ERRORS.

2.3.7   Integrated mod_plsql

The mod_plsql module for handling hypertext transfer protocol (HTTP) requests has been directly integrated into the server in Oracle10g Release2. This eliminates the need to install an Apache listener separately for invoking PL/SQL procedures using the Web-Toolkit API over an HTTP connection by means of an URL.

Summary

This chapter covered the new and advanced functionality introduced in Oracle11g and Oracle10g from a feature-set and solution-set standpoint. The next chapter details the best practices of choice and suitability criteria in terms of the programming languages, platforms, and solution architecture for an Oracle-based embedded programming application.

Chapter 3

Programming Languages, Platforms, and Solutions

In This Chapter

■ Why and when architecture takes precedence over feature set

■ Best practices in terms of Oracle database interaction

■ Best practices for using SQL and PL/SQL only (with HTML, XML via PSP, or Web Toolkit)

■ Best practices for using .NET based languages (C++, C#)

■ Best practices for using Java-based languages (Java Libraries, Java via JDBC, Java via SQLJ, Java via Java Stored Procedures)

■ Best practices for using PHP-based languages (PHP-only, PHP and AJAX, PHP Web pages)

■ Perl in the picture—best practices for the perfect fit and use of Perl in an embedded scenario

■ For better or worse: Application-centric and business-centric key performance indicators

3.1 Introduction

A best-practice strategy for choosing and determining the suitability of an embedded programming solution is governed by a set of essential factors that serve as evaluation criteria for the solution being proposed. These are generic in nature and apply to any technology, architecture, and methodology in consideration, whether it is Java-based, .NET-based, PHP-based, Perl-based or solely Oracle-based (using SQL and/or PL/SQL in conjunction with HTML/ XML). These can be grouped into the following major categories:

■ The *purpose of the proposed solution* in terms of software pragmatics; that is, a generic solution that is more like a product in broad terms, a customer-centric solution, a benchmarking solution (that eventually would evolve into a product or software application), an architectural blueprint (that can be enhanced/extended), and so on.

- The *type of users it is tailored to*; that is, end-users (both technical and nontechnical), researchers, architects (business/functional, technical, techno-functional), analysts (business/functional, technical, techno-functional), and so on.

- The *pervasiveness of the business use of the solution*; that is, enterprise-wide, department-wide, and so on. This in turn determines the number of prospective users who would be using the proposed solution. A key factor in this case is the various business processes involved.

- The *proposed solution deployment*; that is, whether it is a totally new solution, a replacement for an existing solution, codeployed alongside existing solutions (may or may not be integrated with them), or used as part of an existing solution (either embedded or plugged).

It has to be understood that most of the time, there are no fast-start or one-fits-all solutions in any or all of these cases. How well the proposed solution is architected is the key to it being the best-fit for any implementation. The chapter begins by highlighting the importance of an optimally architected solution and why getting the design right first time makes a big difference. The subsequent sections details the best practices involved in determining the right-fit of the embedded programming language options available, starting with a purely SQL and PL/SQL based Oracle11g solution to .NET based, Java-based, and PHP-based languages, and the use of Perl in the embedded programming scenario. The last section highlights the best-of-breed for a best-fit solution in terms of the Key Application/Solution-centric and Business-centric Indicators, converging on the conclusion that *"a best-fit solution is always a win-win over a best solution."*

3.2 Why and When Architecture Takes Precedence over Feature Set

Once the business need has been determined for the proposed solution, the next step is to determine the architecture and design of the solution in terms of the business processes involved from a functional standpoint and the technologies to be used and methodologies to be followed from a technical standpoint that maps vis-à-vis the functional aspects. There is no single easy way to accomplish this; a best-fit architecture is the foundation for a best-fit solution that yields not only optimal system performance but also better business performance and an exceptional customer experience, ultimately leading to a greater customer/business lifetime value.

The "Why-and-When" of architecture precedence depends on the following broader aspects:

- *The level of automation involved*—Design, deployment, management, provisioning, monitoring
- *The solution technology used (to achieve the automation)*—Solution end-to-end as a service (both software and business services), just a part of the solution as a service, the software only as a service, business processes only as a service, and so on:
  - Service-Oriented Architecture (SOA)—Web Services, Software as a Service (SaaS), Platform as a Service (PaaS), Infrastructure as a Service (IaaS), and the like
  - Business Process Management (BPM)
  - Business Activity Monitoring (BAM) and Complex Event Processing (CEP)
  - Continuous Event Processing and Monitoring across the solution end-to-end, enabling business continuity

These act as cross-centric methodologies for solution architecture and application development.

- Enterprise mobility provided without compromising on a superior customer experience.
- Solution excellence and competency overlapped with the feature set supported by the designed architecture components; this is now emerging as the key criteria for the go-ahead for a solution implementation.
- Enterprise-wide seamless communication/messaging—EAI versus ESB versus a software-based messaging engine.
- Enterprise-wide transparent data integration, including accessibility; analysis; modification (of both structured and unstructured data-text, voice, video, click-stream, real-time streaming); and the impact on the solution efficiency in terms of the contextuality of how the textual (or unstructured) data is stored and retrieved; how to measure its effectiveness for both input and results in terms of its usability; and how to define data quality metrics in such cases.

- Security strategies that are one-on-one with the corresponding tools and technologies available. This is especially important in "security-beyond-the-enterprise" scenarios, like wireless environments and endpoint security.

Taking this into account, here are a set of key indicators in terms of why-and-when architecture ranks top on the to-do list:

- Aligning business processes with the technologies (IT processes) involved is one of the primary solution requirements, in the design of which architecture plays a major role. Is the proposed solution the best-of-breed that leverages, to the fullest extent possible, the coupling of technology and business processes to get superior business value? It must not only streamline the business processes involved (through process integration) but also optimize them to provide a win-win for the business case involved. The rule of thumb is to *derive a superior business/customer experience by architecting an end-to-end business process channelization design.*
- The performance of the solution should be optimal and at the same time visible (that is, significantly noticeable and appreciable). Here, performance refers to both system (that is, the solution) and business performance, without compromising on the reliability.
- What you want, your way—Is the solution a "one-size-fits-all," or one that is more specific in nature? Here the key thing to note is that "one-size-fits-all" and "more specific" are references to the scope of usability, meaning whether the solution addresses all users, all data, and all business needs in terms of information presentation and business performance. Ultimately, "what-you-get-is-what-you-need" specific solution architecture is the one to be designed to replace a "one-fits-all" solution architecture.
- Customer return on investment (ROI)—This boils down to a cross-customer *value versus speed versus price versus time* accelerating curve.
- Seamless enterprise-wide accessibility (this includes "right here, right now" access, too) to a wealth of data and information. Here, the phrase "enterprise-wide" is usually contained to a particular customer. This spawns another major task, that of protecting and isolating business/customer data and the same time preserving logical and physical solution (technical/architectural) independence.
- Eliminating architecture silos in the solution—This applies to the number of intermediate solution layers to be designed and

implemented for the end solution and is a driving factor for both application integration and data integration (including data sharing).

- Can the proposed solution meet next-generation capability requirements? This must be taken into account as the proposed solution must be adaptable to future business requirements (i.e., extendable or enhanced in a better-simpler-faster manner and leverage (advanced or changed) technology potential to achieve an optimal performance versus value solution). Here's a list of considerations in this scenario:
  - On-demand and dynamic provisioning
  - Incremental scaling of applications
  - Dynamic load-balancing
  - Zero downtime (this means eliminating planned downtime)
  - Running applications as dynamic services
  - Intelligent data management
  - Hot-pluggable component capability
  - Multicontent "plug-and-play" integration and management (*delivers business value*)
  - Flash interactivity via live end-user controls
  - 100 percent thin client
  - Cross-browser compatibility
  - Shareability—Disk, memory, CPUs (share-nothing, using public or private cloud for a cloud-compatible solution that enables sharing only computing using a high-performance analytic database on the DBMS side; share-something [Disk—Oracle RAC, Sybase IQ]; and/or share-memory—SQL Server).

These in turn decide the architectural design strategy, which includes virtualization of both applications and data stores (databases, data warehouses, data marts, data archives, etc.); application grid; open source solution; cloud-based solution; SaaS-based and on-demand solution (*to achieve "deliver more, cost less", accelerated implementation cycles*); and application of the same design to *Security as a Service and Solution as an Appliance.*

Why not do a customized Solution as an Appliance? This can be achieved by integrating the Oracle11g DB Tier, the application Tier, and the presentation Tier all in one hardware and software box that is very customer-specific in terms of the business (solution) domain. This approach needs to be used more universally across the customer-base.

Why not do a customized solution-as-a-service? This can be achieved by combining Infrastructure as a Service and Platform as a Service, and the end-to-end application Software as a Service. The above stated Solution as an Appliance can be taken to a higher level by virtualization and Web Services to deliver a Solution Appliance as a Service.

Will there be any time delay when utilization of the CPU will be 100 percent? How will you deal with this?

In building a business case for consolidating technologies/systems/tools, the customer/user needs get the first preference as a basis for the selection of design criteria .

Eliminate the burden of integrating disparate technologies and provide for true just-in-time resource provisioning.

- Is an open-source solution on top of Oracle considerable? Or would it be preferable to have an out-of-box or custom-built solution on top of the Oracle database layer? What happens down the line, when the technologies used are no longer market/industry-trendy or state-of-the-art?
- What is the application efficiency in terms of performance, security, scalability, reliability, high availability (24x7), unbreakable, interoperability, and maintainability? Is this a solution that accelerates when web-enabled or deployed in a different but similar business (and system) environment?
- What is the data usability in terms of data protection (avoiding data loss or leaks end-to-end, intrusion in terms of insider threats etc.), integration (cross-data-sources), security, retention (including purging of inactive data—this doesn't necessarily mean redundant data, as sometimes duplicated data is valuable data), and recovery?
- What types of activity monitoring will be used? Possibilities include database activity monitoring, application activity monitoring (this might include user activity monitoring and/or business process activity monitoring in line with system processes activity monitoring and/or auditing), automating the end-to-end monitoring process to enable continuous monitoring, and real-time alert notification.

- How will you deliver operational excellence and realize new levels of innovation by enabling more responsiveness and agility? This largely depends on the appropriate technology/methodology being chosen; for example, an SOA-based solution is a good candidate for achieving operational excellence.

3.2.1   Suitability Criteria from a Business/Customer Perspective

- *Best-fit solution*—The solution should provide what is required: "what you get is what you need."
- *Better operational performance*—Performance should be better, faster, easier, and cheaper and have optimal outreach for current and future needs (in terms of the ability to extend, enhance, and adapt the business functionality vis-a-vis the changes in business and technology imperatives).
- *High business value and superior customer experience* —Attaining TCO and maximum ROI requires accelerating the *value-versus-performance-versus-price-versus-time* curve to gain a competitive advantage and high business value in terms of revenue/profit generation and cost reduction (here, performance involves speed, quality, time-to-value, and business value). Additionally, this trend in customer-centricity is evolving, with business value being measured in terms of ROC (return-on-customer) as the preferred metric over ROI (return-on-investment). The concept of ROC is explained in detail in Chapter 8, in the section titled "Application Development Framework".
- *Agnostic customer view end-to-end*—The solution delivered should bring in an *anonymous and unified* customer-centric view across all interactions and touchpoints (e.g., business-centric, project-centric, solution-centric, end-user-centric, endpoint-centric) of the customer, spanning the entire end-to-end business, that is completely transparent of the business/technical processes and methodologies involved. In this respect, customer-data-centricity—a single unified view of the business's critical and commonly used data—is a high priority.
- Zero-loss downsizing
- Self- or auto-manageability
- *Reliability, availability, security, continuity*—Refers to the best fit technical architecture involved, to enable high availability and disaster recovery, scalability (scaling up and scaling out in terms of

business workload and number of users), visibility and security in and out of the solution enterprise, and ability of the solution to enable business continuity with no or minimal IT intervention after the deployment and post-deployment phases.

- *Usability*—A smart, user-friendly and business-savvy solution not only meets business functionality but also provides user-friendly usability in terms of ease of use, real-time flash interactivity (e.g., auto-complete, auto-fill, personal search enhanced, etc.) and responsiveness (i.e., self-usability as is and down the line). In other words, self-service-driven and self-manageable across the entire customer/user base in context.

Key Business Performance Indicator (BPI):

Choose specifics that are vital to a superior customer-centric experience and best-fit business agility and incorporate them in the solution architecture.

3.2.2   Suitability Criteria from a Solution Architecture (Technical/Techno-Functional) Perspective

- *Better business agility*—Align business processes with corresponding IT processes involved in "live" environments. Business agility drastically reduces soft costs. Agile development doesn't have to mean a fragile enterprise process, but one that's a best fit for:
  - Managing IT/software change
  - Business requirements management
  - Application lifecycle management
- *Software/vendor validation*—Use proactive testing strategies, asking what, how, when, and why. One recommended approach is to do "fire-drill" type testing.
- Elimination of large development cycles
- *Elimination of silos in the application/solution architecture*—This is essential for business agility in terms of right-time solution usability (that is, usability that is real-time, on-demand, and able to incorporate business process changes as they occur), so that the change is visible to the end-user almost immediately (while at the same time being transparent). This goal can be achieved using

SOA-based solution methodologies that enable business-IT processes and data to be exposed as reusable services, end-to-end in terms of operational integration and enterprise-wide pervasiveness. This can be implemented in Oracle11g by using the Oracle Grid Framework for the enterprise solution (infrastructure, database, application)

- *Rapid-fire visual analysis and reporting* using a unified presentation layer—A solution should be intelligent enough to be "smart, savvy, and friendly" at the same time; can it provide some business insight that the user can bank on via the use of intelligent smart boards, dash boards, e-boards, and so on? This type of functionality in turn expands the visibility of the application from the standpoint of the business processes involved.

- *Business process and customer-data-centricity* (functional/technical process/methodology/technology transparency)—This is required for customer-centricity (refer to the earlier section, "Suitability Criteria from a Business/Customer Perspective"). The solution delivered should bring in a single customer-centric view and provide transparency across all of the business and technical processes and methodologies involved, including, most importantly, customer-data-centricity. In this regard, "data agnostic" can mandate a single unified view of *all* (critical, common, enterprise-wide cross-source-system) data or multiple unified views of the same that are less pervasive but still call for consolidation/integration into existing business processes. This adds to the reliability of the solution being delivered.

- *Standards-based, compliance- and/or policies-adhering*—The solution must comply with the business organization's policies and with state and federal regulations, such as Sarbanes-Oxley (SOX), the Payment Card Industry (PCI) standards, the Health Insurance Portability and Accountability Act (HIPAA), and so on.

- On-premise (out-of-box, locally developed) or on-demand.

- *Solution adaptability*—The solution must have the flexibility to add/enhance functionality in line with business requirements.

- *Proactive and pre-emptive testing*—Testing should be planned and proactive, as opposed to reactive testing and troubleshooting. This can be done by a "fire-drill" type simulated test or by using a snapshot of the "live" application end-to-end in the test environment. Oracle11gR2 Real Application Testing and the Oracle Application Testing Suite enable this.

- *Comprehensive application and data protection and disaster recovery* while enabling dual mode (read-only and read-write) access (via a physical standby database for queries, sorting, reporting, and enhanced secure functionality at the application/presentation layers).
- *User-friendliness and business savvy*—The IT solution should adopt intelligent content management techniques to transform it into a solution that is user friendly and business savvy. Consider:
  - Policy-driven self usability, using voice, data or Web (including click-stream), while at the same time ensuring that appropriate security is not compromised at the user, group, or role levels from the end-user standpoint. This plays a pivotal role in CRM by enabling a more efficient customer experience (both engagement and empowerment), and also saves costs. This adds to the ROC measure of the solution by increasing the customer lifetime value (CLV) of the embedded solution.
  - Enabling Flash-based live interactivity (e.g., delivering "personal search enhanced web pages", auto-fill, auto-filtering in real-time, etc.), which gives greater end-user control in terms of flexibility and contextual information analysis.
- *Infrastructure support*—This involves:
  - *Server support* at the hardware, operating system (OS), and middleware levels
  - Client support
  - *Database support*—This is important from the aspect of how well Oracle11g can meet the (business-IT) solution architecture requirements at the database Tier, as well as the cross-compatibility of running other Tier-1 database-based code components (e.g., SQL Server, Sybase, DB2, etc.) inside an Oracle11g database.
  - Portal and/or Web services support

Key Solution Architecture Indicators:

- Solution interoperability
- Data and results archiving and retention with (near-)zero downtime
- Customer-specific isolation of applications and data
- High availability and disaster recovery (using Oracle Data Guard, Audit Vault, Oracle Total Recall)

•Security (application/data authorization/authentication, information/ data protection and control-within and outside of the on-premise solution landscape)

•A unified solution (processes, data, and application consolidation, and a unified view of data isolated by business customer/function)

•Deployment on-premise versus online (including on-demand, extranet Web access etc.)

•Scalability (scaling up and scaling out—key drivers for design)

•Better user adoption (relies on the self-service features incorporated in the solution/application)

Achieving Quality by Design—Quality is not all about 100-percent perfection, but about how the solution can meet and be put to its fullest use across the latitude of desired business-centric functionality. This involves key criteria to be considered at the design/architecture stage from a solution standpoint (end-to-end or otherwise), as listed below:

•Innovation through self-service enablement and adaptability - these add to the business continuity and value of the solution post-deployment

•Efficiency (high-performance and un-breakable)

•Ease of integration into target environment (requires proper design choices for deployment and application integration)

•Ease of use and manageability

•Functionality (commonality, consistency, continuity of events, processes, data/content, standardization, simplification, synchronization [streamlining] and automation)

•Value (primarily better business benefit)

•Implemented solution service and support

3.3 Best Practices in Terms of Oracle Database Interaction

Best practices for Oracle Database interaction typically involve bidirectional data movement between the Oracle11g database and the solution/ application, which in turn might have intermediate layer software (either custom-programmed or otherwise) for varied functionalities such as data integration, sharing and consolidation, migration, and so on. This in turn calls for at least four important aspects to be taken care of—namely, data integrity, data protection, data consistency, and data presentation/storage (data isolation by customer, compatibility, implicit/explicit format conversion, and other issues such as managing unstructured/complex structured data). This necessitates a *data I/O framework* that, when implemented, translates to a best-practices strategy at the database Tier and/or the application Tier(s). Collaterally, the deployment options (such as exposing data as services, etc.) also contribute to some of these aspects, especially data presentation-isolation and data security.

This subsection describes these aspects in terms of *principles-as-best-practices* to be implemented at the database Tier of the solution architecture.

Key Indicators:

Implement a framework-by-design strategy that is reusable in terms of both rules and patterns, as well as their outcomes. The resulting framework can be deployed using options such as Web services and collaboration techniques as part of the process flow.

Leverage the power of the Oracle11g database and its in-built functionality to the fullest possible extent, not only in terms of SQL alone but also in terms of optimal database/data-centric foundation design, metadata design, computation (in-memory or in-database) and efficiency (high-performance and fault-proof).

Here's the list to start with:

- Derive business rules for data I/O, depending on the type of data (transactional or analytical) in Oracle11g. For transactional data, all aspects of data integrity, from uniqueness to eliminating redundancy to referential integrity (RI), should be considered. For analytical data, the RI rules can be omitted, as the data in the analytical database is already clean, quality data. This means the primary focus for business rules derivation of data should be on the user-perception of the same (this aligns with the logical data definitions in place). The typical methods to do this are:
    - Derive them based on the logical data model that's either stored in a data dictionary or a standard metadata definition file. This enables greater flexibility in adapting the rules obtained to fit into the embedded programming language space, as it is at a higher (or rather business-oriented conceptual) level.

- Mine them from the underlying third normal form (3NF) and/or dimensional data model.
- Refactor them into a rules engine based on business policies. The following subsection, "Enforcing Business Rules for Efficiency." discusses the best practices for the same.
- Implement these rules in the embedded programming solution, bypassing the database-level enforcement specific to the solution being architected in terms of data access and data sharing requirements.

- Derive appropriate rules for data accessibility by retro-analyzing the underlying data design model—purely relational, relational-and-OO, relational-and-dimensional, purely dimensional, or purely analytical; having a high-performance access design using clustering, partitioning, parallelization, session-specific, and instance-specific persistent stores such as projections/views, result-set caching, in-memory (custom) data grid, or IMDB cache—and synchronize the same with the embedded programming language capabilities in terms of exposing the data to the unified presentation layer and vice versa. This also decides the data sharing implementation inter- and intra-applications.

- Derive rules for data provisioning, data federation, and data fanning and funneling, as well as further analysis (drill-up/down, drill-thru, and drill-across), advanced analytics (e.g., descriptive, categorical, numerical, predictive) and custom-built analytics (including run-time analytics), data visualization, and end-user interactive metrics/computations.

These rules have to be derived and implemented in such a manner that they don't get hidden in the embedded code—the code for implementing these rules needs to be encapsulated and insulated, but the rules themselves should be inherently traceable. This approach helps in easing consolidation and migration and/or in extending/enhancing the architected solution for future business vis-a-vis IT needs.

- Do not build data-based silos; Doing this will in turn reduce application silos. Oracle11g provides powerful methods such as data and application integration, virtualization, and instant deployment across all access touch points that enable efficient application delivery.

- Provide consistent real-time data availability cross-data-consumers; that is, data that is both contextual and in the desired format at the same time. This means maintaining the data presented in a "current" state-can be real-time update of changed data as-is, and/or refreshing of in-store (fairly static) data-so that the end-user sees the most current data. An emerging approach is to provide an information-as-a-service strategy using data services that can accommodate both data access and integration. Oracle11g supports this using ODI or OWB (at the ETL/EL-T level) as well as using the Enterprise Grid that functions cross-solution-Tier.

- Enable right-time data sharing. As opposed to real-time or near real-time, right-time data sharing provides end-user access to data in information form that is consistent and most accurate, whenever it is needed, wherever it is needed, and by the right user who is authorized for the same. This functionality is akin to on-demand real-time access, the primary difference being that even already-stored data can be a part of this right-time data access in addition to real-time data (that mostly refers to data availability, as it is changed without any efficiency impact). There are multiple methodologies available to achieve this, including (but not limited to) data virtualization in real time using Data-as-a-Service, an Enterprise Information Integration (EII) solution capable of on-demand enterprise-wide data sharing, and right-time data integration that is both easy-to-implement and easy-to-access.

3.3.1   Enforcing Business Rules for Efficiency

If data integrity is a key factor in the solution involved, use trusted declarative constraints at the database level, as far as possible, to implement business rules that mandate data integrity. These are part of the entire solution/application security framework, which involves database security, application security, and network security. And database security involves data protection, which in turn ensures the protection of data integrity.

Nothing can beat the power of Oracle11g (and its SQL engine) when it comes to SQL-based data access/manipulation, and nothing can beat the declarative DB capabilities to enforce database controls (which are the database-equivalent of business rules) when it comes to data integrity.

The database needs its own layer of security, as does the application/solution. Network security is still needed, but it isn't sufficient to protect the database from unauthorized intrusions and changes.

3.3.2   Pre-emptive and Proactive Measures

Prescale the database in terms of data access, data storage and data loading by:

- Allocating the size by a factor of at least 10 of the current size
- Pre-tuning the database using Oracle11g's Self-tuning capabilities
- Automating table, index, and segment rebuild, reorganize, and fragmentation tasks for optimal performance, based on the transactional/analytical functionality of the solution/application in context
- Automating high-performance data access using partitioning, MVS, projections (IOTS or cluster-based), query and result-set caching (on the DB server, in-memory—e.g., in-memory database cache (IMDB cache), in-memory data grid (mostly tied to the application layer or client-side cache), and pipelined functions for data streaming (ETL, data pumps, Oracle streams)
- Automating error checking at the database schema level for server-related out-of-application errors (e.g., suspension of database activity and other resource-related fragmentation, defragmentation, etc.) as well as the data dictionary and database state and synchronization
- Designing and implementing a centralized metadata-based search and reporting service across all the enterprise database configurations that spans all levels of metadata, from the Oracle11g Data Dictionary to any custom-designed metadata layer (including XML metadata). This search-enabled functionality must accommodate all types of data involved, structured to unstructured, including data in collaboration, Web 2.0, and text, voice, and video types. In addition, this should be augmented by a separate (but integrated and transparent) meta-definition layer that holds the data movement processes such as workflow, monitoring, auditing, user-interaction captures etc.

Key Indicator:
All these meta-definitions are to be stored and managed inside of the Oracle11g DB.

3.3.3　Database Interaction: More than Just GB and Data Quality

This is one of the key challenges in any solution involving out-of-database interaction, including one that is based on embedded programming languages. The "must-have" practices in this regard are as follows:

- Use result (data) sets and data binds or bind variables for sharing between the database and the application, ensuring the accuracy of NULLS on the DB side as well as in the embedded language, defaults for NULLS, handling NULL, empty and blank (space) values.
- Never use a programming language variable for the actual *data* passed between the database and application Tier. This has to be done using bind variables. The former can be used only for dynamically passed schema object names.
- Always use Oracle REF CURSORs to share sets of rows (immaterial of whether bind variables are used or not). The interoperability of weak and strong REF CURSORs as well as that of data processed statically and/or dynamically (using arrays, collections, or otherwise) is facilitated by the Oracle11g feature set and its proper mapping to the embedded programming language environment to prevent any data loss or inaccuracy are focus points to be taken care of in this respect.
- Ensure that database interaction is not vulnerable to SQL injection attacks by parameterization of SQL statements and the like that involve user-input values, especially those that involving dynamic binding. A good example of this is validation of the user input login info against a database-implemented business rule based on FGAC policy or a data quality process in the overall implementation.
- Use data identifiers when merging similar and dissimilar data (ensuring the type-compatibility, data type collation, etc.). These enable linkage of the two while simultaneously preserving the

proper context and enabling easy storage/retrieval of the same between the DB to the application. This can be achieved by using NLP (natural language processing) techniques for multilingual databases, refining data by means of standardized data entry procedures, and scoping the latitude and longitude of data to the relevant business use—the right data for the right use at the right time (we shall call this the R-R-R rule, for convenience). For example, we can design metrics (both categorical and numeric) that can measure the upside of good data and mar the downside of bad data. Here, good and bad refer to R-R-R ability of the data. Oracle11g's Content Management Solution is a viable option to implement the above. This is discussed in more detail in Chapters 4 and 6.

■ Design a rich metadata model that acts as a mediator between the physical data source and the end-user access layer by hiding the technical complexities of the accessed data and exposing it a business-savvy, user-friendly format.

Remember that this is an additional metadata module solely for the purpose of information presentation and its plug-and-play use; it is more generic and reusable. This is different from the traditional metadata definitions included for MDM, Data Structure Design, and other business-specific definitions that require metadata storage specific to the customer-centric solution. Again the key indicator here is to store and manage both of them in-database.

3.4   Best Practices for using SQL and PL/SQL only (with HTML, XML via PSP or Web Toolkit)

The most obvious reason for using SQL and PL/SQL only, to architect an Oracle11g based end-to-end business solution is that the customer requirements mandate an Oracle-based solution. This can be for various reasons—perhaps the new solution is to augment an existing solution that is purely Oracle-based, and must either be codeployed or coexist with it. Perhaps a stand-alone solution is required to meet the specific requirements of a specific business/service functionality that doesn't exist at all.

The key usability indicator here is to apply SQL-PL/SQL in Java, .NET, HTML, and other Web-based environments that are Oracle-based.

The benefits of this are:

- Less integration work
- *Seamless operational flow and execution*—Oracle-to-Oracle nativity between the database and the presentation layers
- *High efficiency in terms of scalability, reliability, and performance*—inline, in-memory, and in-database execution of code without requiring platform-specific connectors, adapters, and API
- *Seamless replication and distribution*—by means of sub-databases or datasets without the overhead of intermediate code layers
- *A comprehensive Web 2.0-enabled IDE-based toolset*—for development and deployment. Examples include Oracle Developer Suite, Oracle ADF, Oracle DI Suite, Oracle APEX (for auto-generating applications directly from the IDE), and Oracle JDeveloper for object-based applications (even if they are pure PL/SQL-based)

Based on the above discussion, the best-fit scenarios for using SQL and PL/SQL only, as embedded programming languages in an Oracle-based solution can be listed as follows:

- An end-to-end business solution that is highly transaction intensive, data intensive, and business-logic intensive, and that needs to adhere to high availability and scalability standards and be GRC-enabled, but only needs to leverage the Web-enablement functionality to expose the presentation UI. This can be architected using Oracle11g's full-fledged rich set of features, using HTML/XML/Groovy for the Web interface layer via PL/SQL Server Pages (PSP) or the PL/SQL Web Toolkit, or calling Groovy Scripts directly from PL/SQL.
- A custom-built solution on top of the enterprise-wide one in place; an example of such a solution is one that can be exclusively tailored toward corporate/executive management to meet mission-critical and highly sensitive transactional and/or reporting needs and that is used for research and/or penetration of the business in order to advance to the next level.
- A solution based on the existing solution infrastructure that can be used for doing business as a hosted service. The new solution can derive all necessary input from the enterprise solution in place—be it data, business rules, or complex business metrics—but it is designed specifically for a particular segment of the business domain or user domain, and functions as an SaaS (Solution-as-a-Service). This can be designed using an Oracle11g-based Web-enabled solution and

cloud-based deployment (provided by a managed cloud services provider) or by building additional but simple and easy-to-use virtualized management layer for the same.

- Designing and developing code appliances that can be plugged (statically or dynamically) into other Oracle-based solutions (e.g., Java-, .NET-, or PHP/AJAX-enabled) and can run independently of the target environment. This greatly simplifies the custom-coding of generic business functionality for each target application and at the same time ensures *active-code* augmentation capability for implementing the underlying business logic.

Irrespective of the use-case scenario, the key design strategy is to build a solution that uses Oracle11g for the database Tier and Web-enable the same using an HTML/XML layer that takes care of the user access interface—and a touch of FLASH, if needed.

3.5   Extending PL/SQL to Use Emerging Dynamic Scripting Languages Like Groovy in the Database

Groovy is a dynamic, powerful, and highly flexible scripting language that can add a touch of interactivity or Flash to the user presentation interface. Using Groovy scripts directly from PL/SQL can be an innovative method to expose the database-inherent business logic for front-end user access.

Key focus points include:

- Compounded auto-code generation for testing multiple test-case scenarios
- Auto-creation of SQL and XML templates

3.5.1   Extending PL/SQL to Use HTML/XML

PL/SQL applications can be made globally accessible by deploying them on the Web. Web-enabling a PL/SQL application involves the use of HTML and/or XML and requires deployment using a Web server. Web-enabling PL/SQL essentially consists of coding PL/SQL subprograms (mostly encapsulated in a package) that generate Web content for backend and frontend application processing. This in turn involves generating the GUI using HTML/XML-enabled Web pages and generating the interaction logic for database processing and presentation. The client (typically a Web browser) interacts with the database over an HTTP communication channel. Traditionally, this is done using CGI, in which each HTTP request is handled by a new forked CGI process. Using PL/SQL over CGI eliminates these additional processes and also provides the ability to leverage the power and efficiency of the Oracle database in terms of features that can be used and the optimizations that can be done. PL/SQL in conjunction with HTML/XML can be used in one of two ways, embedded HTML/XML code in PL/SQL or embedded PL/SQL code in HTML/XML.

The code listings below specify the distinction between using the two methods.

Code that uses HTML in PL/SQL:

```
CREATE OR REPLACE PROCEDURE proc_html_in_plsql
IS
BEGIN
htp.p('<HTML>');
htp.p('<HEAD>');
htp.p('<TITLE>Customer Application</TITLE>');
htp.p('</HEAD>');
htp.p('<BODY>');
htp.p('<H1>Customer Information</H1>');
htp.p('<TABLE BORDER="1 ">');
htp.p('<TR><TH>Name</TH><TH>Long Name</TH></TR>');
FOR idx IN (SELECT c.cust_name, c.cust_long_name
FROM cust_tab c
ORDER BY c.cust_name ) LOOP
htp.p('<TR>');
htp.p('<TD>'||idx.cust_name||'</TD>');
htp.p('<TD>'||idx.cust_long_name||'</TD>');
htp.p('</TR>');
END LOOP;
htp.p('</TABLE>');
htp.p('</BODY>');
htp.p('</HTML>');
END;
/
```

Here's an example of code that uses PL/SQL in HTML:

```
<%@ page language="PL/SQL"%>
<%@ plsql procedure="proc_plsql_in_html_psp"%>
<HTML>
<HEAD>
<TITLE>Customer Application</TITLE>
</HEAD>
<BODY>
<H1>Customer Information</H1>
<TABLE BORDER="1 ">
<TR><TH>name</TH><TH>Long Name</TH></TR>
<%
FOR idx IN (SELECT c.cust_name, c.cust_long_name
FROM cust_tab c
ORDER BY c.cust_name ) LOOP
%>
<TR>
<TD> <%= idx.cust_name %> </TD>
<TD> <%= idx.cust_long_name %> </TD>
</TR>
<% END LOOP; %>
</TABLE>
</BODY>
</HTML>
```

The first method involves using HTML in PL/SQL by means of a generic API exposed via the PL/SQL Web toolkit. This approach generates HTML output (including dynamic HTML) that is executed on the Web client. A stored procedure written using the API is invoked as a URL (with parameters, if necessary) that is translated by the PL/SQL gateway and is processed to return database information combined with HTML to the client. This method is suited only for PL/SQL-intensive applications, because the HTML is generated from within PL/SQL code.

Note that most of the Web applications are highly HTML-intensive and mandate the use of dynamic content. This combined with the need to include the results of SQL queries and PL/SQL logic inside Web pages calls for a fast and convenient method to Web-enable a PL/SQL application. The second method of using PL/SQL in HTML is a key code design that can be adopted in this case. This method is done by embedding PL/SQL within HTML using special PL/SQL tags. This kind of Web page is called a

PL/SQL Server Page (PSP). PL/SQL is placed within special script tags known as PSP tags. These are similar to scriptlets in a Java Server Page with the only difference being that they are written in PL/SQL. A PSP can be written in HTML or XML.

The key performance indicator of using a PSP is that it enables inclusion of dynamic content within static HTML to produce cutting-edge Web pages. The dynamic content is generated using PL/SQL logic that is executed on the server-side (that is, the database server) when the PSP page is submitted by a Web browser. This is more powerful than dynamic HTML and also minimizes network roundtrips, thus increasing efficiency. The rich dynamic content gives more flexibility in Web-enabling the application.

Key aspects to focus on are:

- Page-sectioning and partitioning at run-time can be done using dynamic HTML and the dynamic "logic" content inclusion.
- Passing parameters from the Web client to the database can be done using HTML forms or URL links with hard-coded parameter values. The former is a rich and more flexible method that enables input validation and user selection.
- Parameter values can be reused by storing them in non-display elements in the HTML form or in cookies. The PL/SQL Web toolkit has API to set and get cookie information. An alternative to this is a database solution that involves storing these parameters in tables or PL/SQL structures. Concurrency issues must be taken into consideration when using this approach.
- SQL result-sets can be processed dynamically and returned to the Web client using these methods. The PSP technique adds more flexibility, as the output can be directly included in the enclosing HTML without any overhead.
- The Web-enabling process is a two-task process in which the HTML takes care of the presentation services and the underlying PL/SQL package takes care of the processing logic. This provides for inclusion of robust authentication logic of data being input to the subprograms including validation for missing, NULL, invalid, and outlier values. OUT parameters can be used internally within the PL/SQL layer, with the calling subprogram decoding the same

and then transferring the data to the Web client. Error messages from the PL/SQL code can be propagated to the Web client using the HTP.P procedure. However, the PL/SQL subprogram should ensure that effective exception handling is in place so as to prevent inadvertent calls to subsequent procedures or data manipulation operations from taking place.

- Unhandled exceptions in a PSP can be displayed on the Web client as an error PSP by including a definition in the original PSP using the errorPage attribute of the page directive. The current state of data in dynamic Web pages can be preserved by using hidden parameters.

- HTML pages generated by either of these methods can be invoked by external Web programs, such as JavaScript or CGI. Passing data between the various layers should be in strict conformity with SQL and PL/SQL requirements in terms of data type, parameter, and return value mappings.

- The choice whether to use HTML in PL/SQL or PL/SQL in HTML (via a PSP) is governed by the type of application being Web-enabled. If the application solution is HTML-intensive, use a PL/SQL Server Page. If it is PL/SQL-intensive, use HTML in PL/SQL. If the application to be Web-enabled requires a lot of dynamic content (especially database-dependent content) within static HTML, using a PSP provides the optimal solution. Even dynamic HTML cannot handle all cases of dynamic content to be embedded within PL/SQL. This is probably the biggest plus in choosing PSP over HTP. A PSP can be deployed with only the Web browser on the client, making it a handy and easy tool as a front-end for any database application. The inherent PL/SQL code can take care of all other interfacing, database processing, and interaction processes. This gains an edge over using the HTML in PL/SQL method.

- A PSP allows for PL/SQL code that is pluggable after the HTML has been generated. This makes it handy for its use with Web authoring tools, which mostly generate pure HTML. The HTP way of Web-enabling requires the HTML to be generated from existing PL/SQL code, which most Web authoring tools cannot interpret. However, the latter technique is a boon when converting existing PL/SQL applications to a Web-enabled mode.

3.5.2   Generating Web-Enabled PL/SQL Applications Using Oracle APEX/Oracle JDeveloper

This architecture enables integrating Oracle-DB functionality with dynamic Web content generation via dynamic HTML pages to generate a fully usable and scalable Oracle-based Web application that is SQL-PL/SQL based.

Oracle APEX (Application Express) is an IDE-cum-runtime-platform that enables custom solution generation by way of Data Services consumption using Web Services to integrate data/content from heterogeneous sources that can be DB-based (Oracle, MySQL, SQL Server, etc.) or external source based (Excel, Cloud deployments, etc.) and present it via a dynamically generated HTML-based Web page.

Oracle JDeveloper can be used to generate a Java-based Web-service that can be consumed to create a Data Service callable from any PL/SQL stored function.

Rich Internet applications (RIA) with High-Definition GUI can also be developed by incorporating Flash-based functionality, using simple yet robust client-side scripting such as Groovy Scripting, PHP/Ajax scripting, or JQuery.

3.6   Best Practices for Using .NET-Based Languages (C++, C#, J#)

Oracle11g embraces the .NET Framework for application development, including ADO.NET 2.0, the key data provider for the .NET Framework, which marries the database-based data management and the embedded programming language-based data management via a database-to-embedded language connectivity layer based on an established API and managed code. Each and every .NET-based application that uses Oracle11g as its primary data storage and manageability component needs bidirectional data interaction between the Oracle database and the application,, and use the implemented solution to achieve a better business value. The .NET Framework as such provides a host of embedded programming languages, from Visual Basic to C# (that is, C-, C++-based) to J# (that is, Java-based).

3.6.1   ODP.NET: More than Just ADO.NET Rehashed

- Use ODP.NET for an Oracle11g-based .NET solution to get the right value and right results for the right design

Oracle11g's native-managed .NET data provider called ODP.NET leverages the full potential of Oracle11g for optimal data access, management, and interaction, coupled with powerful SQL capabilities, to address issues from language-specific typed datasets, multiple sharable result sets, and discontinuous data to concurrency, multi-tenancy, high availability, and fine-grained security.

Additionally, using ODP.NET provides a tighter integration (and hence implicit and enhanced tighter control) of the managed code with Oracle11g eliminating issues of data type mismatch (native versus language specific); inline execution of .NET code within the Oracle11g database (via .NET stored procedures that allow a mix-and-match of SQL, PL/SQL, XML, and C# code, the use of REF CURSORs and client-side result-set caching for optimal large scale data access and share-ability); enhanced application security using proxy authentication, client identifiers, and parameterization to prevent SQL Injection attacks; and pre-emptive locking to avoid database deadlock.

3.6.2 Leverage J2EE Inherent Server-Specific Benefits with Minimal Cost and Time-to-Deliver

- Use .NET-based embedded programming languages for a solution that involves, to a large extent, augmenting solutions based on the component object model (COM)/distributed component object model (DCOM). Typical situations include building an extension solution component (to be embedded in an existing enterprise-wide IT environment) to cater to extended/enhanced business needs; or a solution that must co-exist alongside an existing solution but needs to be COM/DCOM-enabled.
- Consider .NET-based embedded programming languages for a solution that needs to be delivered at multiple end-use touch-points in context. A good example is a RIA that needs to be deployed as Solution-as-a-Service (using SOA/Web Services), or for on-the-go usage (mobile platform endpoint) that needs to run on Microsoft platforms.

Based on the above criteria, the best-fit scenarios for using .NET-based languages in embedded programming solutions can be listed as follows:

1.   Develop solutions that are Microsoft platform–specific and mandate scalability, a rich UI, and desktop activity—at the database, in the application/mid-level, and on the presentation/UI Tiers. This approach gives a 100-percent managed .NET solution.

2.   Develop solutions that need to be .NET-enabled, which leverages the best of both worlds: heterogeneous, cross-platform interoperability as well as integration of non-.NET-based applications, such as J2EE and so forth, as well as PC desktop enablement. This approach gives a hybrid SOA-.NET solution.

The result is a best-of-breed solution that has true "thin-client" capability for the end user that involves only server and browser; everything in between is eliminated or remains transparent, depending on the implementation.

There are several design strategies to do this:

- Architect an entirely customer-focused solution, as follows:

  Database Tier→Application Tier(s)→Presentation Tier
  ←Oracle11g-based J2EE-enabled→←.NET-enabled object→
  ←Oracle11g DB, Oracle WebLogic Server→←via Web services→

- Using Oracle11g .NET stored procedures is a good technique to leverage this functionality.
- Define code wrappers for the supplemental applications using .NET-enabled "managed" code, and expose them via SOA-enabled Web services. The supplemental applications usually sit on top of the "foundation" (i.e., non-.NET based) application/solution. This is a best-fit for solutions that require the extension of the pre-existing "foundation" solution.
- Componentize the application (code) to be .NET enabled (either supplemental or extracted from the "foundation") so that it is interoperable for execution with the non-.NET based language code implementation. The .NET-enabled component is exposed via Web services. For example, .NET-enabling COM/DCOM (or J2EE) objects, enables leveraging the high-potential of Microsoft SharePoint collaboration functionality. This means the "foundation" application can still be run on a UNIX platform and be J2EE- or non-.NET based, leveraging the full-range high-scale benefits of the same while exposing the more-specific module of

the application on a Microsoft Windows platform to get the end user's desired benefit. And all of this is transparent to the user.

Oracle11g supports both of these functionality using Oracle SOA-enabling and .NET-enabling techniques.

Key Indicators:

•The development, deployment, and integration scenario of the target customer
•Seamless interoperability (EAI, EII, EPM, etc.)
•Customer-focused factors, such as the type of solution desired (supplement an existing "foundation" solution? build a new one? buy an out-of-the-box (OOB) solution and extend?). In the buy-and-extend scenario, .NET enabling the "extend" part saves extra coding required for the additional bells and whistles involved in the extension. Simply componentizing the "to-be-extended" code by extracting it from the OOB solution and exposing it via Web services does the job. This is quite a common case for Tier-1 solutions implemented using industry-standard technologies such as Java/J2EE or for legacy applications that need to use the emerging industry-standard .NET framework for whatever purpose.
•Rich enterprise applications imply rich Internet applications that in turn call for a rich Java presentation interface (using Web 2.0, etc.), a rich .NET presentation interface (using .NET Windows Presentation Framework or WPF, for example), or a rich custom presentation layer. This can be standardized into a unified presentation interface.

3.7 Best Practices for Using Java-Based Languages (Java Libraries, Java via JDBC, Java via SQLJ, Java via Java Stored Procedures)

The power of Java is in its inherent support for heterogeneous and platform-agnostic or OS-agnostic applications. This adaptability proves to be a great asset in leveraging Java (inside and outside the database) for cross-platform integration of custom applications in Java.

Other key suitability indicators for using Java are:

- A greater degree of scalability and reliability, compared to the other embedded languages (e.g., .NET-based C# or PHP/Ajax, etc.). Java scales almost linearly with the Oracle DB and at the application and data levels.
- Oracle11g application infrastructure middleware is primarily Java-based (e.g., Oracle ADF, Oracle JDeveloper, Oracle SOA Suite, etc.).

Based on these facts, the best-fit scenarios for using Java as an embedded language in Oracle-based solutions can be described as follows:

- *Web applications that need to be Oracle-based* and are not restricted to a particular language implementation, as long as the business functionality and state-of-the-art user interface requirements are met. These applications can leverage the high performance potential of both Oracle11g and Java to target a huge user base, which in turn goes a long way towards improving the "business value" of the solution. Such applications can be deployed in any Java-supported OS platform, including Windows, and have the ability to scale to the optimal extent. Both Java and Oracle offer a rich set of business solution functionality, with (distributed) transactional support (e.g., using Application Grid technologies), powerful messaging and transport services (Java Messaging Services (JMS) and Enterprise Service Bus (ESB)), Web Services, and dynamic GUI (via Oracle's ADF components, BC4J Framework, or Java's JSF). *Oracle11g's native compiler for Java is at least 10 times faster than ever and this offers both nativity and managed code in the Oracle-Java environment.*
- *Existing Oracle-based solutions running on multiple operating systems* (like UNIX, Linux, Windows, etc., as well as mainframe) can leverage Java to augment additional functionality (business logic, processes, and/or data/information) using custom Java codelets that can be exposed as Java-based Web services, which are reusable across the end-to-end enterprise. *This hot-pluggable integration makes Java a more suitable embedded programming language of choice.*
- *Large enterprise applications involving multi-Tiers*, like ERP systems or EAI solutions) can be good candidates for using Java with

Oracle11g to gain a wide range of functionality that can include module augmentation, business process implementation, or services-based "anytime, anywhere, anyone" accessibility.

- As a real-world use case, using Java with SQL-PL/SQL for an Oracle-based solution enables the enterprise-based solution to communicate with existing backend applications such as billing and accounting, as Java excels in performance and functionality on the hardware, OS, and application Tiers and hence can better handle a variety of functional/provisioning capabilities by mimicking the existing solution architecture.

- Java can also be used to build custom "application-server" simulators for enterprise or other Oracle-based solutions, to provide interfacing functionality between back-end core solution(s) and front-end Web-enabled clients (such as portals, etc.), thereby enabling interapplication communication, collaboration, and management. All this can be done, no matter what the OS and overall solution environment(s) are. This way, the in-place solution can have easy and efficient access to the server-side business logic and data—especially when it needs to be exposed to external client environments (e.g. over the Internet or via a wireless-enabled device or non-Java client application).

- A good use case is to design a smart code accelerator by embedding Java in SQL-PL/SQL. Real-world scenarios are:
  - Apply the power of Java to tackle complex business logic (enhanced verification and validation).
  - Dynamically mash-up unstructured data and/or external content, such as Google Maps, XML-based content or Visual Data elements, to enable unified information delivery in a seamless and DB-efficient manner. The use of data objects based on JPA entities enables in-database Java persistence, and the mash-up can be done by querying the same using the Java Persistence Query Language (JPQL) along with native SQL and XML-XSLT.

Build Smart Code Design Frameworks, akin to ODI KMs, that use declarative design strategies and arrive at reusable, adaptable, and flexible code design framework or patterns tailored towards a particular functionality. This code can mix/merge SQL, PL/SQL, Java, etc. and scripting languages such as Perl, Python, JavaScript, and so on.

The key focus points are:

- An open and standards-based architecture based on a multitiered design
- Less integration work to be done and with less cost too, especially when the solution in context needs to interact with existing applications developed in other Java/non-Java environments
- The automatic memory management feature of Java, which enables efficient and less memory usage in the application-Tier that is Java-based
- The Java language and its associated Frameworks, which are strong in the areas of high scalability and ability to handle very high-volume transaction applications. Oracle11g-based Java solutions derive the in-built efficiency and robustness of session management, automatic memory management, fail-over, load balancing, and cross-OS application integration on the Oracle DB side as well on the "native and managed" Java side, and all of this being transparently managed under-the-hood
- The ability of Oracle-based Java applications (either using Java in SQL-PL/SQL or Java calling SQL-PL/SQL code) to be scalable and high performing on the Web, not only from the application standpoint but also from the data/information standpoint (the code is IDE and application-server agnostic)
- Processing and/or transformations involving high-volume transactional data, such as ETL or operational data integration, that can be more securely and efficiently managed in Java, especially if it involves enterprise-wide usability
- The messaging services of Java, which are powerful to support any messaging mechanism, including publish-and-subscribe, thus eliminating the need to be tied to a particular messaging process, still capitalizing on the benefits of co-ordination, standards-based and compliance (in fact, Java Messaging Services (JMS) can be used in conjunction with SOAP to improve the efficiency and scalability of Java-based Web Services, as opposed to using HTTP and SOAP)
- The key benefit of a seamless process flow across heterogeneous platforms for portal based information delivery, personalization of applications (like self-services coupled with real-time information availability) in mission-critical and dedicated situations

The key indicator here is that Oracle and Java provide a more flexible and dynamic management architecture for OS-platform and integration independence in terms of hardware, software, applications and/or services; customer-adaptability; scalability (across user base and processing complexity/volume) and performance, that are highly essential for server-side processing as opposed to the client-side.

3.7.1 Using Java via JDBC, SQLJ, Java Stored Procedures or Java Libraries

Using Java via JDBC is an essential requirement for Oracle-based data access to and from Java applications. JDBC is a standardized database connectivity API that provides bidirectional data interaction between the Oracle DB and the Java-coded application/solution, whether it runs inside or outside of the DB. Generally Java via JDBC is used to call SQL-PL/SQL code from Java-based code. Java via Java Stored Procedures involves SQL-PL/SQL code calling Java classes or libraries. Java via SQLJ involves an OCI API to embed SQL-PL/SQL code within Java code.

The key deciding factors are:

- The type of SQL statement being executed
- How data is to be transported to and from the application Tier to the Database Tier via the Data Access driver (i.e., JDBC in this case)
- Whether an additional Oracle-specific client-side driver like OCI is involved (the best practice is to avoid one as far as possible)
- Whether the embedded data access code is fully managed by the database

These in turn determine the efficiency of data access, processing, and delivery in terms of overall throughput, response time, data delivery to the presentation layer, scalability, and ease of deployment.

The best practices in terms of using What-When-Why are listed below:

- Use Java Stored Procedures...
  - *When there is a need for data access and processing that is data-rich, as it can benefit from efficient execution of code that is SQL-intensive.* The greatest advantage of this is that it helps in

decoupling data access (involving SQL) from complex business logic (involving Java code).

- *To extend database functionality not available or not efficient when done using PL/SQL.* As Java implements a safer type system, automatic memory management, dynamic polymorphism, inheritance, and robust multithreading and messaging, the complexities involved in the extension process can be managed more efficiently using Java code running inside the Oracle DB. As a use case, using Java Stored Procedures to build a robust 360-degree messaging module (e.g., e-mailing (including e-mail archiving), queuing, etc.) based on JMS Framework within the SQL-PL/SQL environment enables greater productivity of the application from a functionality perspective and tighter integration with the database.
- Always specify the Java class as public and its methods as public static when defining a Java stored procedure.
- Use fine-grained access control when accessing resources outside of the database, such as operating system files from external stored procedures.
- Use Java via JDBC to call SQL-PL/SQL stored code from within Java applications.
  - Always use Oracle's native Java JDBC API, as these are designed for optimized code compilation and execution and do not necessitate the overheads of type conversion for identifiers (eliminating type mismatch), performance-centric result-set retrieval, calling PL/SQL stored procedures from Java code, and so on.
  - Always use bind variables for formal data parameters in both embedded SQL statements and stored subprograms This ensures SQL statement re-use and also eliminates extra parsing.
- Using Java via SQLJ involves an additional Oracle OCI driver and requires the corresponding client libraries to be installed. The data flow is routed via the OCI driver to the JDBC driver that sits on top of it, and this in turn involves latency, thus decreasing the throughput. This process has a direct impact on scalability. SQLJ is a good choice when the embedded solution needs to interface with existing SQLJ code in which the core business functionality has been implemented.

No matter what the method of Java connectivity and interaction with the Oracle database is, here are some powerful practices that can enhance the application efficiency, scalability and productivity:

- Use database resident connection pooling in conjunction with statement pooling.
- Configure connection pooling with re-authentication.
- Use delegated authorization combined with localized authentication.
- Use bind variables for data parameters to enable statement reuse and enhance compilation and/or execution performance.
- Use Oracle JVM that has been optimized for Java execution in 11g.
- Disable the auto-commit mode as far as possible.
- Enforce row-level security at the DB and the cache levels. This makes the solution highly secure, which in turn boosts the reliability and productivity of the same.
- Tune the SQL-PL/SQL code for optimized access/update functionality so as to enable Oracle-based RPC execution, as opposed to Oracle-based native statement execution. This eliminates re-parsing, statement preparation and type conversions. This can be done by the use of bind variables and the appropriate method of calling the SQL-PL/SQL code based on the type and nature of the statement being called (e.g. Prepare Statement, Execute Immediate, Execute as a Procedure, Execute using array processing etc.).

3.8   Best Practices for Using PHP-Based Languages (PHP-only, PHP and Ajax, PHP Web Pages)

The convergence of PHP and Oracle11g is a best-of-breed combination of using open source scripting languages with a proprietary database like Oracle. PHP extends the capabilities of Oracle11g to enable powerful and dynamic scripting using open source embedded language programming. The standard PHP extensions to Oracle allow for using the PHP Web Framework to generate scripts for dynamic execution on the Web Interface Layer.

The strongest points in favor of choosing PHP are:

- The ease of use of Web PHP Framework, in terms of its flexibility along with its business-IT friendly open source–based licensing terms

■   A rich-feature set for building Rich Internet Applications RIA) based on Oracle DB that can support the enterprise-level demands without compromising on the security of the overall solution

The case for use cases of an Oracle11g- and PHP-based embedded solution can be based on the following:

■   To build enterprise Oracle DB applications that can run in Web environments and use dynamic interfaces for the UI layer. The rich set of PHP scripting functionality and the high performing func-tionality of Oracle11g DB can be married to achieve direct integra-tion and interoperability of complex business logic being made persistent in the Oracle DB and exposed as a RIA via web-enable-ment using PHP.

■   To create rapid and robust application accelerators for dynamic Web interface enhancement of Oracle-based Web-enabled solu-tions that can be reused and easily embedded and deployed. A good real-world example of this is *Ajax-ifying PHP to expose complex objects mapped to Oracle relational structures to the UI Web browser, in a seamless and transparent manner in conjunction with XML.*

■   Taking the declarative capabilities of Web programming and scripting to a next level by using PHP to build declarative list-based selection and drill-down lists, extending the Web interface with partial page refresh, page templates (for a consistent look-and-feel), interactive user navigation (using Ajax if required), and automation of these on the fly—that goes a long way, not only in enabling UI reuse, but also in enriching the end-user experience.

The key focus points are:

■   Tuning the connection parameters in terms of choosing the data access driver closest to the Oracle DB for native support as well as management. The Oracle11g PHP driver and the Oracle-PHP Zend Server are good choices. This means using the oci_pconnect() call in the PHP code for connecting to the Oracle DB allows for optimal scalability. Note that even though there is an OCI call involved, the oci_pconnect() via the PHP_OCI8 driver has been optimized for optimized data access with in-built performance-cen-tric features like DRCP (database resident connection pooling), statement caching, statement pre-fetching using a default array size that can be tuned (similar to fetch array size in SQL-PL/SQL), FAN-based event notification, use of privileged connections using off-DB authentication like OS-authentication, and so on.

The Oracle11g-PHP Zend Server can be used in enterprise environments to enhance existing Web UI by PHP-Ajax, enabling them to provide a full-featured Web 2.0 compliant UI layer while at the same time ensuring the high-performance and security required. This provides a plug-and-play out-of-box PHP intermediate layer to Oracle-based applications that can reside on Windows or Linux OS without affecting the core enterprise solution platform.

- Enable DRCP for persistent connections and statement caching.
- Enforce row-level security at the DB and the cache levels.
- Enable page caching for URL-based caching of HTML output and diagnostics, either programmatically or automatically using Zend Server. This is a huge performance benefit for PHP pages that are dynamically generated by *increasing the Request-Response throughput—one of the primary reasons for using PHP*. Using page-wise custom caching rules adds to this benefit, as the cached pages can also be compressed during creation.
- An Oracle-based PHP application can communicate with Java code using a Java code adapter that acts as a bridge between PHP and Java. If using the Zend server, this can be enabled by installing the Zend Java Bridge during the installation process.

3.9   Perl in the Picture: Best Practices for the Perfect Fit and Use of Perl in an Embedded Scenario

The perfect fit scenario of using Perl in an embedded solution is as an intermediate language to auto-generate SQL/PL/SQL and the embedded language (Java, .NET, PHP) code. This is very useful in implementing code-appliances that either accelerate or enhance the functionality in context.

Other real-world application best fits for Perl are:

- Using Perl to automate access and management tasks via prebuilt Perl scriptlets
- Using Perl to achieve open extensibility and multitenancy:

- Automating the job and process scheduling tasks, for example, for configuration and deployment. This can help in accelerating deployment of solutions as also re-using the scripts for additional similar deployments
- Pre-emptive error resolution and prevention or the ability to pre-identify potential error spots using Perl scripts built out-of-box. This can aid in eliminating (re-)coding of custom scripts and run-time variables oriented expressions. Perl scripts can also be used to automate the reporting of error-notification via alerts, error-resolution, and diagnostics. These are very useful when used as input baselines for error diagnostics during the debugging, testing, auditing, lineage measurement, and services-enablement processes

3.10   For Better or Worse: Application-centric and Business-centric Key Performance Indicators

3.10.1   Focus on the Customer

- Deliver a user-friendly and business-savvy solution. A *best-fit solution* is better than the "best" solution, from a business/customer standpoint.
- Results are key—business value, business performance, and solution performance. You must deliver more with a solution that costs less, is simple to implement, and is faster than before (this equates to the promise of better business value).
- *Key BPI (business performance indicator)*—Choose specifics that are vital to a superior customer experience and best-fit business agility, and incorporate them in the solution architecture: Start with a design based on the user perception of the solution, and let this determine the functionality/technology/methodology to be used.
- Application Adaptability, Functionality, Manageability, Reliability
- Application Usability:
  - Build once, deploy multiple times (on-premise), used by single/multiple users
  - Build once, deploy once (on-demand as a pure hosted SaaS), used by multiple users
  - Build once, deploy multiple times (on-demand, but having a solution-as-a-service capability—that is, both SaaS-enabled

and SaaS-enabling, so that the solution is hot-pluggable or embeddable into other SaaS-based or on-premise solutions), used by multiple users/multiple times.

The build phase can be onsite in some situations; this poses a challenge to obtaining the B-B-B solution. The key indicator here is the reduction of the TCO across the Oracle11g (Database) and Application Development tools employed to build the customer-specific solution.

3.10.2   Application-Centric

Seamless Integration between Enterprise IT Services and Applications

The business agility criterion for solution architecture calls for a seamless integration of applications and the corresponding processes/services driving these applications across the enterprise. This necessitates a flexible, scalable, and distributed integration framework for the same, in terms of a transparent mediation/communication platform that is persistent, pervasive, and at times intermittent; it takes care of the data movement, connectivity, transaction management, and clickstream-like messaging, as well as the monitoring and managing of the implemented framework, ensuring fine-grained security across all applications spanning the IT enterprise.

This can be achieved using an enterprise service bus (ESB), which provides a connecting arc between enterprise applications (existing, legacy) and enterprise services, leveraging a best-of-breed architecture based on emerging technologies and methodologies (e.g., SOA-based Web services, messaging, etc.) to deliver optimal business-IT agility, not only from an integration standpoint but also from an services orchestration and design pattern perspective.

Benefits include:

- Seamless application-to-application and application-to-end user touchpoint integration and synchronization
- Ability to launch/interface with external applications on the fly

EPM-Enabled Solution

EPM-enabled solutions are the convergence of information management and performance management as a framework for unification of business and IT for business (streamlining business processes, information and technology processes across the enterprise to achieve the B-B-B).

Benefits include:

- Integration of disconnected and heterogeneous transactional data sources and/or applications
- Consolidation of multiple databases and/or applications
- Both of the above being performed as a continuous process

Continuous Complex Event Monitoring, Notification, and Handling (including Auditing of the Same)

Oracle calls this Complex Event Processing and Business Activity Monitoring. It involves the tracking and notification of business user activity in terms of event occurrence end-to-end—that is, Oracle11g database-initiated events, events triggered from the application Tier, architecture-related events (including those that are infrastructure-related), and events initiated by user-interaction.

Key Indicators:

The continuous monitoring, notification and auditing of events and processes is needed to improve operational efficiency as well as provide business continuity.

The get-more-for-less business-IT paradigm is a key player in cause-effect application issues. Putting in place a robust problem-solution framework that has the minimal impact on the architected solution as well as on the end user can be at least one of the best-fit resolutions.

Information and Data End-to-End

This is especially important for solutions involving mashed up data content that is mission-critical.

- Databases and data management
- Data integration
- Data migration
- Data quality

- Data enhancements, which are useful for custom analysis-enhancing, or refining, of existing data to gain business insight in terms of decision-making (data-driven decision making and automating the same), expanding the data breadth, and identifying subviews at a detailed/more granular level
- Data federation
- Master data management
- Data governance
- Metadata management
- Multimodal data operation (OLTP, OLAP, online predictive mining)
- Data visualization
- Real-time, right-time data streaming
- Enterprise ETL (data loading [ETL, EL-T], taking into account data breadth, data upload frequency, and data update frequency)
- Data analysis (including anonymous and unified business dimension–linked longitudinal analysis)
- MDX-based analysis (for analyzing multidimensional data using Oracle Objects for OLE-DB and/or XML/A)
- Data modeling, visual data modeling, and data visualization

Efficient Data Archiving and Recovery for VLDB

Keeping transactional data online once closed is expensive, impractical, and often risky. Furthermore, rapidly growing data and document volumes quickly cause system performance and productivity to plummet, frustrating users.

Solutions include:

- Solution virtualization end-to-end—more than just a cost-saving measure
- Solution remote deployment and management—managed services, hosted services, SaaS-enabling capabilities (pluggable into existing pure hosted and/or stand-alone applications), cloud-based SaaS, and automation and/or streamlining of the management of these.

See Figure 3.1 for a typical Oracle 11g-based solution scenario.

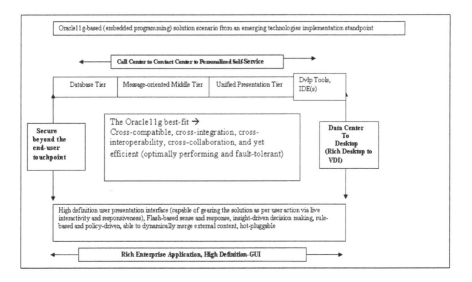

Figure 3.1   Typical Oracle11g-based (embedded-programming) solution scenario..

Summary

This chapter described the best practices in terms of "what to do" and "based on what" criteria for the various embedded programming language–based Oracle11g solution architectures. Stressing the fact that architecture is the key to any solution to be put into practice, the sections that followed highlighted the primary criteria to consider while determining the suitability and right choice of an embedded programming language, from SQL and PL/SQL to those that are .NET based, Java-based, and PHP-based, and also identifying ways that Perl can help in this scenario. The last section is an asset to this chapter and lists the key application-specific and business-specific indicators involved in the overall determination.

Chapter 4

Best Practices for Data Structure Management

In this Chapter

- Data representation: database versus programming language perspectives
- Best practices for using heterogeneous data structures: arrays, array lists, lists, maps, enumerations
- Best practices for using LINQ to objects (in Oracle11g)
- Best practices for using objects as data structures
- Best practices for metaprogramming: use or eliminate

4.1 Introduction

Data structure management plays a primary role in managing data from the time the data is captured until it is transformed into presentable information, and it becomes a key driving factor for the efficiency of the (enterprise) solution being architected. As part of data integration or otherwise, data structure contributes a lot to the way changes are made in the database via applications. The proper selection of data structures and their use for the synchronization of data management optimizes the efficiency of the application. The union of co-existent technologies and deployment platforms calls for a "solution for coexistence" (e.g., using SOA-based services) for data management, that in turn escalate to efficient data structure architecture.

Data treated as services, especially for exception handling at the application and database levels; transaction auditing and logging user activity/business activity—including audit activity—by the second; and event streaming are all part of application streaming, which includes data streaming in real time. Using functions that are callable from any programming language to enable group policy–based security in addition to row- and column-based security contributes to the big picture of the solution framework and a unified computing platform. An emerging and next-generation scenario that exemplifies this is the collaboration of cloud computing and the consolidation of data management and integration (which reroutes implicitly to data structure management), including but not limited to data federation, data masking, and enhanced data encryption. And all of these depend on the data structure as a major factor for data definition to achieve optimal data access, manipulation, integration, and management.

A solution architecture suited for efficient business functioning of the database can be based on the following aspects:

- A unified solution framework that involves a unified architecture framework, a unified integration framework, and a unified presentation framework from the standpoint of anyone-anytime-anywhere accessibility without compromising on efficiency and productivity, and has the ability for SOA enablement as well as having SOA-enabling capability so that it is embeddable in any existing SOA-based services platform.
- The foundation for such a solution calls for a data management framework in line with the infrastructure management, capable of on-demand data services and portability. *Data structures are the design foundation for data* and play a critical role in the architecture of the data management framework.
- *The coordination and synchronization of the data flow depends on how the code is written—security of data depends on security of code,* and this in turn propagates to the security of the whole solution being architected. *The primary indicator is to use solution accelerators composed of code accelerators that encapsulate efficient data structure design. This gives optimal code performance in terms of modularity and ability to handle high-volume data flows—which in turn ensures that structured information is available at the right time at the right place for the right user.* Oracle11g database high-performance and high-availability features of group policy invocation; column-based fine-grained access control; encryption at the tablespace level (as of 11gR2), which enables an entire application to be encrypted in one pass; fine-grained dependency control; implicit design; and self-tuning capabilities can accelerate data optimization. The best practice is to design the data flow in sync with the business process flow, so that it not only aligns in terms of IT processes but also provides business continuity, eliminating the need for IT intervention in the long run. This adds to an ideal solution technology infrastructure flow, all the way up to the end-user presentation

layer for data availability and access. Oracle11g provides some of the greatest and largest technologies, such as enterprise data integration, application integration architecture, enterprise performance management, enterprise service bus, and so on, to implement this.

- One of the key design indicators is easing the data practices implemented to be extensible across the enterprise. Here, "enterprise" means the business space of the solution being architected, in terms of usability and requirements, high data availability, and flexibility for collaborating with existing applications. *Using appropriate data structures helps a lot in creating modular embedded code accelerators that can be plugged in on demand without affecting the existing in-place applications and solutions.* This capability contributes toward providing a superior customer experience from a solution standpoint as well as a user standpoint in the business domain.

The primary goal is to present data that becomes meaningful as information, and at the same time simpler to integrate more quickly, for the end user to play with it. This aids in the users' ability to drive decision-making based on the data. The user interactivity so involved helps drive the business functionality based on the data, turning discovered data into actionable information for current and future use.

Combining solution and infrastructure components to enable an extremely flexible architecture requires the convergence of Platform-as-a-Service and Infrastructure-as-a-Service in the design of a custom solution Software-as-a-Service; this approach provides a 360-degree fit in terms of a superior customer experience and business requirements.

The other aspect is integrating high-volume unstructured data, such as video, audio, and click-stream data, and propagating it in a streaming fashion for the right data–right time–right user accessibility.

4.2   Data Representation: Database versus Programming Language Perspectives

The representation of data in a database (Oracle11g) and in a programming language structure (like Java, C, C++, C#, etc.) can be analyzed using the following criteria:

1. The type of data to be represented

    ■ Single type data versus multiple type data
    ■ Structured versus unstructured data
        ■ Structured types [numeric, character, date, time, Boolean, etc.]
        ■ Unstructured types [textual (ASCII, Binary), geospatial, multimedia and content-based (video, music, image, graphics), multidimensional]
        ■ Complex Structured types [hierarchical data, unstructured data "flattened" into a single type like XML type, etc.]
    ■ Linear versus nonlinear (composed of multiple data types in a single value) [arrays, lists, etc.]

2. How the data is stored

    ■ Persistent versus transient
    ■ Flattened "table" row/column representation
    ■ Support for non-atomic and heterogeneous data in a row/column cell
    ■ Creation of the data structure (table) using SQL DDL

3. How the data is accessed/updated (create-retrieve-update-delete, or CRUD, operations)

    ■ Using a unified standards-based relational database management system (RDBMS) language (SQL) for DML, DQL operations
    ■ Using programming languages alone (3GLS like C, object-oriented programming languages [OOPLs] like C++, Java, C#, etc.)
    ■ Using a hybrid method by means of language-based interfaces that extend the functionality of SQL 4GL to enable 3GL and OOPLs to interoperate with each other for CRUD operations on data as well as on data structures.

4. How the data can be presented for end-user access: *The primary indicator here is how meaningfully the data (regardless of its format) can be transformed into information that will enable the end-user to derive insight on what the data represents and how useful it is for further business use.*

Data stored and processed in-database is very efficient. This efficiency in turn cascades to data structures that are resident in the database and operated upon in the database. This approach requires a common language interface for both the database and programming language data structures, and hence for the data to be stored/processed/operated upon. One of the key indicators in choosing data structures is how the contained data is used. As an example, to store nonobvious relationships between data such as social text aggregations, we need a semistructured or complex structured data structure with a flex-field component.

Taking into account the above stated analyses' criteria and the key efficiency indicator, Table 4.1 explains data representation and storage from an Oracle11g DB and embedded programming languages perspective:

Table 4.1   Data Representation and Storage: Database versus Programming Language

	Oracle11g database	Embedded Programming Languages
Type of data	Structured, semistructured, unstructured, multi-representational (linear, nonlinear,), binary, multimedia, rich format data	All of the types that an Oracle11g database supports.
How the data is stored	All of the data residing in the database is stored in "flat" row/column format table structures that are native to the Oracle11g DB. This is true even for storing "object" data (storing data and its associated behavior), semi-structured data, unstructured data, etc., that is also leveled to a flat table row/column format. These follow either a totally relational model or an ORM (object relational mapping) model. Any (portion of) data outside the limits of in-data	In language-specific storage data structures like structures, unions, enumerations, arrays (in C/C++), Objects, classes and inheritance constructs in OOPLs (C++, Java, C#, J#), XML Types, and other special types. As OS files that are mostly portable across OSs. As managed or unmanaged object components that provide greater flexibility and interoperability between heterogeneous applications.

Table 4.1   Data Representation and Storage: Database versus
Programming Language (continued)

	Oracle11g database	Embedded Programming Languages
How the data is stored (cont)	base table storage is stored in either a different segment or in an OS file. For object data and nested data (data within data), the in-database table structure is abstracted to a higher logical level to create the object that can store methods for behavior of the object too. And a different category of data structures called collections enables storage of linear and nonlinear multi-type and multidimensional data using Associative Arrays, Nested Tables, and Variable Arrays. And "rich-format" data, such as text, multimedia, and geospatial data is stored in Large Objects (LOBS) and/or specific text, XML, and geospatial formats. The data residing in databases is highly persistent in terms of retaining the created data for almost any amount of time, unless it is deleted or otherwise lost. The database method for CRUD operations is based on transaction management, optimized data access by leveraging optimized data structure design, and ensuring implicit (declarative or nonprocedural) database (both data structure and data) security, integrity, consistency, concurrency, maintainability, monitoring,	The data in these cases is mostly transient as opposed to the continuous persistence offered by databases. The programming language way of ensuring the same criteria for CRUD operations involves a lot of coding, either manually or using IDE. The key differentiator here is the power of the programming language to leverage the potential of UML and a "true" object-oriented based Model to create a highly flexible, easier and efficient application system. Even if a programming language doesn't support the type of objects a particular application

Table 4.1   Data Representation and Storage: Database versus
Programming Language (continued)

	Oracle11g database	Embedded Programming Languages
How data is accessed/ updated (CRUD operations)	and tuning, thus providing a greater degree of reliability and accuracy with minimal external management. The robust transaction, analytics, and performance management potential (in-memory - IMDB cache, Flash cache (in 11gR2), in-database, or a hybrid approach) of an RDBMS coupled with the extreme flexibility of objects help an ORDBMS-based data and data structure storage, access, and management gain the leading edge over non-database-based "pure" (embedded) language applications. To achieve the 360-degree flexibility of "true" object orientation, one has to resort to an object-oriented DBMS, wherein object orientation is an inline feature of the data model itself, based on which the database design model is derived. An ORDBMS like Oracle11g, though, supports OOP features by means of user-defined types, methods, functions, and inheritance; it is still based on the relational model of an RDBMS at its core, but only extending/ exposing it to achieve a certain "level of abstraction" of object orientation. This object support in the DB merges the programming capabilities of OOPLS and the DB capabilities of persistent storage of un-structured/object data in	needs, the "object" approach is flexible enough (in fact, it is more flexible) to handle these use cases. 1. Programming languages can be used alone (3GLs like C, OOPLs like C++, Java, C#) for applications that do not require to interact with a back-end database. 2. A universal data transport language like XML (that preserves the semantics of the data in addition to the data itself) can be used, but is constrained to an XML DTD/ Schema, as is the case with Oracle11g. 3. A specific or unified framework-based API can be used, such as Java J2EE Framework API, .NET Framework API, and code wrappers that allow seamless communication between them.

Table 4.1   Data Representation and Storage: Database versus
Programming Language (continued)

	Oracle11g database	Embedded Programming Languages
How data is accessed/ updated (CRUD opera-tions) (cont)	native DB format and uses SQL-based language to query/ update this data, eliminating the need for a separate API layer to achieve the same result. 1. The data structure creation for storing the data and all data access/manipulation opera-tions is done using a standard, unified and declarative SQL that serves the purpose of pre-serving data identity, integrity, consistency, concurrency, and efficient any-query, any-time access. User-defined types for storing object-based data, too, are treated in the same manner. Rich-format data types use the same mechanism. 2. A hybrid method is used by means of language-based inter-faces like Open Database Con-nectivity (ODBC), Java Database Connectivity (JDBC), and Oracle Call Interfaces (for C/C++) to extend the function-ality of SQL 4GL, enabling 3GLs and OOPLs to interoper-ate with each other for CRUD operations on data as well as on data structures. This allows flexibility of bidirectional data exchange between Oracle11g DB and the application by enabling seamless synchroniza-tion/compatibility of the inher-ent data structures at each of these Tiers.	

Table 4.1   Data Representation and Storage: Database versus
Programming Language (continued)

	Oracle11g database	Embedded Programming Languages
How data is accessed/ updated (CRUD opera- tions) (cont)	3. Oracle has its proprietary 3GL extension to SQL via PL/ SQL, which enables the cre- ation of user-defined functions that can coexist with other db objects. 4. Oracle also allows in-data- base execution of Java rou- tines, .NET-based language routines, C/C++ routines, Groovy Scripts, and Web 2.0- based HTML/XML/PHP/AJAX code in a seamless manner by implicitly taking care of the proper data type and data structure compatibility, JIT compilation (Just-In-Time Compilation), data exchange, and exception handling in addition to transaction man- agement and the power of in- database, in-memory compu- tation. It also has a common interoperability framework called Application Develop- ment Framework (ADF).	
How the data can be pre- sented for end-user access	The key here is how the user wants to see and use the pre- sented data. For the data to be presented in a meaningful, user-friendly, and application-friendly for- mat, a semantic metadata layer needs to be designed and implemented, that unifies the	All of the data presentation options are valid for program- ming language solutions, too. The key difference is how effi- ciently and accurately this can be done, based on the capabil- ities and limitations of the (embedded) programming lan- guage involved.

Table 4.1   Data Representation and Storage: Database versus
Programming Language (continued)

	Oracle11g database	Embedded Programming Languages
	different types of data into a single, centralized repository and transforms the data into information that adheres to business-terminology and enables the user to better inter-pret the same (without having to bother about the nitty-gritty technicalities involved).	
How the data can be pre-sented for end-user access (cont)	Sometimes, data is presented using various visualization ele-ments (interactive/non-interac-tive, graphic, photo/image/map-based, and/or a mash-up of external data to merge trans-parently with the presented data) to create a superior user experience. Breaking down complex struc-tured data, semi- or unstruc-tured data into a uniform format provides a consolidated semantic/single view for the purposes of customer-centric isolation of the "global infor-mation pool" based by busi-ness function and/or industry domain; or for live streaming/surfing of the same. The data can be presented as reports in a variety of formats, including PDF, XLS, RTF, XML, HTML, and the latest-and-greatest RDF (Resource Defini-tion Format).	

To encapsulate the pragmatics of data and data structure representation in Oracle11g DB and "pure" non-database-based programming language data stores, the following subsections highlight key aspects of both.

4.2.1   Database Implementation

Oracle11g is an object-relational database, and its data representation preserves the key criteria of a RDBMS by allowing the following:

- All data to be represented in a "flattened" row/column format
- Row/column values to be atomic
- Each row to be uniquely identifiable
- All values in a single column to be of the same (data) type
- The order of columns to be insignificant by default
- The order of rows to be insignificant by default
- Each column to be identifiable by an unique name

In addition to this representation, Oracle11g has extended its database semantics to support complex data and "object" data in the following ways:

- Non-atomic and heterogeneous data in a single column (non-atomic data includes multiple values of the same data type being stored in the single column value)
- Object support via user-defined types and associated behavior inside the database
- Multirepresentative data and binary data (such as text documents, audio, video, images, and Web-based semantic structures) by means of collections, large objects (LOBs), geospatial object types, XML types, and so on

The object support in the database merges the programming capabilities of OOPLs and the DB capabilities of persistent storage of unstructured/ object data in native DB format. By using SQL-based language to query/update this data, there is no need for a separate API layer to achieve the same result.

This way, all types of data can be stored, accessed, and updated using one seamless, standard SQL-based and declarative data definition (via SQL-compliant and efficient data structures), manipulation, and control language.

4.2.2   Programming Language Implementation

In the "pure" programming language scenario, all data is primarily stored in specific language-inherent data structures, which are object-based or can be mapped easily to an object representation. Applications based on these benefit from the high functionality and full-featured semantics of these languages. All types of data can be accommodated in these so-built object structures, allowing a greater degree of flexibility, not only in terms of being a data store but also in terms of collaborating with other similar language-based applications in a simpler, faster, and better manner.

The demerits of such an implementation are:

- Such data is transient and, for persistent storage, mandates the use of an external file system and/or an object-oriented database that can handle all the complexities of true object-orientation (the non-object data handling being implicitly taken care of).
- Data management gets too complex, and data I/O to and from interconnected application components leans towards a new programmatic API for storing and retrieving object- or non-object-based data, which in turn needs additional programming to expose it to the end-user presentation level. This is a dramatic downside for large-scale application systems, whether they are for high-volume transactional processing, or for analytic/reporting purposes.

Here's a list of recommended guidelines before exploring best practices for data structure management:

- Leverage the pre-existing Oracle functionality
- Adding powerful lookup and enhancement routines to programs
- Use search capabilities as seamless as Google Search (or as close to it as possible)
- Use data services for data quality
- Ensure that the data service can be accessed by a simple XML call
- Emphasize total data quality integration, encompassing all embedded programming scenarios (including profiling, cleansing, parsing and standardization, matching, enrichment and monitoring, data escalation, data continuity, and validation of object data as a whole using de-parsing
- Provide a flexible, effective solution for master data management (MDM). *The rules for the same are to be defined by the business and*

*not by the MDM architecture. The design and implementation of the
same should only consume these rules based on the data type and content.*

- Ensure an affordable, full-featured enterprise data integration platform

4.3   Best Practices for Using Heterogeneous Data Structures: Arrays, Array Lists, Lists, Maps, Enumerations

Deciding what kind of data structure to use and when depends on the particular solution in context. However, there are generic "rules" across the
major embedded programming languages that can be put into practice to
achieve optimal functionality and efficiency. Here's a list of must-haves in
regard to what you should and shouldn't do when it comes to using heterogeneous data structures such as arrays, array lists, lists, enumerations, struc-
tures/unions, and the more generic classes to start with:

- Use Oracle's native data access drivers for each embedded programming language implementation. For example, use ODP.NET
11gR2 (version 11.1.0.7.2.0, as of the writing of this book) for
database interaction with .NET languages (C# is the best choice).
This takes care of the Oracle11g inherent optimization for the particular language in context. For example, in the case of data structure management, it provides transparent syncing between the
Oracle and embedded language code in terms of contextual
parameterization, binding, deferred execution, and so on.
- Choose a data structure that can talk to the Oracle11g database
without any data loss, type-mismatch, type-conversion overhead,
parameterization limitations, or SQL injection vulnerabilities. The
best fit for this is to leverage the Oracle native data type support
coupled with the dual advantage of the Oracle Data Access drivers/
components for Java/J2EE, .NET, PHP, and C/C++ programming
frameworks, which are maximized for framework-specific efficiency and for Oracle DB-centric efficiency. As a use case, arrays or
array lists can be chosen to consolidate multiple elements of data
into a single structure that can be used as a "bind" host variable for
processing. This gives a huge performance gain as well as scalability
in handling large data-sets having heterogeneous data elements.

- Choose a data structure that enables data serialization via data-type casting and/or consolidating data in multiple formats. A good example is the XMLTYPE, XMLSTREAM in Oracle11g, which can accommodate almost any kind of data from simple numeric data, ASCII text, or dates to binary text, documents, multimedia, and graphics, including XML-formatted data. The important point is that this can be done using the declarative SQL interface that can benefit from the full potential of in-database performance metrics. The XML type, along with ODP.NET user-defined types (UDTs), can also be used to simulate a LINQ to Entities generic API, based on the ADO.NET Entity Framework (Entity Data Model) for language neutrality for CRUD operations.

This is a key indicator for the forward engineering of the solution architecture, as consolidating data in multiple formats means more than merging/converging the data values: The resulting data should be able to inherently "join" the business semantics of the different types of data being merged. In other words, what's presentable is a solution that seamlessly integrates the business meaning of the underlying data, which the end user can visualize in terms of information that helps derive business insight/value.

- Choose a data structure that optimizes bidirectional data flow between the database and the application, cross-application program result-set sharing, data aggregation, and SQL-based declarative data accessibility for the purposes of presentation. Good examples are the PL/SQL REF CURSOR type and SQL CURSOR expression type, which in combination optimize data/result set sharing between all the above-mentioned embedded programming languages.

The REF CURSOR is the optimal data structure for database interaction involving embedded programming languages (that are non-Oracle based). Oracle11gR2 supports REF CURSOR pre-fetching in .NET-based queries that fetches the first rows along with the REF CURSOR pointer in a single round-trip to the DB. This reduces the overall round-trips for fetching the complete result-set (a performance improvement).

- Choose the best data structure for array type based data. Oracle11g-based .NET solutions can also use PL/SQL associative arrays for data I/O between the database and the .NET-based program via ODP.NET for Oracle11g. The array and list data structures in C# can derive optimal performance benefit from this.

- Use user-defined types (UDTs which are analogous to objects) to interact with OO-based embedded language objects one-to-one when complex unstructured data is involved—for example, spatial data, click-stream data, and so on. REF objects can be used to map object data to relational-table data.

- Use collections inside the DB (VARRAYS, NESTED TABLES) for manipulating PL/SQL-based logic for data management. This is useful for handling programming language–specific data structures like arrays, lists, array lists, enumerations, and so on.

Oracle 11g has provided seamless interoperability of each category of embedded programming languages—Java-based, .NET based, PHP/Ajax-based, or HTML/XML based— in addition to PL/SQL with SQL and/or PL/SQL, by:

- Executing Java, .NET, PHP/Ajax, and HTML/XML code in conjunction with SQL-PL/SQL using stored procedures/functions inside the database. This is Oracle11g calling embedded programming language code.

- Declarative and native Oracle-based API using Java Database Connectivity (JDBC) for Java, Open Database Connectivity (ODBC), Oracle Data Provider (for .NET) and Oracle Database Extensions for.NET, and the PL/SQL Web Toolkit for (HTML, XML) to share/interoperate data/result sets from Oracle11g to the respective embedded programming language environment, bi-directionally. The native compatibility enables additional overheads in the processing/transfer of data/row sets between the database and the application Tier and also takes advantage of the high-performance SQL-PL/SQL functionality inherent in Oracle11g, such as dynamic cursor variables (REF CURSORS), passing entire result sets between different embedded language programs, cursor sharing, result set caching (including that on the client side, which is especially useful for .NET applications using Oracle11g at the DB Tier), and connection pooling/caching.

- Enable native language–specific API-based applications (like those that are purely Java/J2EE, .NET, PHP/Ajax, or HTML/XML-based) to seamlessly interact/interoperate with Oracle11g DB.
- Using Oracle-specific Rapid Application Development/Rich Internet Application integrated development environments (IDEs) such as Oracle JDeveloper 11g, Oracle APEX, and extensions like Oracle Developer Tools for Visual Studio .NET, and ODP.NET, which have in-built functionality to auto-generate code (or code stubs) that, to some extent, leverage optimal data structure selection and inclusion. Oracle11g also supports the Eclipse framework and the Ruby on Rails framework. All of these provide optimized database-application interaction and enhancement, including solutions requiring advanced scripting languages and Flash-based features.

4.3.1   Design of a Code Accelerator that Uses Optimized Data Structures for Efficient Data as Well as Data Structure Management

This section describes the design of a code accelerator that uses a common data structure, the XMLTYPE, XMLSTREAM, to enable efficient data I/O between the Oracle11g DB and the embedded programming language application.

Code accelerators serve as performance enhancers for the overall solution in terms of automating the optimization of code performance, and also as reusable code components via libraries (obfuscated binary code that's portable). The corresponding code-bases are easier to maintain.

Here are the pragmatics for the same:

- Use the Oracle11g XMLTYPE data structure—as a multicolumn-based structure or as a row-based table structure—via the CREATE TABLE … AS XMLTYPE SQL statement. These are part of the XML DB technology that enables high-performance XML storage and retrieval and seamless interoperability between XML and SQL (CRUD operations).
- Use the various prebuilt XML constructs/functions such as XMLTABLE with XMLELEMENT (DOCUMENT or CONTENT type data), XPATH constructs, and so forth to serialize and/or cast

data involving multiple data types like NUMBER, VARCHAR2, CLOB, BLOB, BFILE, and so on. If necessary, use conversion functions like TO_CHAR, TO_BLOB, BFILENAME(), and so on.

- For data aggregation, use the XMLTABLE function and the PIVOT XML clause, and/or prebuilt SQL aggregations such as ROLLUP, CUBE, and so on. This enables segregation of data output based on different types/levels of data summarization.

- Encapsulate the entire code in a packaged function having a parameter of REF CURSOR. The actual argument to this function is passed via a CURSOR expression.

- Using Oracle11g dynamic SQL interoperability between native dynamic SQL (via the EXECUTE IMMEDIATE declarative statements) and the API-based DBMS_SQL package, manage the resulting data returned to adapt to dynamic execution that enables converged result set data sectioning by business function and/or criteria.

- Enable Oracle's array processing capabilities on the embedded language application layer, especially the dynamically controllable row size and the fetch size, to self-tune the database read/write access.

- To enable embedded language-based specifics on the client side, Oracle DataAdapter interfaces can be used. For example, if a .NET client application requires System.XML support, then it can used on the application client side, still benefiting from the XML DB usage that is server-based *(the perfect choice for data management and hence for data structure management)*.
The following code snippet illustrates this:

```
SELECT XMLTABLE(...)
```

By using an intermediate XMLTYPE store and then applying Oracle11g functions for uniform transformation of multi-format data enables the bidirectional data transport. The use of the package takes this to the extent of making the multi-representation seamless by providing a layer of abstraction that is minimally prone to dependency invalidations, and also improving performance.

If using Oracle11gR2, enable and automate the new feature of storing the .NET application state inside the Oracle DB. This reduces the overhead of redoing the data management processes (which includes the data structure syncing, too) by representing the last application state "as-is" (i.e., something similar to application state caching). Examples are "My-Favs-List" on a Bookstore/ Media site or the famous "Shopping Cart" feature in online purchasing sites—these can be visited again with their most recent state restored.

4.4   Best Practices for Using LINQ to Objects (in Oracle11g)

Language Integrated Query, or LINQ, is a prebuilt .NET Framework technology that provides language querying/update functionality from virtually any data source, not just limited to SQL-based databases. It is one unified and optimized data access/manipulation language for databases, XML data sources, or object collections (this is the case in "pure" programming language data stores). It's NOT similar, in terms of analogy, to the SQL 4GL for querying any RDBMS or ORDBMS, but is a standards-based and common syntax–, semantics- and pragmatics-based programming language for CRUD operations on a unified XML-based data model schema definition, but *only for the .NET environment.* The key indicator is that it is a metadata definition for describing the underlying source data, while being agnostic about how that data is stored. So it transforms data from several disparate sources into a common Entity Data Model schema definition (that is XML-based), irrespective of how each of the individual data components is stored on the respective data source. And finally, it exposes the same using Entity SQL (eSQL—a SQL-like language) for entities.

OOP functionality, involving classes, objects, and methods as data structures tier together, has its own native definition for data access and integration. The .NET LINQ enables using one programming language with rich metadata, compile-time syntax validation, static typing, and IntelliSense, all of which are pre-integrated to be used with all .NET-based languages like C#, VB.NET, ASP.NET (that is, it can be used just like using any C#, VB.NET, or ASP.NET inherent syntax and semantics). The LINQ Framework includes LINQ for SQL (MS SQL Server), LINQ for Objects, and LINQ for XML for the SQL Server RDBMS, object collections, and XML data sources. The query framework for XML is termed XLinq and supports high-performance in-memory XML processing using XPath/XQuery functionality in the embedded programming language. The equivalent framework for relational data, called DLinq, leverages SQL Server–based database schema/efficiency functionality in the .NET run-time CLR system (from strong typing of table data to query path and execution optimization). LINQ for Objects provides the benefits of high-performance query/update over in-memory collection of objects.

Using LINQ, .NET-based LINQ-enabled languages like C#, VB.NET, ASP.NET can filter, enumerate, and create projections of several types of SQL data, collections, XML, and DataSets by using the same syntax. The resulting SQL is dynamically generated.

4.4.1   How does LINQ fit in the Oracle11g-.NET space?

- Microsoft .NET LINQ Framework provides 100-percent managed code inside the .NET Framework and was primarily designed for "pure" .NET-based applications interacting with MS SQL Server RDBMS. Managed code eliminates the need for making external calls outside of the .NET environment. So there is no need for additional client components outside of the .NET environment. This is a key indicator for high performance and scalability.

- Oracle11g, by being an ORDBMS, has direct native data storage/access/manipulation language support for Objects in the database via UDTs and collections (Variable Arrays and Nested Tables). ODP.NET 11.1.0.7.2.0 have simulated the LINQ Framework functionality and integrated it into the ODP.NET native Oracle11g managed provider for .NET.

- Although ODP.NET 11g doesn't directly support DLinq, XLinq, and LINQ for objects in terms of 100-percent managed code without the need to have Oracle client libraries, the rich feature set and robust performance-enabled functionality in ODP.NET 11g can provide the "best-fit" LINQ-like programming capabilities for "querying" collections of objects, XML-based data with pre-integrated native XMLTYPE and XMLSTREAM data structures, and native declarative .NET API for object collections, including arrays of arrays, nested tables, Object REF data structures, variable arrays, and native declarative data access drivers for .NET DataSets.

- This can be used to work on embedded programming language-specific data structures like arrays, lists, array lists, and enumerations, as well as the DataSet data structures, by using a native set of query functions/operators/constructs that are Oracle SQL-PL/SQL compatible and thus enable procedural coding for complex SET operations like array/list filtering or data value summarizations on elements in a collection as well as on collection sets. This is analogous to the SET operations on nested table collections in SQL-PL/SQL introduced in Oracle10gR2.

The best-fit for LINQ in the Oracle11g domain is threefold:

•For existing Oracle-based .NET applications already designed and developed using the LINQ Framework, Oracle11g enables seamless migration to ODP.NET 11g without having to change application code or compromise on functionality, efficiency, scalability, and productivity. The Oracle11g ODAC client installation is now a simple single-file click install. The only downside of this is that, as of the writing of this book, there is no direct support in ODP.NET 11g for DLinq to Oracle and the Entity Framework of the Microsoft .NET core LINQ Framework. However, other data providers for Oracle have this additional capability, the primary ones being DataDirect Connect Managed Data Provider for Oracle from DataDirect Technologies, and Devart dotConnect for Oracle from Devart.

•For new .NET solutions that are Oracle11g-based, the current release of ODP.NET 11g provides the full range of LINQ Framework functionality (except the Entity Framework) and in fact, additional richer functionality in terms of Oracle-specific high performance, portability, RAC, Object Collection support, and client-side result set caching that improves reused query execution on the client side and can improve the disconnected data source performance via the DataSet data structure. A DataSet is a .NET application data structure that functions as a disconnected data source (i.e., when the .NET application is decoupled from primary data (base) source, the client-cached data in the DataSet can still be used to run queries on the application side). Any updates to the original source data pertaining to that in the DataSet are auto-synced by ODP.NET 11g, using its inherent manageability capabilities.

•Thirdly, ODP.NET supports the full stored procedure capabilities of LINQ for SQL (Server) on the Oracle side, including auto-code generation of SQL queries and parameterization, returning result sets as strongly typed collections, distributed, and more. This is analogous to the declarative DML support of collection of nested tables using SQL directly, but extends it a bit further by doing the same on the .NET layer and saving the changes back to the DB.

4.4.2   Best Uses of ODP.NET LINQ to Objects in Oracle11g

- *In applications that are data-transaction intensive and/or distributed and mandate CRUD on data stored in heterogeneous data-model representations, for high performance, scalability, reliability, and advanced security* .
- *In C#-based embedded programming solutions, to facilitate object collection–based set operations like conditional subset extraction from a collection; and to simulate SQL-based JOIN operations on object collections using Oracle-declarative SQL syntax (something like a Query Expression in LINQ).* This is analogous to the CURSOR expressions feature in PL/SQL, which proves handy and efficient in eliminating complex joins by performing in-memory computation. This in turn simplifies data access involving multiple RI relationships by enabling direct (random) access to the set members' objects in the collection. These correspond to the child tables in a parent-child relationship. The same holds true for set member creation/update/deletion. Use the custom DataContext class and its member methods via the ODP.NET Data Access Components API to store and initialize the collection set members, enabling seamless compatibility and synchronization between Oracle types and C# types.
- *In applications that use .NET-based code subprograms SQL embedded in them.* ODP.NET allows the same to be directly callable SQL-PL/SQL code by storing and executing them in the DB using .NET stored procures. (This is akin to the LINQ to SQL feature to use stored procedures rather than SQL calls.)
- *By using LINQ-simulated Query Expressions in ODP.NET as a viable data structure in combination with .NET stored procedures.* This best-fit practice gives a double benefit: the native manipulation of object collection in C# and the execution efficiency, integrity, and security of in-database stored code. Use the Data-Context custom class and define the stored procedures as methods of this class. ODP.NET generates strongly typed arguments and strongly typed object collections for the parameters and the output returned, respectively.

4.5 Best Practices for Using Objects as Data Structures

Objects as data structures extend the semantics of the object programming languages (such as C++, Java, COM/DCOM objects, etc.) to provide full-featured database programming capability while retaining native language compatibility, by seamlessly mapping object programming language objects one-to-one to database objects. Oracle11g is an object relational database management system (ORDBMS) and has a flexible mechanism of in-database object management on the lines of object-oriented (OO) programming objects via object type creation (that corresponds to a Class) and extending the functionality by using object type instances as column objects or row objects, and using objects and collections as interoperable data structures inside the DB and exposed via SQL/PL/SQL. This inherent mechanism simplifies the way embedded programming languages involving objects can interact/integrate with the database. All the interlinks—associations (relationships), generalizations (super-type/sub-type hierarchies), and compositions (relationship dependencies), as well as SELF links on the same object—to be specified, used, reused, and un-used, if necessary, are preserved.

The native Oracle data drivers for object languages like Java, C++, C# etc. provide API for the same. The API support both feature-rich and compute-rich functionality optimized for transparent data access, manipulation, and application processing. Object data resides in the database and is manipulated collectively with queries in a query language. Oracle internally levels down the object structure to a flat table row/column representation. Object relational mapping (ORM) enables serialization of object data between source and target. Here's a list of recommended practices for using objects as data structures:

- Use objects as data structures for applications that mandate representation and presentation of complex data or objects in persistent form. "Pure" object-oriented programming language (OOPL) objects hold "transient data," such as that found in executing programs. The relationship between such data is still driven by the data itself at the database level by means of native Oracle-specific object REFs. All Oracle11g-based embedded languages, such as Java, .NET-based C#, and C/C++, support data access components that synchronize one-to-one with the programming language object API in context, allowing efficiency at the database level as well as at the language tiers.

Oracle11g objects seamlessly merge the operation and manageability of persistent data (as in a relational database management system, or RDBMS) and "transient data" as found in executing programs. All of this is transparent to the application solution and involves no (or minimal) changes to the application code.

- Use objects as data structures to design code accelerators. Typical use cases that can be implemented are:
  - Consolidation of data based on type granularity to provide a unified view at the presentation level (for example, time data encloses an hierarchy of sub-elements like Time Zone, Year, Month, Week, Day, Hour, Minute, Second, and Fractional Second; the use of custom time object(s) as data structure(s) greatly simplifies the creation and management of the same to the finest granularity)
  - Building multidimensional arrays
  - Simulating nested table set operations using embedded languages

4.5.1 Code Accelerator for the Consolidation of Data based on Type Granularity

The code accelerator algorithm for the consolidation of data based on type granularity can consist of the following steps:

1. Create an object type that has all the sub-elements as its members.

2. Define methods for the "business-required" functions to be tied to each of the granular sub-elements.

3. Expose the access and management of these via native Oracle-based object API for the particular embedded language in context.

4. Consolidate the results for the desired output using the following methods, single or in combination:

5.   Use SQL directly to create a unified view based on the persistent object data, specific to the output desired. The output can be presented using another common object data structure (on the lines of the code accelerator described in section 4.2 using the XML-TYPE) via REF CURSOR and CURSOR expression or using SQL nested table set operations.

6.   Expose the constructed SQL via Oracle11g provided the JDBC, ODBC, Oracle Call Interface (OCI), external procedures, and ODP.NET API, depending on the language in context.

7.   Use a common collection-based object API (e.g., object data structures, methods, logic, etc.) using OBJECT types and collections that expose a declarative custom-built object API mapped to custom classes. Oracle11g JDBC/ODBC API, .NET API, and PHP API all provide custom class creation, update, and access capabilities. Also, embedded language stored procedures can be used in this process.

8.   In a .NET-specific application solution, use the ODP.NET object functionality using query expressions (LINQ-analogous) to perform set operations directly on object collection members.

Using objects in the database enables the mapping of database objects and programming language objects to an appreciably reasonable extent (if not a one-to-one mapping or one that provides a 360-degree flexibility) by implicitly leveraging the database-specific functionality for data structure and data management as well as the extended programming capabilities of 3GL and 4GL languages inside the database, thus providing embedding and interoperability of SQL and (non-SQL) programming language code for process-intensive, computation-rich functionality.

The linkages between the complex object data are implicitly maintained and thus become self-inherent, eliminating the necessity of join operations in cases where multiple/hierarchical relationships are involved. As the data access is still based on a declarative SQL query, the ORDBMS is smart enough to take advantage of the query optimization features of the RDBMS and make them work on the underlying objects and their methods, delivering results with high performance and greater scalability.

4.6   Best Practices for Metaprogramming: Use or Eliminate

Metaprogramming, from a database and application development stand-point, is all about collecting and consolidating functional data element definitions and business rules into an unified "superdata" definition and language format, so that the end-to-end business users have a single common ground for defining and communicating across disparate functional units, each with its own data definition and business interpretation of the same.

To implement metaprogramming in action, the database needs a *metadata* repository or schema to be created that subsumes all the different business data definitions and business rules into one common format that can be stored in the same format as the database in context, without compromising logical and physical data independence. This metadata layer is a consolidated data definition schema that implements a centralized design of all the different units of business data definitions and their associated business rules and stores them in this schema to provide an integrated table definition.

As database design progresses from "pure" relational to object-relational and involves the embedding SQL and/or PL/SQL code in 3GL & OOPL code and vice-versa, meta-programming in terms of the meta-data layer on the database side (both data definitions & business rules) and meta-program layer on the application side (for additional unified code modules that cannot be accommodated in the meta-data layer, especially non-declarative and complex rules that specific to the embedded programming language and business function in context) comes close to becoming a standard definition/programming interface for Oracle11g-based embedded programming solution modeling, design, and development.

Figure 4.1 illustrates the importance of having meta-data and meta-programming.

Here's a list of recommended practices for the use of metadata and metaprogramming:

- Always include the metadata and metaprogram design in the solution architecture. The metadata definition should be capable of consolidating data at the single- or multisource level (as identified by the necessary business entities) into a single data definition

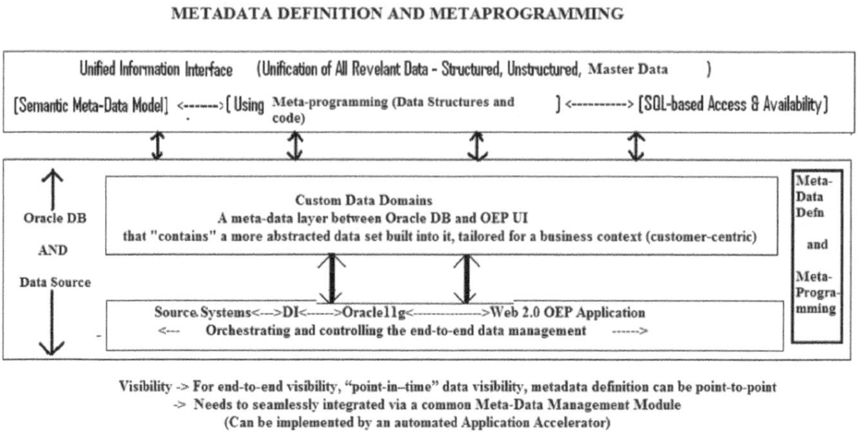

METADATA DEFINITION AND METAPROGRAMMING

Figure 4.1   Importance of Metadata Definition and Metaprogramming.

schema. This serves as central store for all of the solution processes involved. To start with, this corresponds to the business solution in context that sits on top of the base multisource operational (mostly transactional), primary lookup and reference tables. This layer is required for the interfacing of disparate data sources with the Oracle11g database so that data from all of them can be loaded into a "unified" (from a business functionality point of view) data definition schema.

■ There can be a second level of metadata definition, corresponding to the business solution in context, that sits on top of the base metadata corresponding to the high-level data isolation/segregation demands that are on par with the business specifications. In this case, the final data presentation involves the redirection of the second layer metadata to the base database schema (which acts as the data source for this) to derive the desired output.

■ Always derive the metadata definition based on the base (source) tables, columns, relationships (linear RI, hierarchical, self-referencing) by cross-mapping them to the *functional business components*—that is, the business entities, their attributes, and any additional derived attributes to be added. The derived attributes can be implemented as virtual columns (especially in situations that demand high-volume SQL-based data access).

■ Metaprogramming is required when aligning the programming side of the solution with the consolidated metadata definition.

This ensures that the consolidated data is presented as meaningful information that provides a consolidated view of the underlying data. *This is a key indicator for end-user decision making in terms of deriving insight to gain business value.* The code accelerators discussed in the earlier sections of this chapter all involve metaprogramming in terms of the common object data structures coded, as well as the underlying logic via member methods or stored procedures. The code itself doesn't constitute metaprogram, but the underlying code design pattern does, as it describes "code about code."

- Use metadata definition to design a comprehensive, consistent, and coherent MDM architecture that pools business-specific master data in context with the corresponding source data, transforms it into a common definition for use as a single "logical" view, and stores it in a persistent centralized repository inside the Oracle DB. Metaprogramming can be used to federate this unified master data coupled with the business transactions/operations data based on business-driven rules.

Summary

This chapter described the best practices for data structure management in terms of optimal design for data access and CRUD operations that align with the various embedded programming language data structures. Presenting the data structure as the design foundation of data management, the starting section described the data representation and the key differentiators from a database and programming language perspective. The subsequent sections highlighted the best recommended practices for handling heterogeneous data structures like arrays, lists, array lists, and enumerations; the benefit of using objects as data structures in embedded programming scenarios; and the role of LINQ in embedded language programming and the best fit of LINQ in the Oracle11g ODP.NET domain. Code accelerator design algorithms for using best-fit data structures to arrive at a more generic data access/update involving embedded languages were presented.

The next chapter describes the best practices for error detection and handling in terms of error tracking and trapping, event-based notification of the same via alerts and asynchronous mechanisms, and best practices for preventing improper error escalation.

Chapter 5

Best Practices for Robust Error Detection and Handling Management

In this Chapter

- Best design practices to reduce the probability of errors and enable quick resolution
- Techniques to obtain complete error information
- Techniques to customize the error information returned
- Techniques for halting further processing on error occurrence

5.1   Introduction

Error prevention, detection, and resolution are indispensable to any IT application/solution quality, and in turn drive the durability, scalability, efficiency (performance and unbreakability combined), security, and usability. In this way, *error management is both a requirement as well as an asset to the solution being implemented.* And *secure code contributes to a secure solution,* the development of which in turn depends not only on the best programming practices for error and exception handling incorporated into the application, but also on the associated best-practice design. Secure code design and hence fault-tolerant code means the solution is minimally vulnerable to run-time errors that can be one of the following: technical glitches in the solution design, coding, logical errors due to violation of business rules, poor performance, unauthorized access/modifications, or other unhandled exceptions.

A robust error management design in place ensures the integrity and reliability of the end-to-end solution, enabling minimal or no impact on the integration, componentization, modularization, and the Software-as-a-Service (SaaS) enablement (Web services, application services, information services, etc.) of the same.

The development of an embedded programming solution based on Oracle11g requires the use of application programming interfaces (APIs) to interact and interoperate between the different layers or tiers of the solution: namely, the database Tier, the intermediate or middle Tier (if any), and/or the application/presentation Tier. Also, it might involve interaction with additional URL-identifiable sites. This kind of Web interfacing (may also be needed sometimes on the-fly) can make the solution more error-prone, primarily as the solution in context has no control over the extraneous Web layer. This situation also holds true for external data sources interfacing with Oracle11g.

Runtime errors can be classified into the four broad categories:

- *Database-related errors*—These include errors due to failure of embedded SQL statements, errors due to failure of in-database stored logic called from the embedded SQL program, errors due to failure of transactions or inconsistent transaction states, and internal errors due to uncommon reasons—for example, a system or database crash. Most of these errors are implicitly raised, and Oracle handles these situations primarily via predefined named exceptions and un-named DB server exceptions. The developers' role is to trap, resolve, and/or propagate these errors upstream.

- *Programming language–/application-related errors*—These include errors due to failure of SQL-PL/SQL– and/or programming language–specific code, and errors due to failure of application logic, such as application-level validations due to improper input/action from the end user or violation of business rules. These can be handled using custom routines that translate, transform, or merge the DB-related logical error info and the pure language-specific error info. Even customized error codes and messages can be used, if needed.

- *Presentation interface–related errors*—These include errors during display of information and/or visual components at the end-user GUI, inconsistencies between Web-exposed browser states, invalid object resolution between Web-enabled application services, and/or HTML/Flash-based Web pages.

- In addition, errors due to ripple effects, multiple programs losing scope and state across the different tiers of the solution, and so on can also be raised.

Oracle11g and the associated embedded-language API/functionality provide different methods to code exception handlers for obtaining the error information to the most granular level possible. Of special mention are the techniques to customize the error information returned as per application requirements by extending the exception model with additional logic, at the database as well as programming-language levels. To take it further, Oracle allows halting of the application execution and, simplifies the overall error management process by means of in-built declarative API (that can be used to derive a unified error management framework to work across the solution end-to-end), cross-technology compatible debugging tools and IDEs.

5.2   Best Design Practices to Reduce the Probability of Errors and Enable Quick Resolution

The best practices to minimize errors associated with the database, application, and presentation layers are:

- Leverage Oracle11g DB and solution functionality to implement existing features that are both powerful and efficient.
- Pre-analyze the scope of potential errors and their resolution by conducting design reviews, peer code reviews, and improvement of the same.
- Do an iterative "fire-drill" simulation test of each program/application module, beginning in the development phase; this ensures that the solution module in context is as error-proof as possible, even before it goes to other phases of testing. A good way is to capture "live" snapshot of relevant data and inputs and perform the testing. This enables Agile Testing by way of iterative test cycles on an as-is basis.
- Learn from production deployments by capturing the errors and their diagnostics and resolution practices, and use these as baselines for error management. This enables a means of quantifying errors akin to measuring their impact; it can help in determining pre-emptive actions for error prevention in future runs or deployments.
- Take the best practices pragmatics to the next level, by creating *error instance templates (visual and/or categorical) by using the so derived baselines and their analyzed results.*

A testing framework that can be used as a "benchmark by design" results in a solution that is less error-prone while at the same time enabling quick debugging and fixing of any errors that do arise. This framework can be implemented using a layered approach to error prevention, detection, debugging, and resolution. .

Any Oracle11g-based embedded programming solution primarily can have the following n-Tier structure:

- *The database Tier*, comprising the Oracle11g Database.
- *The intermediate Tier*, comprising the middleware software that enables interprocess and data communication/collaboration between the database Tier and the presentation Tier. This Tier can be optional in certain cases.
- *The presentation Tier*, comprising a Web-based rich user interface (UI) that is both user-friendly and business-savvy, enabling both technical and nontechnical users to interact with the solution in a seamless manner via push-button actions, click-and-go information visualization, Flash-based user action-response, personal search features, and the like.

The key indicator for a robust error prevention, detection, and resolution strategy is to architect a framework that seamlessly integrates across each of these Tiers. A proactive and pre-emptive framework methodology involves a Fast-Actionable-Synchronized-Tested (FAST) validation, monitoring, debugging, and testing architecture that supports the multi-cycle, in- instant Agile testing paradigm, and can be implemented using built-in code modules, in combination with existing Oracle11g-supported tools and functionality, to accelerate this process. After all, the purpose of a solution is to store, access, process, and present "data, data everywhere" without "dropping" on the business (and hence IT) value of it.

Table 5.1 shows a typical design architecture that can be followed as a best practice.

Table 5.1   Typical design architecture for best-practice error prevention, detection, and resolution.

	Error Prevention	Error Detection	Error Reporting	Error Resolution
A C R O S S A L L T I E R S	Validation	Validation	Notification via alerts	Debugging (using Oracle11g native functionality)
	Extended Validation	Trapping (by leveraging native functionality) and logging/auditing the same. Event-based continuous monitoring of the solution via automatically triggering events across all solution touch-points, including end-user activity—and integrating this process into the overall workflow.	Define alert clusters by (dynamically) profiling alerts based on domain-specific and customer-centric (e.g., for each business context, client-user, etc.) segmentation as well as IT-specific contexts (e.g., what data, process, code module, triggering event, etc.) and correlate each of these to the error in context. Finally, consolidate the resulting alerts into a single alert. This eliminates alert redundancy and can be implemented via a code accelerator for Master	Handling (of the errors using code modules) The key here is to fix the error and log the exception handling logic without affecting or changing the business rules in place. An approach similar to alert clustering can be used for error handling and logging too. Typical Master-Error-Management (M-E-M) components can include automated error-bots for custom error notification federator; error archival and retrieval catalog; and the like.

Table 5.1   Typical design architecture for best-practice error prevention, detection, and resolution. (continued)

Error Prevention	Error Detection	Error Reporting	Error Resolution
		Alert Management (M-A-M) (including automated custom tagging to the individual alerts). This eliminates using a new alert for each point-to-point notification, while still preserving the business pragmatics of the same.	These are discussed in the subsection(s) that follow.
Ensure application-level code (both SQL and non-SQL) aligns with the specific business rules tied to it	Tracking (the source of the error, by leveraging Oracle11g-specific and language- specific features, and logging of the same)	The custom alert clusters can be adopted as alert templates for future use or as measurable error severity meters by correlating them based on their type, context, and frequency of occurrence across a timeline.	Reports output (documenting the error trapping, tracking, debugging and handling details in the form of (preferably) well-formatted reports)

Table 5.1   Typical design architecture for best-practice error prevention, detection, and resolution. (continued)

	Error Prevention	Error Detection	Error Reporting	Error Resolution
	Pre-emptive measures (error resolution and prevention by pre-identifying potential error spots, using error-diagnostics baselines)	Scheduling of jobs/processes to automate the above three functions		Baselining (reusing the error diagnostics captured as input baselines for pre-emptive measures, which in turn helps embed pre-coded modules via extended validations based on the error occurrence and resolution patterns)

<---------- Support Batch and Online Solutions --------------->

These code modules can serve as code accelerators and can be built using:

- Business policy-based validation and extended validation routines on all the Tiers. This also includes nonvalidation-related error tracking, trapping, alerting (in a business-friendly manner), and handling.
- Continuous monitoring and event notification routines using real-time alerts that synchronize (propagate) the "cause-effect" scenarios across all the Tiers with minimal impact on solution performance. *A good option is to mimic a "relay" design that cascades the same.*
- Special validation/monitoring routines specifically tailored towards database activity (to-and-fro). This ensures a pre-emptive way of measuring not just data quality, but also the performance of the live database, on an as-is basis. This is critical to any Oracle-based solution, especially one that involves an application layer using

embedded languages. *This in turn should take care of database and data security, quality, blind spots in the data as well as in the data flow (again stressing the AAA paradigm in terms of data storage and accessibility), unnecessary or "stale" data, and so on, as well as the data presentation and modification at the presentation Tier.*

Have scheduling, reporting (includes error-notification via alerts as well as producing documented reports that can serve as input baselines for error diagnostics, debugging, and testing), debugging, auditing, and services-enabled componentization of the overall implementation to provide cross-Tier lineage of the so-designed framework.

These code accelerators function as the database-application layer analog to achieve push-button, one-touch (click-and-go) functionality at the presentation layer.

5.2.1   Design Pattern for a Typical Error-Handling Code Accelerator

A set-based policy can be declaratively and/or programmatically incorporated at the database and/or application level using custom stored functions, user-defined operators, and so on. They can be called from SQL and/or the embedded programming language using the language-specific API, still maintaining Oracle nativity, compile-time and run-time dynamism, and reusability. The set-based policy can perform a validation event, an error tracking/trapping/notification/handling event, or a testing/debugging event, and can be grouped by business function, data set and/or data object, user space, or a combination of these. The key focus points are:

- A variety of query types, especially those that are criteria based and time bound, are more vulnerable to SQL injection attacks, which can lead to unauthorized user access to the application as well as incorrect/inconsistent data access and updates. In addition to using bind variables, each query can be parameterized to prevent illogical queries being dynamically generated in an effort to eliminate such attacks.
- Running embedded language–based stored procedures from within Oracle11g makes the application more error-prone due to

the asynchronous design nature of these two environment frameworks. This boils down to the fact that the "best practice" code for an embedded language that is high performing may not be necessarily the "best practice" code for the same language when executed inside Oracle11g. This a-syncing is a critical contributor to the probability of error occurrence, and subsequently to fixing it.

Oracle11g has great code optimization features for Java, .NET, PHP, and HTML/XML code running inside the DB. A best practice is to use these features to write high performing code with built-in "seamless-streamed" error-handling routines for the embedded language involved, so that it executes as closely as possible to an Oracle-specific SQL/PL/SQL stored procedure. By being both seamless and streamed, it provides a coherent (or consistently phased) code design pattern for a free-flow execution of the error-handling code, thereby maintaining a freeflow process for error dissemination and resolution across the solution Tiers. Using the Oracle11g Java-enabled, .NET-enabled, and PHP-enabled features enables efficient error handling. For example, the ODP.NET specific functionality of FAN (Fast Alert Notification) for .NET based solutions enables pragmatics similar to the "divide-and-conquer" approach by having specific error-handling code accelerators at each individual Tier and at the same time streamlining all of these for a coherent and consistent execution.

- Errors generated from inconsistencies in the processing of multi-content-based data, such as semi-structured data (EDI data, e-mail messages), Web data (graphs, visual models, etc.), multimedia data (audio, video, binary documents: PDF files, Word files, etc.), or integrated external data—for example, external files and the like stored in Oracle-compliant format(s) like CLOBs, BLOBs, BFILEs, XMLTYPE data structures, and so on—need to be properly trapped, alerted, and diagnosed, as some of them are located outside Oracle and might depend on the OS file system. A real-world scenario could see errors resulting from unauthorized access to the OS files for BFILEs or other out-of-Oracle DB resources (triggered by Oracle11g fine-grained network access [e.g., via SecureFiles, etc.] functionality).

At the database Tier, use Oracle11g native database functionality, like enhanced programming language specific features, as well as the inherent database features for error prevention, online detection and debugging, and fixing of the same, to achieve efficient database functioning as well as application-contextual data/information accuracy, reliability, and efficiency.

The key indicator is to build a design that, when implemented, has minimal impact on the database and application functioning and at the same time involves no (or minimal) changes to the management of the same. And Oracle11g and its cross-language-compatible native capabilities are the "best fit" to be leveraged to get such a result.

Oracle11g's SOA functionality can be leveraged to build a data services engine that can incorporate the above-stated validation, event notification via alerts, and database-based error trapping, handling, and propagation routines and expose them via services for a more pervasive and enhanced usability.

At the application layer, programming language–specific code layers can be designed to augment the default functionality provided by Oracle11g. *An intelligent code design is to use the Oracle11g In-Memory Database Cache (IMDB-cache) on the application Tier and write connectivity/accessibility code to enable faster access/updates to data at the end-user level. Oracle11g automatically takes care of the synchronization and coordination of the in-memory cache and the underlying database.*

An end-to-end unified error tracking, reporting, and handling engine can be designed, similar to the data services engine mentioned above, t perform a similar function, using the data services engine as one of its components, and managing seamless coordination across the database, intermediate (application) and presentation Tiers.

Custom Error Notification Federator

For error events notification via alerts, Oracle11g exposes the Oracle-DB-integrated Advanced Queuing (AQ) mechanism to the embedded solution space. .NET, Java, and/or OCI-based applications can use this for streams-based queuing, de-queuing, and notification of error messages or other categorical messages (and at the same time store them persistently). For errors related to high-availability failures at the network, DB-server, or DB-instance levels, use the appropriate callbacks for this events notification and then custom-code for the handling of the same. For Java-based applications, Oracle11g provides a native JMS/AQ mechanism/API for improved performance.

Custom Error Archival and Retrieval Catalog

The Custom Error Archival and Retrieval Catalog is a key error management indicator for the overall solution. The architecture-by-design to implement this should focus on:

- A centralized error-log repository for all errors (implicitly or explicitly raised), including Alerts fanned to notify the same.
- Integration into the database Tier, with the flexibility to be incrementally extensible (if needed) without modifying the solution
- Seamless streamlining of the end-to-end error management process (creation, federation, semantic error-info mapping [technical-to-nontechnical details], notification, tracking and trapping via continuous and automated monitoring)
- Indexed retrieval and personal-search capabilities based on multiple error-centric filters—using the Master-Error-Management categorization criteria—such as Keyword, Tags, Text, Domain (Business Area, Application, User-Session, User-category, User-privilege), all of these relating to the Error Type, Text, and/or Severity, Alerts. etc.
- A robust retention and recovery policy that enables auditing of the errors as well as the events that initiated them and the remediation processes to handle them.
- IT-friendly and business-friendly error reports that are secure and can be shared, internally and externally (via, export, e-mail, publish-subscribe or other collaboration-platform based methods).

For existing Oracle11g-based applications

- Oracle Database Vault ensures data protection at the application level
- Embedded languages like PL/SQL, C/C++, Java, C#, and PHP can use the respective programmatic extensions to IMDB cache to leverage the benefits of IMDB cache with little or no application code changes.

The as-designed code accelerator can leverage

- *Oracle JRockit JVM for Java/J2EE based solutions* to accelerate Java-only applications running against Oracle11g. This provides direct integration of internal as well as external server-side specific Java class libraries with Oracle11g. *The generic JDBC driver can be used to access non-Oracle data sources via JDBC callouts in conjunction with the Oracle SAX and DOM parsers.*
- *Oracle Weblogic Server* for Web-based solutions to accelerate Java-based rich Internet applications (RIA) running on the Web (via the Application Grid).
- *Oracle ADF (Faces)* for a unified collaborative and interoperative application/solution development framework that is cross-embedded programming language–enabled (Java, .NET, PHP, Web services, etc.).

5.2.2   Best Practices in Terms of Tracking and Trapping Errors

Proper exception handling not only depends on the type and severity of the errors, but is typical of the source of the error. In an embedded-language programming solution with Oracle as the backend DB, several invalid references can lead to source of the error—for example, NULL values, pointers to NULL object REFs (also termed under the generic name NULL references), and so on. Although this is a case-by-case scenario, there are recommended practices that can be generalized across the database, application, and presentation layers of the solution that, when implemented, will enable "error scoping" that leads to an access path to the source of the error.

Here's a list of the best-of-breed in regards to the same:

1. Enable declarative Oracle11g-based features for prevention, detection, and resolution of errors

    - Enable Oracle11g compile-time warnings by setting the PLSQL_WARNINGS initialization parameter as follows:

```
ALTER SESSION SET PLSQL_WARNINGS = 'enable:all';
```

    This highlights any inconsistencies in the code pertaining to errors during the compilation process.

- Exception-enable every Oracle11g-based stored subprogram with a default exception handler, as follows:

```
EXCEPTION WHEN OTHERS THEN
-- Either RAISE or RAISE_APPLICATION_ERROR
-- has to be used
            RAISE;
        -- RAISE_APPLICATION_ERROR(…);
```

With compile-time warnings turned on, the PLW-06009 WARNING is displayed when a PL/SQL-stored program is compiled without a WHEN OTHERS exception handler, containing either RAISE or RAISE_APPLICATION_ERROR statement calls.

- Enable Oracle11g-based JDBC/ODBC logging by default. This can be disabled programmatically in demanding situations.

- Enable transaction-level auditing; it is a good way to measure the success and failure of each DML statement being executed, irrespective of the source from where the particular statement is issued. This can be done by setting the AUDIT_TRAIL initialization parameter to the value EXTENDED_DB. Oracle allows toggling between on/off states as necessary.

- Track application-user context info using Oracle11g DB application contexts (which can be at the session or GLOBAL level for each database). .NET-based embedded languages also provide client identifiers to ease this process. An alternative way to this is to auto-enable auditing at the database level and user-profile level (that helps tracking the sign-in and sign-off information. Also, custom user Context Lists with Attributes can be created and used for this purpose.

A key indicator in error handling is how the error is represented in the presentation platform. This might sometimes necessitate producing/consuming an error-hierarchy in context.

2. Presenting the error raised at the database and/or application Tier to the presentation interface can be accomplished in a number of ways, alert notification being the most common method. However, in certain situations, this might not be sufficient to communicate the cause-effect relationship of the error more meaningfully. As an example, *logical errors* (i.e., non-Oracle-server-related or other nontechnical errors) can be very well represented graphically as (single/multi) colored bars and/or showing the support/confidence impact of the error visually, in terms of staying-within-limits/best-results interpretation. Ideally, this error measurement information is presented in an insightful manner for better handling of the errors. Oracle11g and the associated embedded-language technologies support SIEM as a methodology for visualization and interpretation of the measured error. This is doable using configuration scripts that can be custom-modified based on requirements criteria. The next level is to transform (via code) the underlying logical error into a viewable display with interactive controls enabled, so that the end-user can play with the error measures shown and tweak/shift/shear the same to arrive at a conclusion for a better resolution. This goes in line with the reusability/baselining best-practice stated earlier, and the code accelerator can include an *extended validation* routine to implement the same. Scripting languages such as *Perl can be used in combination with regular embedded languages for coding the same.* (Refer to the section entitled "Perl in the Picture" in Chapter 3.)

3. Identify application code involving NULL values and OBJECT references (or REFs) as they can result in "Null References" exceptio:n

`System.NullReferenceException`

This error can occur when object-based data structures are used for processing, especially for unstructured data and semistructured data and the interconversions involved (e.g., sharing content-based data from the Oracle DB/DD via embedded-language API, creating application-specific custom docs to serve as extended application help, etc.).

4. Identify the code associated with push buttonñenabled execution and scope it separately. Common errors associated with this are:

    ▪ Errors raised from validations involving restricted data display, especially default values, based on end-user privileges. This is primarily due to incorrect code that needs to be modified to accommodate dynamic refresh and display of valid data based on user access. To generalize, this scenario can be extended to incorporate smart validation policies for interdependent data between columns in a single row, across rows, or across tables. Typical ways to do this are using row-level security and custom set–based policies tied to user authentication, authorization, and auditing (key error, user, and application information logging) at the database Tier, and dynamic data refresh on the application/ presentation Tier, with minimal side effects.

    ▪ Errors occurring after clicking the *submit* button (e.g., the resulting screen is not refreshed or becomes frozen). The key tracking indicators here are to see if large result sets are being output to the screen and to test the same functionality on smaller sets, to see whether it works. This error can also be a DB locking issue after fetching a certain number of records; it could also be due to resource contention. This can follow the iterative testing approach that enables agile testing.

    Sometimes the cause of these errors can be hidden, in the sense that the error message displayed does not directly reflect the cause of the error. The error was raised due to the cascading effect of an inconsistency, as with invalid parameter values, parameter settings, and so on. Recognizing and dealing with this issue is critical for debugging, especially when dealing with objects and object references (as is the case with SQL-PL/SQL and Java, .NET, C++, and PHP/Ajax–based embedded solutions).

5. Another potential error-occurrence scenario is the consistency factor, when there are different dataset display representations that involve end-user interaction. Identify all such windowing-based operations on multiple disjoint dataset displays (e.g., via

tabs or displays derived from these tabs, such as graphs, plots, subdisplays, and so on) and ensure that no inconsistency exists when the same are moved, closed, minimized, maximized, or are not dangling. This again directly points to the code underneath and needs to be *handled using dynamic data display and coherence capabilities.*

6. Identify SQLs that are prone to inconsistent execution times. Typical real-world scenarios are:

   - A batch program runs in 20 minutes, whereas it takes at least an hour to run the same SQL, given the same parameters, data set, and database environment. This is due to the fact that batch mode is faster, as there is no complex rendering/delivering of the results (in most cases, it writes to an OS file or to specialized tables). When it comes to retrieving the results on the application side, SQL has to fetch and deliver (either incrementally or fully) and this to-and-fro iteration can take more time (and resources) than the click-runstore execution of a batch process (even when initiated from an application UI).

     Identify data uploads that are done transparently (during off-peak hours) via scheduled batch jobs. Although every aspect of the solution is back to normal after these loads: *what's not visible is the amount of data that has been loaded.* Hence, a query that took two minutes on a Friday at the end of the day might run "forever" on Monday morning at 9:00 A.M. And all the end users' frustration ultimately reflects on the IT/technical team. This is where a coordinated team effort is needed, with the DBA notifying the development team that the data volume has changed *n* times.

The key indicator here is to design the query (before the test/tune/tweak) by running it in a pregrown database whose size is estimated to be some n times the actual size of the current database.

Oracle11g makes this process easy by way of Real Application Testing (for load and stress testing), in which you can take a snapshot of the "live" production DB and use it as a baseline for pretesting queries and tuning to scale optimally in case of incremental data-loading situations that affect the corresponding query runtime. And this job too can be automated by scheduling at periodic intervals of time—for example, during weekends after the data upload has finished. Finally, the results of the test can be converted to meaningful information and the users notified by alerting them of performance impacts (if any).

7.   Identify errors caused by the deletion of rows from the application (when embedded-language API calls are invoked to do the same). This typically happens when the application tries to access the row that it has just deleted. Oracle11g takes care of this by providing exclusive row-level locking, but the primary problem is that the row is being deleted due to the execution of the programmatic code and hence, somewhere, read consistency is being compromised. The resulting exception is usually a

```
System.ApplicationException
```

8.   Another common scoping problem is seen in errors that occur due to auto-defaulting of row values after committing a particular row from the application interface. This relates to a pure application error that involves introducing some extending validation to refresh the status once the given row is submitted.

9.   Identify code involving specialized types, such as XML Types, Large Objects, and so on, and ensure that the respective elements in the type lineage are accurate. As an example, when using XMLType, both its element type and the XMLNodeType should be in sync. Otherwise, this results in the following exception:

```
System.Xml.XmlException
```

This holds good for code on the database Tier as well as that on the application Tier.

10.   Be prepared for errors arising from nonavailability of resources due to inactive solution components, "denial-of-service" due to "denial-of-access" or otherwise, or abnormal termination during code execution.

Typical errors in this category include:

```
<....>: The specified <resource> is not
available.
     <....>: Insufficient privileges to access the
     specified <resource>.
     <....>: Internal error. Execution of <....>
aborted.
```

Here <resource> can refer to a memory insufficiency, or a workflow task that is inconsistent with the business process flow, or an abnormality in code execution due to an internal error (an error that cannot be specifically classified as belonging to any of the predetermined server errors) in the runtime execution flow.

Whereas the cause, effect, and resolution of the first two types of errors can be determined with a variable amount of ease, identifying the same for the third "internal error" can be quite cumbersome. This is where the process of automated and continuous monitoring of the solution helps, as does the systematic diagnostic and troubleshooting of the same by a teamed effort of the system administrator and the DBA, using the various logs of event and activity monitoring.

5.3   Techniques to Obtain Complete Error Information

Applying a layered approach to error trapping and tracking is a predominant factor in obtaining the complete error information across the end-to-end solution. A good starting point is to follow a methodology for Master-Error-Management similar to the Master-Alert-Management practices outlined in Table 5.1. Here are some best practices for the code design pattern for the same:

■ Identify code patches or outlier-code that has been extracted from elsewhere and merged into existing source programs. This can lead to the code being wrongly interpreted (as it is less visible in terms of what it does and why it is there), which in turn exposes a potential risk of being untraceable in the long run.

■ Track the source of the error using built-in database and programming language exception handling routines. Examples are using the

PL/SQL DBMS_UTILITY.FORMAT_ERROR_BACKTRACE in conjunction with DBMS_UTILITY.FORMAT_ERROR_STACK and SQLERRM; this combination can enable obtaining the line number at which the error occurred, in addition to the error message, and the error stack. *In a similar manner, using the embedded language–specific exception handling routines and the corresponding Oracle11g-provided interfacing API, the complete error information can be obtained.*

- Use canonicalization transformations to unblind details about the error source in case of object-based data obtained from the tracking results, by means of an Oracleembedded-language API for decoding and unmasking, as the same cannot be directly exposed as error text for representational purposes.

- The complete error details obtained can be logged persistently or exposed via data/information services for baselining in addition to being transformed into a customized error message for notification to the end user.

- Oracle provides the famous REF CURSOR type to dynamically "stream" error messages across the different tiers, which helps streamline error processing. This REF CURSOR type is supported by Java, .NET-based C#, and/or PHP code using an Oracle-native API that is optimized for performance and resource utilization. This technique comes in very handy to implement the *Custom Error Notification Federator and Error Archiving and Retrieval Catalog* described in the previous subsection, "Design Pattern for a Typical Error Handling Code Accelerator".

Always use Oracle11g-based stored procedures to expose the error information to the end-user environment, regardless of whether such information pertains to a database-specific error, a programming language–specific error, or a combination of both. This is very important, especially for errors related to validation of business rules, violations of data and application integrity, inconsistencies between different object references, and so on.

- Using DBMS_JAVA.SET_OUTPUT in combination with DBMS_UTILITY.FORMAT_ERROR_BACKTRACE and DBMS_UTILITY.FORMAT_ERROR_STACK enables coding a robust error-tracking mechanism in Java-based environments.

DBMS_JAVA.SET_OUTPUT enables redirection of DBMS_OUTPUT.PUT_LINE output to the Java environment.

- Inconsistent session management, in terms of both user sessions and session state, can be handled by using the relevant declarative features as described in the section "Best Practices in Terms of Trapping and Tracking Error Information" in conjunction with Oracle11g's inherent support of the native embedded-language technology, such as Java/J2EE, .NET, PHP, and Perl, for ensuring browser-based and services-based session stability and preventing scripting languages vulnerabilities like cross-site scripting (XSS), cross-site request forgery (XSRF), and so forth. The storage of the application state in the Oracle11g database and the overall session management can also be cataloged in the DB and managed for restore/analyze tasks. SIP (or Session Initiation Protocol) based mechanisms can be leveraged to analyze the best-fit scenario(s).

5.3.1   Tracking Error Information for Database Errors (Occurring in Any Tier)

To delve into the details, complete error information for implicitly raised exceptions can be captured using an exception handler and by tracking the error code, the error message text, the error line number of the first occurrence, the error execution stack, and the call execution stack. The call execution stack is a superset of the error execution stack that aids in tracking execution steps during debugging. The error execution stack displays the sequence of program steps that lead to the error that originally occurred, including the line number. The technique of obtaining complete error info can be implemented using code encapsulation in the form of packages (primarily PL/SQL-based) that provide the API for getting the error information (which includes all of the previous information listed, excluding the call execution stack).

The steps involved in creating such a package are as follows:

1. Define a record type or an object type (for a more robust and unified data structure) with global scope that contains the error message text (error code is part of this), error line information, and the entire error execution stack. The error line information contains the program owner, program name, and error line number for each line in the stack—where "program" refers to one of the called subprograms in the top-level program of the stack hierarchy.

2. Define a function that processes the exception info, populates an instance of this record or object type, and returns the same using REF CURSOR. An optional parameter to flag the inclusion of the entire error execution stack can be added.

The function for getting complete error info is to be used in all embedded-language programs and application modules, irrespective of the error logging and/or UI presentation mechanism. The core work is done by the DBMS_UTILITY.FORMAT_ERROR_BACKTRACE and DBMS_UTILITY.FORMAT_ERROR_STACK functions. The former returns the actual line number in the source code that failed the execution process the very first time; the latter returns complete error message without any truncations.

5.4   Techniques to Customize the Error Information Returned

The visible, useful components of the complete error information returned are the error code, error message text, and error execution stack.

5.4.1   Database Errors

In this case, the error message text begins with the error code prefixed by ORA. To customize this information, use the following sequence of steps:

1. Extract the error message text alone from the output returned by SQLERRM or DBMS_UTILITY.FORMAT_ERROR_STACK. This can be done using SQL-PL/SQL at the DB level.

2. Parse the error execution stack returned by DBMS_UTILITY.FORMAT_ERROR_BACKTRACE and obtain the original line number from the entire error stack, along with the program name in which the error occurred. The parsed info can be logged in a database table or file for persistent storage.

3. Transform the Oracle server error message into a user-friendly error message. Based on the error code, assign a customized error message from a lookup array object cached in the embedded language or stored-or-cached in the DB. *A one-to-one mapping of the Oracle error code with a custom error ID is a recommended practice and enables specialization of the error code instances specific to a*

business function. Note that the same SQLCODE can map to multiple instance IDs in this scenario.

4. Throw, trap, and handle customized error messages based on application-specific requirements. This also includes associating programming language–specific exceptions with these customized error messages that correspond to logical errors.

5. Escalate to the embedded-language environment using Oracle-native API for the language in context and/or the programmatic features of the same. This can be done by using an object structure at the application program level to make the parsed info transient and a (bidirectional) mapping from DB object to program object.

5.4.2   Programming Language–Specific Errors (Not Related to Oracle Server Errors)

In this case, the error message consists of either a system exception or an Oracle-based native language exception such as those related to null/invalid object references, invalid XML, messaging services errors, and OS-specific exceptions that pertain to the particular embedded language in context. The easy way to resolve these errors is to follow a similar methodology to that stated for database errors:

1. Trap and extract the error information using {throw…catch} notation.

2. Parse it using the language-specific string or regular expression functions.

3. Implement a mapping routine to transform the technical error into a customized "user-friendly" format, like serialization, enumeration, projection, and so forth.

4. Expose the same, using embedded language–specific GUI features or otherwise.

A best practice is to retrofit the converted error information as a parameter to an Oracle-DB stored procedure or a persistent object data structure that can be called from the particular embedded language using Oracle-native API or method invocation. To achieve this, code a "generic" stored procedure using an Oracle-compatible but standard ODBC/JDBC driver that can be used as a template for the stored procedure callout. This stored procedure can be used exclusively for this purpose only. As Oracle11g provides interoperability between Java, .NET, PHP/HTML/XML and SQL-PL/SQL, this strategy seems practically implementable. This can be part of the error-bots described in previous sections.

5.5   Techniques for Halting Further Processing on Error Occurrences

An important aspect of exception handling is what to do when an error occurs. This raises three options: Should we halt further execution when an exception occurs, ignore the error and continue processing, or let the exception fall through and handle it elsewhere? Of the three, halting the execution at a critical error-point is of significant relevance. As an example, errors resulting from high-severity validations and business rules cannot allow the application to continue processing beyond the point of occurrence. Ignoring the error can be useful when it does not impact the control flow of the application from one logical point to another. This is true even if the error is at the application code level only. The third option, letting the exception fall through, should be employed when exception occurring is handled at a later point of time, but should not be let loose until the outermost calling program. This is done by re-raising the exception in each of the enclosing code-blocks. If there is a sequence of subprograms calling one another resulting in a call stack, the exception that first occurred should be re-raised in each and every subprogram and handled by either raising it in the outermost calling program or handling it otherwise.

PL/SQL provides a packaged procedure called DBMS_STANDARD.RAISE_APPLICATION_ERROR that halts further execution from the point this procedure is called. This procedure causes the termination of program execution at the point it is called, in a manner similar to an unhandled exception. This means the entire error execution stack is displayed similar to the output of DBMS_UTILITY.FORMAT_ERROR_BACKTRACE. Additionally, this enables the use of a customized error message using a pre-assigned error number that doesn't represent an Oracle server error number. In fact, Oracle has reserved the range of numbers from −20999 to −20000 for use as the first argument to this procedure. These are the only numbers that can be used when calling this procedure

This can be used on the database Tier whenever an application needs to raise an error with a customized error message and stop execution at that point or when a customized error needs to be raised, trapped, and handled in a more robust manner, as necessitated by application/user requirements.

Summary

This chapter described the best practices for error management in terms of prevention, detection, resolution, and presentation across the end-to-end solution involving the database Tier, an intermediate and/or application Tier, and the end-user presentation Tier. Starting with a comprehensive description of the best practices for error management in terms of design that is both efficient and extensible, it focused on key concepts, such as techniques for obtaining the complete error information (which includes the complete error message text, the actual line number where the error first occurred, and the complete error execution stack), customizing the error information to enable application-specific representation, and halting execution at a particular error-point. A Master-Error-Management methodology consisting of code accelerator–design algorithms that describe best-fit technical procedures and code-patterns (such as custom *alert severity meters* described in Table 5.1 earlier) to arrive at a more generic error management implementation involving embedded languages is presented. The next chapter describes the best practices for data management in terms of best-fit design and development pragmatics. based on the best practices for data structure management and error management as the design foundation for the same.

Chapter 6

Best Practices for Data Management

In This Chapter

- Database management using embedded programming languages; design practices for best degree of fit
- Best practices in terms of connectivity to and interactivity with the Oracle database
- Techniques to connect to multiple databases simultaneously using same metadata
- Best fit for Oracle in the ADO.NET Framework—ODP.NET, ODE.NET
- Best practices for data retrieval
- Best practices for data manipulation
- Best practices for using LINQ to SQL
- Best practices for data validation
- Best practices for using XML
- Best practices for handling unstructured data
- Best practices to protect data integrity and special cases involved

6.1   Introduction

Data: Good, Better, and Best is the foundation for business information processing, delivery, presentation, in-flight interactivity and querying, and analysis that can be put into action for business operational continuity, better business value, and actionable decision-making. Knowing the data and its business meaning in terms of the usage scope plays a primary role in managing data end-to-end, from source data integration to an unified, consistent, and persistent presentation that enables anytime-anywhere-anyone availability and accessibility. Then follows the task of protecting the data from leakage, breaches, threats, and unauthorized access, both within the enterprise solution domain and beyond the enterprise. Once again, the *Right*

Design the First Time is the key driving factor for efficiency of the (enterprise) solution being architected, and goes a long way in promoting optimization, effectiveness, and efficiency of the solution.

As part of data integration or otherwise, this factor contributes a lot to the way changes are made in the database via applications. The proper selection of data source(s)/data elements for the synchronization of data using an optimized source data integration strategy is a practical challenge, as the data sources encompass an union of heterogeneous, homogeneous, and file-based data. The unification of data and content into a seamless information view-let enabling a visualized presentation augmented with the tasks of end-to-end user activity, database activity, and in-transit data monitoring spin off a huge set of tasks that have to interoperate transparently via event-based service-driven processes and in an automated and time-scheduled fashion. Finally, the data management design should be flexible enough to be adoptable and adaptable for current and future business needs.

This calls for the use of multiple co-existent technologies and deployment platforms to achieve an integrated solution (e.g., using SOA-based services for data management etc.), which in turn escalate to data management submodules. Treating data as services, especially for exposure to external applications and shared-computing platforms like the cloud, at the application and database levels; transaction auditing and logging user activity/business activity by the second; and event streaming are part of application streaming, which also includes data streaming in real time. Using functions that are callable from any programming language to enable group policy–based security in addition to row and column–based security contributes to the big picture of the solution framework and a unified computing platform. An emerging next-generation scenario that exemplifies this is the collaboration of evolving technologies such as cloud computing, virtualization, Web Services, and automation; for data management and integration, that includes data federation, data masking, enhanced data encryption, and operational data replication, to name a few. The goal is to achieve optimal data access, manipulation, integration, and presentation—*for lateral visibility into the business value of the same.*

The architecture for efficient data management can be based on the following aspects:

- *A unified data centralization framework*—a unified data integration framework at the source data level as well as at the data/content delivery stage—results in unified information presentation from the standpoint of anyone-anytime-anywhere accessibility without compromising on efficiency and productivity; it should have the ability for SOA enablement as well as having SOA-enabling capability by way of Data Services that can be embedded in any existing SOA-based services and/or on-premise platforms.

■ *A seamless workflow* that is event-based and is in line with the infrastructure management, capable of real-time and on-demand data services, and portability. As highlighted in Chapter 4 on Data Structure Management, the proper choice of data structures, as well as the methodologies for data storage, processing, and representation, is critical to the architecture of the data management framework. Efficient methods to organize the data use partitioning by business dimensions and advanced compression, followed by parallelized execution of queries and transactions, streaming data to make it available in real-time to avoid idle latency, and so on.

■ *Security of code*—How the data flow is coordinated and synchronized also depends on how the code is written. This has a ripple effect; the security of data also depends on security of code, and this in turn propagates to the security of sensitive and customer-specific data throughout the end-to-end solution, both internally and externally: protection from unauthorized user access (and insider threats) for both static data and data in-transit; data breaches; data loss prevention; robust database, user, and network activity monitoring; and audit-logging of the same (bidirectionally). Oracle11g's pre-integrated Advanced Encryption and Masking, Secure Backup, and Advanced Security; Oracle Database Vault and Label Security; and Oracle Configuration Management for Security, Audit Vault, and Total Recall provide a "defense-in-depth" methodology for achieving bulletproof security of data, end to end.

The key indicators are the business drivers significant to data management, to know the specifics of the data—who, where, why, when, how. The optimal performance indicators are based on these key indicators in terms of ability to handle high-volume data flows—instant response to query requests based on temporal effects in data; flattening unstructured content and merging it with external content; real-time availability; high-throughput in the case of transactional data updates; and so forth. This in turn ensures that information is available at the right time at the right place for the right user.

- *Data management and optimization*—Oracle11g database high-performance and high-availability features—such as group policy invocation, column-based fine-grained access control, fine-grained dependency control, transactional data consistency cross-data-bases, and the implicit design and self-tuning capabilities—can accelerate and automate data management and optimization. *The best practice is to design the data flow in sync with the business process flow to ensure that they not only align in terms of IT processes but also provide business agility, eliminating the need for IT intervention in the long run—and leaving some scope for extensibility and innovation.* This adds up to an ideal data infrastructure flow, up to the end-user presentation layer, for data availability and access. *Oracle11g provides some of the greatest-and-largest technologies, such as enterprise data integration, dynamic data provisioning, and Dynamic Data Services based on SOA-Web Services, providing both agility and mobility of information within the enterprise and beyond, as well as in-memory data replication and processing for ultra-high performance.*
- Interactive search capabilities on all kinds of data/content, using declarative, direct SQL-based full-text or regular expression-based searches that yield meaningful results while maintaining the lowest response time.

The goal is to ease the data management practices implemented, ensuring that they are flexible across the enterprise in terms of usability and requirements, ease of deployment, high data availability, extensibility, online/offline collaboration with existing applications, the ability to be up and running for the lifetime of the business and the technologies involved, and (last but not the least) easily adaptable to the changing/emerging technology and business landscape.

Creating modular and embeddable data processing accelerators that are event-based and can be plugged on-demand without affecting the existing in-place applications and solutions is one way to achieve this simplicity.

Figure 6.1 shows the typical data management landscape and the key design indicators that can be focused upon for a best practices implementation.

Seeing the landscape pictured in Figure 6.1 from an IT implementation perspective, the architecture for a best practice data management design for an Oracle-based embedded programming language solution can be visualized as shown in Figure 6.2.

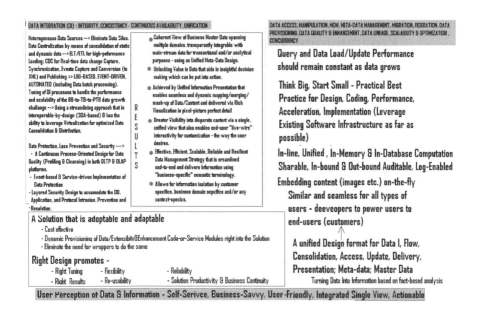

Figure 6.1   Data management landscape and key design indicators for best practice pragmatics.

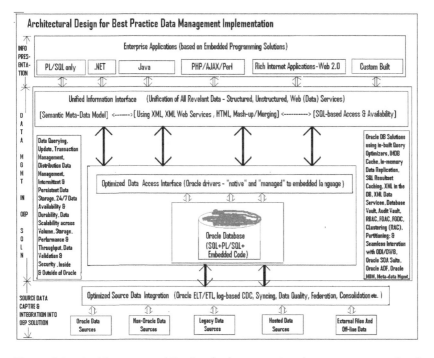

Figure 6.2   Architecture and Design for best practice data management implementation.

6.2   Database Management Using Embedded Programming Languages: Design Practices for the Best Degree of Fit

Combining methodology and infrastructure components to enable an extremely flexible architecture requires the convergence of Oracle Database technologies, robust information unification and presentation technologies (Rich Information Applications [RIA], Web 2.0, Oracle ADF, etc.), and the merging of Software as a Service (SaaS) and Infrastructure as a Service (IaaS) into a consolidated data services platform, resulting in a custom solution as a service that provides 360-degree data management capability in terms of customer-centricity, data isolation by context-specific domains, and high-definition presentation using business semantics—a best-fit for a better business value. This section explores the recommended design practices for the same for best degree of fit in terms of managing data or content, unprecedented end-user visibility into the data/information presented, and localized end-point security. These are listed below.

- *Data-driven RIA*—A consistent, global framework
- *Unstructured information consolidation using active document abstraction*
- *Alignment of data management design with data reality*—How the user sees the data depends on how the data needs to be presented at the user interface (UI) level, and this in turn depends on how the data representation and management architecture—using customized meta-rules—is designed. This in turn dictates how the data needs be to input (stored) in the DB and output (transformed and conformed).
- *Data profiling and enhancement* that allows cross-solution, system, application or source analyses
- *Cross-transaction consistency and* partial transaction partitioning (ACID vs. BASE)
- *Event-based traceability for managing persistent and intermittent changes in data and the related processes*—These changes can reflect an evolving pattern in terms of business functionality or business-to-consumer growth.
- *Unification of replication and transaction processing in the n-Tier solution - that can be components based or otherwise*—For example, CORBA and/or component object model/distributed component object model (COM/DCOM), etc.

- *Application-specific data replication*—Used to improve performance and availability
- *A logical interface for DQL, DML, presentation, and mash-up*—Using a unified "Intelligent Information Programming" code design to ensure continuous availability and performance (Anytime, Anywhere, Anyone (A-A-A) availability), which in turn mandates an integrated cohesion/mash-up and query mechanism of all kinds of data—unstructured, semistructured, structured, and/or externally-imported data at run-time.
- *Coding context-aware capabilities*—Such as context-enabled data/ text search, context-enabled data interaction, and visualization. This in turn calls for a solution that enables this by design.
- Implementing interactive controls for data input and visualization for "live" end-user interactivity and responsiveness
- *Using code accelerators for efficient text search capabilities in Oracle DB*—for example, personal search enabling, ensuring data lineage in searches based on un-ordered data hierarchies, clustering search results, and the like.
- *Implementing a querying code accelerator* for extracting a portion of content-based data (e.g., multimedia graphics data, graphs, images, etc.) or one that is based on text-based search results of a stored PDF document.
- *Proactive and pre-emptive protection against security and integrity lapses due to session data dependencies in RIA.*
- *Supporting dynamic interaction and interoperability among Web-based information content*—This is a *key indicator* in the design of metadata, metarules, and metaprogramming.
- *Supporting a robust and secure interface for data residing beyond the end-to-end solution space*—for example, access to data residing in public clouds or otherwise
- Synchronization of database-enabled data and XML-only enabled data
- Implementing querying of interprocess/intercomponent messages
- *Enhance, extend, and automate detection of vulnerabilities in embedded code interacting with the Oracle DB*, such as Java components, .NET components, and the like.
- *Using code accelerators as performance enhancers for external/un-managed component-based solutions*, whose source code is unavailable (e.g., Java-based or .NET-based components)

- *A unified Data Services Framework to manage data-intensive SaaS-based deployments* in terms of estimating computation times and action-response latency

- *Efficient data sharing between the different Tiers of the solution—* Intra-application, interapplication, and on the Web

- *Using code refactoring* to boost performance in terms of throughput and access times

- *Using data virtualization for data consolidation of disconnected data sources* like independent desktop application data and/or Web-based information delivery; Data Services play a key role in implementing this strategy

- *Creating a "unified information structure"* by dynamic combination of business data–specific data structures (linear, nonlinear, or composite), and Web-mediated delivery of the same using "business-friendly" semantics; metadata design plays a key role in this implementing this.

- Enhancing data management using a context-specific "data-processes-by-example" self-service interface built in to the solution .

- *Dramatically improving data administration* to enable reliability, scalability, and disaster recovery, as well as easy and secure data migration.

- *Implementing a version control system for each deployment version of thecomplete Data Definition Language (DDL) and related database build scripts.* Either this can be table-driven via validation of the scripts being executed in the development/test database (these scripts must have the same version number as part of the code as in the corresponding value in the deployment version table), or it can be achieved by integrating with Oracle11g-specific built-in versioning tools. In the former case, if the build number in the dev/test db is not greater than the build number in the new scripts to be deployed, they are simply not executed. If multiple database schemas are involved, a super-user table can be used for updating the version number for each db/schema in context, enabling the corresponding timestamp in Oracle11g TIMESTAMP format (this allows fractional seconds to be stored) to be more accurate.

- *Agility and efficiency through test-driven pragmatics*—putting the practical design into action.

The key indicator here is to measure the usability of the best design practices not only in terms of performance, reliability, and stability, but also to see how flexible the design is for reusability and adaptability—resulting in a Fast-Actionable-Synchronized-Tested (FAST) design.

- *Online (disk-to-disk) secure data backup.*
- *Overcoming performance challenges.* such as:
  - Consolidation of distributed transactional systems
  - Consistency and durability of concurrent distributed transactions
  - Eliminating data silos using optimized design for data integration
  - *Protecting data integrity of essential data that is stored outside the database*—For example, PDF files or Excel-based reports sent as e-mail attachments and offline archived data.
- *Data migration, data quality, and data enhancement*—Useful for custom analysis, enhancing (refining) existing data to gain business insight in terms of decision making (data-driven decision making and automating the same), expanding the data breadth, and identifying sub-views that are at a detailed/more granular level.
- *Using data federation to collect and disseminate data from disparate sources,* consolidating data in multiple formats including master data using optimal metadata design.
- *Optimizing data loading in terms of data upload and update response times and throughput,* and scheduling of the same.
- *Improving the analytical strength of the data* by incorporating anonymous and unified business dimensions that are linked across and also hierarchically—and providing the flexibility of longitudinal analysis. De-identification of sensitive data, proper data modeling, and interactive data visualization can significantly aid in this process.
- *Granular visibility into the performance of the Oracle database and the application behavior* by monitoring DB-to-application activity, user interactions, and the network—data, events, and process flows. This process can be automated and self-service-enabled to eliminate IT intervention and remote management capabilities.

In-built services, managed services (such as security services, data protection services, remote accessibility services, etc.), event streaming and systems integration are all solution enhancers.

6.3   Best Practices in Terms of Connectivity to and Interaction with the Oracle Database

- Align database column types with embedded language code types across all tiers of the solution, including composite and nested data structures. This can be done by using the %TYPE anchor in code involving SQL, PL-SQL, and the compatible embedded language type in the application code. This ensures logical data type independence between the database and the rest of the solution as also improves performance by eliminating implicit data type conversion and faster access/updates to data.
- Use an A-A-A design that is optimally scalable (scale-up, dynamically scale-out, and scale-in), efficient (speeds up—minimal time-to-delivery) and involves reduced cost of delivery/deployment.
- Build a semantic metadata layer that translates the technical details into "business-friendly" information and expose it to the presentation interface; this is a key factor in driving business value of the solution. This can be done by exposing the semantics using a Semantic Mark-up Language like XML.
    - A conversion function can be used to align the application grid-based row index (or a "logical row id") with the physical ROWID. This can be defined as a PL/SQL packaged function that takes the logical row id as an input parameter and returns the corresponding physical ROWID of the row in the database table. Taking this a step further, this can be added as a declaratively feature, whenever possible.
    - The code execution strategy also decides the performance efficiency of the solution, especially in case of data-intensive processing involving SQL, DQL, and DML. In these situations, the following best practices can be followed:
        - Performing a parallel query partitioning for read access. In this case only a part of the data file/table/data partition is read in each slave process by splitting the data based on size

and dividing these subsets over each slave, yet ensuring that the primary data file/table/data partition is still located on a single file system/database.

■ Partitioning by data, as opposed to database table partitioning by design)

■ In case of parallelizing application-specific SQL code, *a custom partitioning-by-example* algorithm can be designed to simulate the same by partitioning the SQL involved into data ranges using the MOD operator in conjunction with bind variables representing the node # and # of nodes.

■ The partitioning-by-example strategy can be used to achieve application-specific data replication to pivot, merge (un-pivot), aggregate, and segregate data by solution-specific requirements using stream processing (real-time data streaming) by way of pipelined table functions in SQL, which enables collation/cohesion of input/output data across individual clustered data sets, each tailored to address a particular SQL read/write operation. This boosts performance and improves efficiency of the overall data I/O.

■ Create dimensional data (be it SCD or lookup data) for populating fact tables available in the cache by using the IMDB cache on the DB Tier or application Tier (a kind of cache preloading option) *in* case of analytical queries in data warehousing and/or BI solutions. Change data detection and measurement. The ability to detect changes in a data source is a key indicator for data integration. Oracle11g provides both synchronous CDC (change data capture), which uses DB triggers, and asynchronous CDC, which is log-based. This in-built functionality can be extended to automatically "detect" the changes occurring, using events that log data changes while also measuring their impact on the DB, on application load/performance, and on the business context. Then, the CDC escalates the results via live/incremental event streaming and exposes the results to the IT team/business users via Fast Alert Notification (FAN). The impact analyses can be based on comparing rows in the most recent data stream (the changed data) against those in an earlier one (the reference stream), identifying and outputting the differences. The simplest way to do this is to add audit columns to the underlying tables and use parameterized queries, based on the date of data change, to filter the rows that have changed since the last commit/check.

This strategy can be extended to a more generalized *Database Activity Monitoring Framework* to encompass the end-to-end monitoring of the database events and actions.

- Minimize the number of network calls. This applies primarily to Web applications that pull data from a database. Each database call incurs some overhead in terms of CPU cycles, I/O, and memory. For Web-based applications, which are huge hitters in terms of user requests, scalability issues can be overcome by optimizing the Web page load time in advance. In addition, Oracle11g enables returning multiple rows in a single instance via a single stored procedure call. Corresponding to the embedded language involved, there are native result-set objects by the respective Oracle-based Data Access driver. Using these, data can be shared between the Web page and the database in an efficient manner.

The design of the code accelerators can be based on the following options:

- In addition to the generic Information Access Interface, like a query interface as described in one of the above bulleted lists, custom code connectors can be used to "capture" the underlying code, computation, flow, and (hence) the results into a single code-appliance, so that it can be reused in other solutions/applications in place, either co-deployed (i.e., embedded) or co-existent (i.e., standalone execution)
- Synchronous or in-line code appliances determine how the implemented code accelerator is used in the overall solution. The best practice is to use an in-process code appliance via a common coding interface language like C/C++ that is in sync with Oracle11g "native" compatibility. This has two advantages: better performance, as it runs inline with the process base of the server engine; and less set-up and monitoring on the server side, as the code is based on in-server execution and handling of the related events directly inside the server space. The results can be seamlessly exposed using a generic output-enabled metadata language, such as XML or RDF. This is really useful for an in-place solution that is Oracle-based and has an intermediate database-solution interface layer to decouple the processing from the subsolution/presentation tiers.

- Stand-alone or asynchronous code appliances can be coded in the specific embedded programming language, such as C, C++, Java, C#, and are embeddable into a corresponding existing target application. This is because these code enhancers have the ability to run on their own and so are more distributed in nature. They can be installed in solutions running on multiple configurations, as long as the application supports the code compatibility required for specific embedded language in context and syncs with the Oracle database at the back end. The integration of the two can done using an interface bridge. Oracle11g provides both of these capabilities by the in-built "native" providers for Java, .NET, C/C++ that are API-based, as also in-database execution of stored C/C++ code in conjunction with XML outputting capabilities

- A more global solution for end-to-end business activity monitoring can be implemented by using Oracle Business Activity Monitoring, which does the same across the database, solution/application and/or presentation Tiers. This is described in Chapter 7, "Best Practices for Application Management."

- Dramatically reduce the need to code custom scripts using predefined code snippets or predefined expressions—declaratively using virtual columns or procedurally—just plug and execute.

- Leverage DB package benefits like execution time, maintenance time, and minimal vulnerability to schema dependency errors (FGDC)

- Dramatically accelerate mass deployment of embedded code (packages) by using automatic validation and consistency of Oracle SQL-PL/SQL code in conjunction with embedded language code.

- *Fine-grained* auditing and activity monitoring of user/process/transaction level activity at the lowest possible granular level—by individual user task, transaction, and item (table/row/column), using an intelligent Alert notification framework for the same—can done using FAN techniques (Fast Alert Notification) in Oracle11g that support self-execution of the related processes to enable real-time/right-time alerting.
  - Use code accelerators to automatically reroute these alerts via e-mail messages to the appropriate (group) list of users when code packages fail to execute correctly.
  - Use code accelerators to automatically warn the user of poorly performing SQL code via FAN alerts or e-mail alerts notifying

them of the probable latency involved. Simultaneously, warn the DBA/DB Solution architect of the same. Oracle11g has self-tuning capabilities to tweak poorly performing SQL code, and this can be augmented with a custom-built Data Access Performance Analyzer and Enhancer, using in-built mechanisms such as SQL plan baselines.

■ Use code accelerators to create a 360-degree anonymous (de-identified) customer view of cross-functional, business-specific data.

■ Special validation/monitoring routines specifically tailored towards the database activity (to-and-fro) ensure not only a pre-emptive way of measuring data quality, but also the performance of the "live" database, on an "as-is" basis. This is critical to any Oracle-based solution, especially one that involves an application layer using embedded languages. This in turn should take care of database and data security, quality, "blind spots" in the data and in the the data flow (again stressing the A-A-A paradigm in terms of data storage and accessibility), "stale data," and so on, as well as the data presentation and modification at the presentation Tier.

6.4   Techniques to Connect to Multiple Databases Simultaneously Using the Same Metadata

It is possible to easily and seamlessly integrate large volumes from diverse data sources using built-in Data Transformation Accelerators to enable data cleansing for data quality and master data management (MDM) applications.

ETL (extract, transform, and load) operations are essential processes for collecting and consolidating source data. High data volumes, multiple and heterogeneous data sources, data quality inaccuracies, different data model implementation schemes (such as relational star and snowflake schemas), slowly changing dimensions, and multidimensional design are key factors to be considered.

Fast, reliable and actionable decision making is enabled based on the consolidated information, which encompasses all the relevant data.

The following best practices are the primary best-fit design indicators for heterogeneous data integration that ensure concurrency, currency, and scalable performance:

■ Use information contexts that contain only specific actionable data/content pertaining to a context (e.g., business domain, user-request, specific business process, etc.) from large volumes of data, and seamless integrate and automate the same. This provides continuous data availability, in real-time and at the right time

- Use dynamic data visualization by way of 3D and Web 2.0 functionality to create a custom data/content set for each custom information context. Place the control of the same in the hands of the customer/end-user via drag-n-drop interaction. This not only gives the user access to data/content stored across locations, but also the flexibility of using the same on-demand, or at any point-in-time, and most importantly, in any desired manner, that is specific to the business context
- To make the implementation of the above seamless, transparent and reusable, the relevant data/content can be virtually converged into a view structured using the same single meta-data dictionary, that is dynamically managed inside the database or (in-memory if required). 3D visualization of the same can be implemented in a similar manner – and all of the logic and workflow involved is stored and processed in the Oracle database – and can even be exposed as a callable DB-Web Service, in other words, a Contextual Information Service (C-I-S) that gets streamed into the overall DB workflow (on-demand or otherwise)

The CDC techniques in Oracle11g can be applied to the data synchronization and replication processes using the common (custom) meta-data, thereby resulting real-time data integration of both OLTP, OLAP, and external data.

The Key Design Indicator is to zero-in the data-intensive computations into where the data is actually going to be stored, i.e., the Oracle DB. This means segregating the underlying logic into context-specific packaged procedures, that are stored, compiled, and executed inside the Oracle database. In addition, taking advantage of implicit in-lining of sub-programs (as of Oracle11g), can aid in one-pass data I/O. These two optimizations enable improved performance, especially when semi-structured and/or unstructured data sources are involved in addition to relational data sources.

6.5   Best Fit for Oracle in the ADO.NET Framework— ODP.NET and ODE.NET

.NET Framework 3.5 builds incrementally on the new features added in .NET Framework 3.0—for example, the feature sets in Windows Workflow Foundation (WF), Windows Communication Foundation (WCF), Windows Presentation Foundation (WPF) and Windows CardSpace. In addition, .NET Framework 3.5 contains a number of new features in several technology areas which have been added as new assemblies to avoid breaking changes. They include the following:

- The deep integration of Language Integrated Query (LINQ) and data awareness will let you write code in LINQ-enabled languages to filter, enumerate, and create projections of several types of SQL data, collections, XML, and datasets by using the same syntax.
- ASP.NET Ajax lets you create more efficient, more interactive, and more highly personalized Web experiences that work across all the most popular browsers.
- There is new Web protocol support for building WCF services, including Ajax, JSON, REST, POX, RSS, ATOM, and several new WS-* standards.
- Full tooling support is available in Visual Studio 2008 for WF, WCF, and WPF, including the new workflow-enabled services technology.
- New classes in .NET Framework 3.5 base class library (BCL) address many common customer requests.

6.6   Best Practices for Data Retrieval

Reduce database costs significantly by adopting *heterogeneous database architecture (in-memory replicated data sets)* and implementing Oracle11g for a large part of business-critical and operational applications. The IMDB cache feature and the SQL-PL/SQL result-set DB cache and client cache feature for embedded language applications add to in-application support in terms of data access/update performance in production environments. Consider these proactive data access key performance indicators:

- *Self-service querying capabilities*—Ad-hoc querying and the ability to store the results in a custom fashion (e.g., slice, dice, burst, section, redirect to multiple destinations, etc.)

- *Data mining techniques*—Predict anomalies in transaction data; a pre-emptive data quality measure that can be implemented via code accelerators
- *In-solution performance capabilities*:
  - IMDB cache and result-set cache enabling on the solution Tier and/or client Tier in addition to the DB Tier
  - Leveraging *codeless self-tuning options of Oracle11g* by proper configuration and scheduling of the same
  - Dynamic data virtualization for data integration (cross-platform) to data availability to data manipulation to data visualization to Data Services
  - Using Database Resident Connection Pooling for embedded language solutions to enable connection sharing that in turn dramatically increases the scalability of the solution
  - Using disconnected data sources that simulate the IMDB cache feature to act as a fully functional and persistent data source, with the actual Oracle DB decoupled from the application/solution.

The key performance indicator of in-solution performance is its ability to retain optimal performance irrespective of data and user growth (scalability); its A-A-A accessibility; its optimal data throughput in terms of number of transactions processed, data traffic, and response times (to avoid latency) in servicing end-user requests for data (or information) availability; and its optimal CPU usage (e.g., exploiting the full potential of computing resources).

- *Data analysis*—The solution should enable rapid business insight into all kinds of data—operational, historical, strategic, whatever you need to see. This can be done with Oracle 11g's dynamic analyses features, using NDS to construct dynamic analytical queries that can run in-database and then cache the results on the client side, and the like.
- *Database design*—The design should be tailored toward seamless scalability, enabling near-real-time data streams to be processed, stored, and then accessed for operational/tactical analysis purposes. This can be done using log-managed CDC and continuously (or rather intermittently) running "live" feeds of changed data as well as other necessary "data snapshots" based on windowing time frame.

A Key Data Access Enhancer is query prioritization, based on response time as well as business importance. A balance needs to be achieved between running queries with subsecond response times and those with mission-critical importance. This can be implemented by a Custom Query Accelerator that can be built using a query monitoring and tuning framework based on business domain and user context. Oracle11g adds some self-tuning capabilities in the form of automation and scheduling of SQL query plan baselines and query result statistics in terms of CPU and I/O utilization; parsing, fetching, and delivery; response time; and overall throughput. Also, the Oracle11g Real Application Testing functionality can be used to replicate a snapshot of user queries and their diagnostics, analyze the same and create prioritization lists based on analyses.

- *Incorporation of powerful performance-centric techniques*, such as:
    - Pre-aggregation of data (data summarization (by business dimensions) using MVS and custom projections; and data consolidation—a pivoting technique to collapse rows into columns of a derived table
    - Advanced compression of data for optimal data I/O in addition to storage efficiency
    - Partitioning of data to leverage dynamic partitioning pruning on tables/views—this helps in better data/information lifecycle management for both OLTP and OLAP environments
    - Parallelization of queries and/or streaming by means of pipelining (using table functions)
    - Query refactoring to enable reuse of subqueries in super queries, in a single SQL statement
    - Query rewrite techniques using materialized views (these can be partitioned, too)
    - Time-sensitive data access, like as-is queries in near real time, point-in-time queries as of a certain timestamp, and what-if queries for pre-emptive/predictive analysis
    - *Query auditing using autonomous transactions and ASH (Active Session History info)*—Custom log tables joined with the v$active_session_history dynamic performance view

- *Easy-to-use, Web 2.0 interfaces*—These speed and simplify critical business analysis efforts, from information presentation in a unified business-oriented view to on-the-fly integration of external content based on the information delivered to derive an enhanced (and visualized) intuitive view.
- *Integrated in-memory analysis*—This provides powerful performance and actionable "business-oriented" information delivery, right where you need it (R-R-R-R).
- *A relational OLAP design*—This design enables high-volume data analysis by providing multiple views of information using the Web or Excel—without compromising system performance.
- *Continuous data availability and management across the business solution space*—The most relevant data for business operations (active data) can be online, and the rest can be archived in a manner that ensures the same or almost similar response time. The Oracle11g features of dynamic provisioning of datasets in the application Tier, the database grid, parallelization, and the pipelined execution of queries on data residing in-database, in-memory, or in other delegated efficient storage enables seamless scalability, linear performance, and continuous availability.
- *Distribution of retrieved data across different target platforms*—This is another vital aspect of data access best practices, which can be done using various techniques. The ones having the best-of-breed pragmatics are:
  - Federated queries based on a unified view of consolidated data or on multiple coherent views of business-domain specific and/or strategic contexts
  - Federation of Data Services implemented using Oracle SOA methodology to enable real-time or on-demand delivery/publishing of the same
  - Combination of data virtualization and automation. delivering information on-demand to multiple/disparate end-user-device end points in the form of the contextual business information view-let.

6.7 Best Practices for Data Manipulation

Use SQL array processing for massive data updates via the embedded language code or directly in the database via stored procedures using

SQL-PL/SQL. In this case, it is important to identify the typical time-out in seconds for the embedded language solution in context (i.e., in Java, .NET, or PHP/Ajax-based solutions). The average timeout is approximately 25–30 seconds (though this parameter can be controlled by a configuration specific parameter). As Oracle11g locks the table being updated, updates on multiple columns and involving huge row-sets can dramatically impact the performance of the Web-based application, as this also increases the size of the transaction log/rollback segment. In this scenario, Oracle11g allows to leverage SQL array processing based on an insert/update/delete statement so that the data change is done in batches of size n, where n is a reasonable positive number chosen to balance the dataset volume being updated, the disk I/O, the CPU-intensive metrics involved, and most importantly, the size of the PGA or program global area (that is reserved for application code).

Typical values for n are 100 or 1,000. A value greater than 1,000 can also be used, but keep in mind that the larger the value, the more PGA resources consumed, even if the response time is fast.

For each update batch, a commit is to be issued so that it resets the rollback segment and a scheduled job via event processing can take online backup of the transaction logs as the updates are committed for each batch.

Here is a code snippet that illustrates the same with a batch size of 1,000:

```
BEGIN
 LOOP
 UPDATE appl_tran_tab SET depend_val1 = :1,
 depend_val2 = :2
 WHERE tran_code = :3 AND ROWNUM <= 1000;
 IF SQL%ROWCOUNT = 0 THEN
 EXIT;
 END IF;
 COMMIT;
 END LOOP;
END;
```

/

The same code can be encapsulated as a packaged stored procedure and called from the embedded language, such as C#, C/C++, Java, etc. Alternately, it can be directly used as an anonymous PL/SQL block in the embedded language code. Using a packaged stored procedure improves the scalability and efficiency of the code.

Use dynamic code generators to implement repetitive database actions such as Data Control Language (DCL), Data Defintion Language (DDL) statements. Code generators can be used to implement the running of statistics at the database or schema level for all tables, to rebuild, to reorganize indexes after data loads, and to grant or revoke user authentication permissions on a subset of tables/db objects, based on certain conditions. To ensure fast response times for Web-based requests involving high-traffic volumes that are densely distributed, a recommended best practice is to use the partial transaction partitioning mechanism, that works for regular Web-based as well as Web-Services based distributed transaction environments.

6.8   Best Practices for Data Validation

As the embedded language solution interacts with the Oracle database for bidirectional data flow, several processes take place implicitly within the database as well as within the application. The primary processes are data access; data movement; data transformation/processing; data loading; data consolidation; data delivery and presentation in a unified format; data manipulation both implicitly (by the DB and the application program) and interactively by the end user; and data persistence via commit operations.

Data validation is the primary mechanism to ensure and preserve data integrity throughout the database solution. Though each one of these processes involves some kind of validation, the validation of data is vital to the processes of data loading, data transformation/processing, data consolidation, and data manipulation. This section highlights the best practices for the same in terms of identifying "bad" data and cleansing of the same, data de-identification as a measure to anonymously present sensitive data, and various other parameters and procedures encompassing the data validation landscape.

The key data validation performance indicators are content and context. Content refers to the actual value(s) of the data and the format in which it is stored or represented. Context refers to the relevance of the data with respect to the business domain, business process, and/or IT process, which in turn decides the usability of the data in the particular context. Data validation must be performed for content as well as for its contextual scope and use to ensure and protect data integrity end-to-end.

Key indicators for data validation are:

- Volatility indicators
- Comparator indicators
- Additional indicators

Volatility variables include validating input data for errors (functional, technical, missing values)—invalid data, and missing data. These variables enable the determination of the functional limitations of data, which in turn cascades to the technical limitations of such data being input/processed/stored/output.

Locate the "blind" spots in data by way of clearly differentiating empty values from NULL values (from a business function perspective). For example, an empty field value in an input data source might be a valid value from the business case standpoint; loading it into an Oracle table column constrained as NOT NULL needs data masking of the same in a manner that is acceptable to the business-centric use of the same.

Identifying data that is "corrupted" due to missing links or dangling references. This might entail some post-processing steps, such as reorganizing the database structures to fix the broken links. However, this needs to be done transparently to the user and the application. Oracle Data Integrator/Oracle Warehouse Builder, with its inherent enhanced Data Profiling and Quality features, can drastically reduce the implementation effort involved. This can be architected as an intermediate component between the Oracle DB and the application and streamlined as a service or scheduled process via automation.

Comparator variables include

- Using data filters, optimized validation algorithms, and data quality test iterations to identify disparate patterns in data, comparing the relative deviation in the data from normal to abnormal values, and classifying the results as outliers, "unused" data, and sparse data (i.e., due to too many missing values or due to uneven distribution of values) that is critical to the business solution.

- Design for autodetecting data endpoints—the floor-ceiling values for range-bound data and automation of the same (in most cases)
- Validation of underlying business rules in the Oracle embedded solution in context. This requires cross-column data validation to test for interdependencies, cross-row data validation to ensure accurate interrelationships, and/or cross-table data validation/comparison to verify cross-functional business (data) integrity. A typical use case for this is during data migration from a legacy/external data source into the Oracle database.

Additional variables include

- Preserving the integrity of the business keys related to specific entities implemented by corresponding tables. This can be done by assigning artificial keys (as opposed to surrogate keys) that are database-mapped equivalents of the respective business keys and implementing the same using primary, unique, and/or foreign keys. Surrogate keys can be used for further granularity when required (e.g., in database systems that are primarily for read-access and analysis)
- Performing collective validation; a combination of columns taken together as a tuple for validation can result in being marked as "valid data," but one or more of the individual column values might be declarable as incorrect data. *This is very significant in the case of contextual validations.*
- Automating data quality processes to manage "invalid" data on an ongoing basis
- Turning unstructured data into meaningful information that enables insight-driven actionable decision making.
- Providing database and thereby solution scalability in terms of explosive data growth and user base by performing pre-emptive estimation and allocation of database size so as to enable DB pre-growth for the best degree of fit.
- Leveraging clusters and grid computing to get optimal efficiency for the same database-grid, application-grid, real-time "data" streaming for processing and "information" streaming for availability (A-A-A).

6.9   Best Practices for using LINQ to SQL

.NET Framework 3.5 builds incrementally on the new features added in .NET Framework 3.0—for example, feature sets in Windows Workflow Foundation (WF), Windows Communication Foundation (WCF), Windows Presentation Foundation (WPF) and Windows CardSpace. In addition, .NET Framework 3.5 contains a number of new features in several technology areas that have been added as new assemblies to avoid breaking changes. They include the following:

- Deep integration of Language Integrated Query (LINQ) and data awareness. This new feature will let you write code in LINQ-enabled languages to filter, enumerate, and create projections of several types of SQL data, collections, XML, and DataSets by using the same syntax.
- ASP.NET Ajax lets you create more efficient, more interactive, and more highly personalized Web experiences that work across all the most popular browsers.
- New Web protocol support for building WCF services, including Ajax, JSON, REST, POX, RSS, ATOM, and several new WS-* standards.
- Full tooling support in Visual Studio 2008 for WF, WCF, and WPF, including the new workflow-enabled services technology.
- New classes in .NET Framework 3.5 base class library (BCL) that address many common customer requests.

6.10   Best Practices for Using XML

XML has emerged as a unified and universal data representation and storage format that is OS-agnostic, solution/platform agnostic, and more importantly technology agnostic. It has its own schema and tag definitions that can contain descriptors for data or content being stored, can have data represented in a hierarchical fashion, and *is more tailored for incorporation of custom semantics.* It can have external code snippets embedded into it as well. Starting as a next-level language to HTML for Web pages, it has evolved into a data representation and storage model of its own, encompassing a wide range of technologies from relational database data and data model management and object-based data unification (be it Java/J2EE, .NET, PHP/Ajax, C/C++, etc.), to SOA and Web Services, to name a few. Oracle11g has an XMTYPE data type that can be used to store XML data in a table column just like any other scalar data type (e.g., NUMBER, VARCHAR2, etc.). It also has the flexibility of declaratively querying and manipulating XML-based data using XSQL, XPath, XQuery, and native API for the same for embedded languages.

Using XML has the following benefits:

- Seamless data and content (structured and unstructured) consolidation into a unified, simple, and easily interpretable information format for presentation to the business user. As an example, XML can be used to integrate/mash-up internal text data or binary document content from the database with a picture or map by transforming the same into a unified format.
- It is standards based, highly flexible, extensible, and customizable for any kind of data representation, as long as the basic XML structure is maintained.
- It works across multiple technologies, platforms, and operating systems and easily aligns with next generation information architectures like those using service-oriented architecture (SOA) and Web Services, virtualization, cloud computing, data, content and event streaming, real-time integration, and the like.
-

From an embedded programming perspective, the XML advantage comes as an efficient and effective data/content/information access, update, delivery, and presentation mechanism. Here's a list of best practices for use of XML in an embedded programming solution based on the Oracle DB:

- *Use XML as an intermediate storage and processing platform for bidirectional data flow between heterogeneous databases or applications and SQL-based declarative API.* This eliminates the overheads of using temporary tables or intermediate data transformation engines. In addition, the entire process is in-memory, which increases performance and scalability.
  The derived benefits are a balance of speed and quality while presenting data/content from multiple formats as a single unified information view that enables intelligent decision making without losing any of the format/logic associated with the business rules corresponding with each individual piece of data/content.
- *Use XML to accelerate contextual content searches.* As an example, XML can be used as a pivot layer to hold multicontext search

results in one single format that can be processed using a generic rules engine; the results of the same can be federated to multiple targets, each relevant to its context. This improves the performance of such search queries. A classic example of this is searches based on language-based content translation.

- *Use XML coupled with SQL for accelerating federated data access.* This is implementable by constructing contextual views of the data as logical, XML-based, semantic information packs. SQL-based XML data retrieval can be applied to distribute the results to context-specific user requests/application-modules.

- *Use XML Data Services to accelerate (distributed) transaction processing.* Read and update transactional data, using XML for optimal performance and low latency. This is of particular value in the case of distributed transactions, in which data integrity is of critical importance. These Services are interoperable and reusable by design and can be used in existing solutions to protect data integrity.

- *Use XML for disparate data/object binding.* This can be implemented using custom information containers that can be designed as follows:

  - A component containing the organizational structure of the data/object

  - A component containing the storage structure of the data/object (i.e., the actual dataset of values)

  - A component containing custom tags that can refer to context-specific attributes or metadata

The design pattern for the overall implementation can consist of the following steps:

1. Use a code accelerator to build custom information containers for each data/object context that needs to be bound. This can be represented in a specific embedded language object format or in XML format.

2. Tie and bind these containers together using a generic XML-based API to result in a single integrated XML layer.

3. Expose the unified information content using Oracle11g based SQL.

Figure 6.3 presents a visual snapshot of this design.

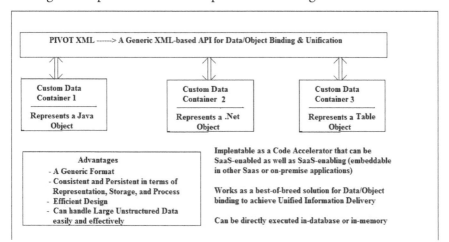

Figure 6.3   Design pattern for data/object binding and unification using XML.

- *Use XML Web Services and SOA as the design choice for real-time data integration.* Here are the design steps for to integrate digital content (images, media clips) in real-time:

   1. Use an input custom code adapter to extract and transform the input content into XML and publish it as an XML Web (Content) Service (WS).

   2. Add an additional component to the above XML WS, which is an event to execute the Web Service that stores the XML-formatted content and also adds a link to its content. *This event itself can be converted into XML.*

   3. Use an output custom code adapter to transform the XML-formatted content into its original format.

   4. This enables the content as well as the link to it to be stored in the Oracle11g DB. Publish the generated link via the same Web Service so that it is exposed for online sharing and collaboration.

   Oracle11g SOA Suite enables this implementation. The XML Web Service can be directly integrated into the DB itself and the input can be fed from the embedded programming language application.

When implementing a Business Rules Accelerator, the rule of the thumb is that it should be extensible or reprogrammable for refactoring purposes.

- Use XML to help simplify underlying data; this in turn helps reduce the complexity involved in analytic data/content.
- Use XML for e-mail consolidation and persistent storage, so that it can be retained for longer periods of time and in an efficient and reusable manner.

6.11   Best Practices for Handling Unstructured Data

Unstructured data includes enterprise data that does not conform to a particular predefined or standard data structure, but needs to be stored, accessed, and manipulated inside the Oracle DB. Examples include documents (Word, PDF, presentations, Excel files, thesis, large docs), graphics, images and maps, audio/video clips, EDI files, data models, Web pages, and the like.

These convey a lot of meaningful information to the business analyst or domain specialist for a wide range of solutions such as information consolidation, content mash-up, complex custom searches on documents, and so forth.

The primary management indicators for unstructured data can be classified as follows:

- Synchronization of solution-level unstructured data with appropriate master data and/or the merging of disparate unstructured data. This is a key performance indicator both from the business and the IT perspectives. A better, faster, easier approach to implement this is to use a custom metadata definition and programming module as an application accelerator, dynamically streaming and streamlining the unstructured data and the relevant master data. Running this directly from the Oracle DB eliminates integration latency and consumes less I/O and CPU cycles, thereby enabling increased efficiency and hence increased productivity.
- Granular visibility of the data at the end-user level, using data visualization, content mash-ups, and live-wire freeform user interactivity (instant action-response), all delivered using business-savvy, user-friendly terminology. This can be achieved by implementing

an additional semantic metadata interface to enable IT->business language processing.

- Personal search capabilities based on context-based, case-based, like/unlike, file-name-based, full text searches, or mix-n-merge modes of filtering.
- Click-stream data access/manipulation and transaction control (including synchronous and asynchronous commit). Asynchronous transaction control involves in-memory data replication that enables subsecond response time for the transaction taking place, still preserving the ACID-based two-phase commit consistency. Oracle11g's Enterprise Grid, comprising the Database Grid and Application Grid, can be used to achieve a similar kind of functionality.

The update operation on unstructured or semistructured data can involve dynamic reorganization of the same in a different format. This calls for the adaptability of the data processes in place to meet on-the-fly alteration/manipulation needs. This can be done by channelizing the data movement/transformation processes using a common "Unstructured Data Service Engine" that can be implemented as a code accelerator and deployed and r-used as a Data Service for unstructured data. A good example is to process a voice data component from a customer call center using XML. The input to the engine is data in audio format, and the output can be in any format, such as PDF, Visual, or the like, with XML being used as a data messaging/mediation/transformation base.

- Protection of the data within and beyond the enterprise solution space. This involves prevention of unauthorized access/update as well as data abuse/breaches by privileged users such as DBAs. The key to securing data against mismanagement from privileged users is to enable grant/revoke of permissions using an external user interface/application module without giving backend (direct) access to the application/DB. Fine grained access control can be used for row/column level security (including group set–based security policies) and Oracle11g column-level, tablespace-level encryption can be used for tighter control.
- Auditing of all changes to unstructured data in the DB and the access/update of external file content. The former can be done at the application/module/user-schema/transaction level, using CDC

in conjunction with Oracle11g-based audit trails and/or business activity monitoring (BAM) and Fast Alert Notificaiton (FAN). The latter can be implemented using Oracle Secure Files. CDC combined with event scheduling/publishing can be used to automate the processes involved. The key indicator here is that the audit results should be made persistent so that custom searches for active/dormant users, data (most frequently accessed/updated data, least used data, and the like.), activity involving access to resources outside of the DB (like the OS file system), and/or a combination of these criteria can be done.

- On-demand integration. The Oracle-based embedded language solution must have the ability to integrate any type of unstructured data on-the-fly. In other words, any such data component should be embeddable inline with the information delivery interface or persistently storable in-database, on-demand, and in-context, not just in near-real-time but also at the right time it is needed. Oracle11g-based SOA/Data Services can be used in conjunction with proactive scheduling and automation for the Data Services Component to be published, to meet this on-demand integration need.
- Efficiency and Scalability
- Anytime Accessibility

Oracle11g provides prebuilt data types for storing such data as CLOB (Character Large Object) for ASCII or Unicode text data, BLOB (Binary Large Object) for all binary data like Word, PDF, presentation, spreadsheet documents, visual data like graphics, images and maps, and all multimedia content-based data like audio/video clips, animated graphics etc. Oracle 11g also has the XML data type for storing these types of unstructured data in a uniform data structure format for delivery and movement of the same between different and disparate application systems (both homogeneous and heterogeneous).

In addition, Oracle Content Management and Oracle Text enable SQL-based unstructured data storage and retrieval based on:

- Storage based on optimized data structures involving object, large object (CLOB, BLOB, BFILE), of XMLTYPE that enable SQL-based CRUD operations on unstructured data. As an example, LOB-based data partitions can be created with the primary dimension or partition key column being the LOB column and a partition key column (acting as second dimension) being a hash-function based identifier that ensures that data is evenly distributed in each partition. either during data loading or otherwise.

- Prebuilt optimized algorithms for text-based document searches using regular expressions in SQL (the power of Unix-like shell scripting directly using SQL and tightly integrated into the Oracle DB) – *for case-sensitive, context-sensitive, pattern-based and Boolean-condition searches*
- Optimized "native" Oracle Types in each of the embedded languages (Java, C/C++, C#, PHP) that enable efficient data I/O and transformations, corresponding to the SQL-based unstructured data types

---

A key indicator for protecting content generated from Oracle like file-based reports, sensitive information extracts can be secured using the 's' suffixed file extension of the appropriate file type inherent in the Oracle Information/Content Management feature-set (e.g., .pdfs for a PDF generated file etc.)

This is very useful for protecting authenticated data beyond the boundaries of the enterprise solution, as the 's'-suffixed file can neither be accessed nor decrypted by any user not granted the required privileges

---

6.12 Best Practices to Protect Data Integrity and Special Cases Involved

Data integrity is an essential requirement of any software solution from the business and IT standpoint. A solution that offers the highest levels of data protection, secure accessibility to all data all the time, and integrity of the same harvests a huge business value by providing consistent, reliable, and highly available information that is bulletproof 24/7, and goes a long way in sustaining the business continuity of the solution.

Ensuring and protecting data integrity involves splitting the data security and protection frame of reference into two planes:

- User interaction with data (and hence with the database)
- Application interaction with data (and hence with the database)
- Data archiving and recovery (to protect the data itself)

6.12.1   User Interaction with Data (and hence with the Database)

This section is concerned with the user accessing/using the application solution or the database. The user can be an end-user with proper authentication and authorization privileges or a privileged user with data administration authority. The typical ways in which a user can compromise data integrity are:

- *Unauthorized user access to the database using a privileged account login credentials.* This involves direct access to the database via a backend interface such as an SQL-enabled session, using the username/password of another authorized user obtained by hacking upper-level Tiers such as an application server or cross-session scripting.
- *Gaining access to encryption keys and using them to retrieve/change sensitive encrypted data.* This is possible when a privileged user like the system administrator compromises the key information and manipulates sensitive data based on the encrypted key.
- *Insider attacks.* These are unauthorized data retrieval/manipulation operations performed by super-users like the database administrator, the system administrator; or internal employees compromising the login credentials to critical databases or using tampering mechanisms to bypass the in-place access control layer to gain privileged access.

Access control as a process is the single source of truth to ensure the optimal level of secure user interaction with the data. Automating the same accelerates the solution reliability and consistency in terms of continuous data integrity.

Oracle has several approaches to restrict user access to and control of the DB and the application, enforcement of DB policies, and implementation of multilayered security, thus protecting the data from abuse and misuse. These are:

- The first level of securing access is at the network and system level. This can be achieved using high-level network and OS security mechanisms such as LDAP directories and enabling Oracle single sign-on capability.

- Role-based access control (RBAC) coupled with fine-grained access control (FGAC) use row-level security at the individual column and row levels. RBAC ensures that the access control is enforced by the system, rather than by the DB superuser or administrator. FGAC custom security policies based on access control lists (ACLs) or otherwise can be implemented declaratively or using packaged API, based on user roles that can grant access to only particular data in the database—provisioning data access at a more granular table/row/column level based on user privileges. The security policies can also be group-based to include a predefined user group.

An access control list is a preregistered list of user-role-object-privilege values that restricts the user from access to specified database objects/ operations by using the list to validate the user's access rights. This can be used to provide authentication, authorization, and end-to-end user session audit.

- Oracle11g's Identity Management solution provides an integrated and secure Web-based set of tools and frameworks that enable the automation and management of user access privileges end to end—that is, to physical systems and databases as well as electronic data, in both on-premise and virtualized (on-demand) environments. It also provides an audit trail for end-to-end user interaction with the database/enterprise.

A robust Data Integrity Protection and Management Solution (DIP-MS) is based on an ACL-based security model combined with a centralized database for maintaining user access privileges and for editing. ACLs, bidirectional database activity monitoring, user and business activity monitoring, and auditing and reporting, exposed via a lightweight Web-based application console, will work throughout the enterprise and even outside it by using SOA-based secure Web Services for the same. Oracle has centralized and consolidated identity management solutions that are based on consistency, commonality, and repeatability—thus ensuring bulletproof reliability and availability of the enterprise solution.

Best Design Practices for Implementing the DIP-MS

The following describes the recommended design practices to implement the so-described DIP-MS for data security, access control, and centralized management—one that not only secures the data from breaches but also prevents de-escalation of the same, resulting in data/information availability, access, and modification that ensure the highest possible level of integrity:

■ Implement data protection and security as a business IT process that aligns with the operational flow of the database and application solution. This not only takes the level of security beyond the designed set of fine-grained polices and access controls, but also provides continuity. This approach is especially useful when the data integration needs to expand or the underlying technology is augmented with newer technologies to keep pace with the ever-evolving IT landscape.

Implement this using a database activity monitoring and security (DAMS) process as part of the solution workflow, automating the security controls as well as the user end-to-end session activity. This can take care of provisioning and deprovisioning of users at various privilege levels for data/database access/update.

■ The access control policies and procedures must be data-driven, meaning they have to be framed based on pre-identified data patterns (e.g., regularities/irregularities in the data, any peculiarities in the data, temporal effects in the data, etc.). This data-driven approach ensures that the policy framework is in line with what the data means to the users, who is going to use it, how it is going to be used, and how it can be enhanced and presented to derive higher value from it. *These qualifications drive whether the policies should be role-based, time-bound, restricted to particular table/column, grouped as a set, and/or event-based.* Then implement the same using the appropriate technology (e.g., declaratively, role-based, using ACLS, SOA-based, and/or using a centralized interface). *Oracle11g allows the policies to be highly granular and customizable.*

- Use custom data-masking code to de-identify sensitive and personal information at the row/column or cell level. For example, a hash algorithm can be used to mask values referring to Social Security or credit card numbers, allowing users to work on the data without being able to see the actual values. *The rules of the thumb are that masking must be consistent with the original value of the data, must be irreversible, and should enable the masked column to be used as part of foreign keys. Iteratively changing the masking rules enhances the strength of the security being enforced.*
- The key indicators here are:
  - Data-masking should be defined as part of DB policy enforcement and automated.
  - Data-masking is also useful for ensuring data is viable for portability outside the solution space. A stronger technique of storage-level encryption enables complete protection of data downloaded to external devices but doesn't impose identity access controls to the database.
  - Oracle11g enables table-level and tablespace-level encryption in addition to row/column level. Incorporating this into the database configuration and administrative functions of the DB can prevent unauthorized access as well as protect the data from abuse.
- Do consider federated identity management as an option for protecting enterprise-wide data integrity/security.

Federated identity management is now a practical reality, at least to the extent that it has been deployed and is being used by businesses—and at least to the extent of assuring a level of comfort as far as the "trust" factor goes.

Federated identity management is in good compliance with the segregation of duties aspect of governance, risk, and compliance. But the greatest risk involved in this is insider threats. Federated Identity Management can still be followed by having a "centralized user access, monitoring, control and audit console" (eliminating the backend channels that give direct access to the system/DB) to ensure that the security processes reside "where the authorized responsibility is" and are not controlled by anyone with database administrator privileges. Oracle's Identity Management Solution includes federated identity management under the hood.

Federated identity management can be implemented via RBAC and FGAC using Oracle11g's Identity and Content Management Solutions to consolidate policy-based enforcement and access control. It can be exposed using a Web-based unified information access and control management GUI. This piece is also embeddable in existing software using any proprietary/third-party integration software. This practice insulates the database and the application from threats from both internal and external attackers and narrows down the risks associated with abuse of administrative privileges.

- Use the same login credentials across database solutions and physical systems. This can be done by using Oracle's SSO (single sign-on). SSO binds a user's privileges to the OS of a particular machine. A more prudent approach is to create custom user credentials by business function and role that are unique to each user (including privileged users) and have a broader scope depending on the user's access privileges. Oracle11g provides for creation of client identifiers along with custom tags for embedded language applications that can be used to check who the user is and which application/table/row/column is being accessed. This works when using proxy authentication to pass actual end-user IDs to the server for validation of user identity against the Oracle DB. In combination with connection pooling, this can facilitate identity access on a per-user basis.
- Using Oracle Virtual Private Database is another way to restrict user access. This is useful for client-side validation based on client identifiers in case of proxy authentication.
- Similar to the SSO methodology, narrowing down superusers' privileges by binding each such account with specific (high-profile) jobs protects from the insider threats risk. To take this to the next level, binding user authentication with OS-level services or jobs adds an extra layer of protection from the identity access and data integrity perspectives. The last two features address the risk of losing integrity due to cross-platform data portability.
- Enforce strong password policy mandates and enable Oracle11g's Automated Password Management to protect privileged passwords.

This feature not only encrypts the passwords in a separate database, but also binds the encryption to the OS file system where the corresponding data files reside.

- Track user activity as it happens by using the golden-oldie method of capturing user keystrokes and logging them. These logs can later be back-tracked to note each and every command during user interaction.
- Schedule automated database vulnerability scans to align with the DB configuration in place. Simulate a hacker's scenario by doing penetration testing using SQL Injection, proxy calls routed via the Web application, and the like.

6.12.2   Special Cases Involved

- Identify information elements that are of greater relevance to specific solution problems and rank them according to most frequent occurrence. Backtracking the table and column associated with these information elements and the corresponding logic tied to them (via declarative business rules or otherwise) enables the detection of particular data columns or records, along with the data values in them, where integrity has been compromised.
- Look for antipatterns in user queries—abnormal queries/requests initiated by the end-user. A good example is to query profiling by the type of data requested and the type of database objects being queried, and to cross-verify the business role of the user with the query profiles executed by that user.
- Insider threats have a direct implication on data integrity, as discussed in the beginning of this section, and can also involve SQL Injection attacks at various levels and database communication protocol misuse, in addition to compromising DBA privileges. These two aspects are discussed in the next section.

6.12.3   Application Interaction with Data (and hence with the Database)

Database Connectivity to the Embedded Programming Solution

Choosing the right data access driver for a particular embedded programming language code to interact with the Oracle11g DB during execution ensures that the bidirectional data flow, including the messages in data transmission, is in tight integration with the DB so as to enable foolproof integrity of the data. It also ensures that there are no data leaks during data exchange in the process of internal synchronization of the embedded language–specifics with the corresponding Oracle "native" driver implementation, such as type definition, type conversion, the accuracy of the data representation and format, and proper handling of NULL values. Of special mention are the cases of object-based data. data type mismatch (strong types and weak types), incorrect type conversion and buffer overflow, and the like.

The best practices in this context are:

- Choose the driver that is closest to the Oracle11g "native" functionality and "managed code" execution with respect to the embedded programming language in context. This achieves a huge performance gain by eliminating an intermediate "middle-Tier custom data access layer" on top of the driver for data interoperability. For example, the ODP.NET data provider is an ideal choice for an Oracle-driven .NET-based embedded language solution. It implicitly leverages the rich and powerful data security features of the Oracle11g DB.
- Authorize database connections based on user/domain/application and database contexts.
- Enable database resident connection pooling and statement caching.

Accelerating Data-Intensive Processing Performance

- Use the right type of Oracle11g "native" API calls for the right SQL statement to achieve optimal data transfer and transformation efficiency (e.g., Prepared Statements for transaction-based SQL, etc.) and to avoid the overheads of statement adaptability, type conversion, format incompatibilities, and memory allocation/de-allocation.
- Use set-based processing, especially while managing large-volume transactional data. Leverage the power of REF CURSORs and their interoperability with dynamic SQL to share data/object sets across solution layers.
- Use in-database execution by coding stored procedures in the embedded language involved wherever applicable—especially in scenarios that mandate integrated processing of Oracle-specific PL/SQL logic and non-Oracle-based logic. This implementation will better handle compute-intensive tasks that use Java, C/C++, and the like-by leveraging optimized mechanisms inherent in the

corresponding technology-that in turn improves execution efficiency (e.g., using JMS as opposed to SOAP/HTML messaging, etc.). Also tasks that require access to OS resources or need to execute OS-specific programs from inside the DB can benefit from in-database execution.

The advantage to this comes directly from the tight integration of the application logic (via the stored procedure) with the Oracle11g DB Server and SQL/PL/SQL. This applies not only to Java, but also to C/C++/C#, PSP/Ajax/Groovy, XML/HTML, and so on.

- Use enhanced IMDB-cache features such as constructing application data–cache grids that allow for distributed caching and data replication. This gives huge performance gains in terms of speed and throughput for transactional data (which gets processed in the primary buffer cache) as well as the instant response, high data availability and durability, and maximum scalability required for high-volume SQL-based query processing—ad hoc, in real time, or reports-based.

The pragmatics to follow include using the in-memory data replication feature of Oracle11g on the application Tier (i.e., Application Grid) and result set caching on the client running the embedded language application (i.e., any end-point client device or browser).

SQL Injection

SQL Injection is a way of gaining access to unauthorized data for retrieval/modification using SQL statements that written to trick the database. These statements are functionally incorrect, but syntactically and semantically correct; when executed, they allow granting of unauthorized privileges or performance of unauthorized operations on data.

Direct SQL Injection occurs when logically invalid values are input for login credentials, but the values pass the test from the Oracle DB technicalities. This is especially the case when the underlying SQL code involves concatenation of the passed "invalid" values to the queries being executed.

This can also occur when an entire SQL statement is passed as a parameter to a stored procedure.

Indirect SQL Injection, also termed "lateral" SQL Injection, is the case where SQL Injection occurs due to illogical DATE and NUMBER values as opposed to VARCHAR2 values (in the case of direct SQL Injection).

The best practices to resolve SQL Injection risks are

- Use parameterized queries inside embedded SQL.
- Use bind variables for data values passed to DML statements and parameters passed to parameterized queries and stored procedures. This also applies to SQL statements executed using native dynamic SQL, including dynamic PL/SQL. Do not use concatenation to substitute actual parameter arguments or for SQL statements at built at run-time.

Using Native Dynamic SQL and PL/SQL

This involves a direct vulnerability threat, that of SQL Injection, used to exploit the Oracle11g database by way of a "mirrored execution" of code that passes the syntax, semantics, and database authorization criteria and is executed—thus exposing sensitive data to the attacker. The explanation lies in the fact that Oracle stored procedures run with the privileges of the owner of the procedure, not the rights of the user running the procedure. So executing DDL statements via native dynamic SQL to gain unauthorized access rights, or regular SQL statements for which the owner of the procedure has DBA rights, enables the invoker of the procedure to retrieve/alter/update data or table structure(s).

Using bind variables for formal parameters in the NDS statement definition resolves this issue.

Using Stored Procedures in Embedded Language Code

This process, too, preserves the integrity of the data, as Oracle executes these procedures with definer rights by default. Therefore, computations involving highly sensitive data (e.g., financial transactions) can be defined in stored procedures, with the default definer rights privileges and execution rights for them granted only to business-specific privileged users (at the same time disabling backend access).

Encapsulating every SQL query using a function (standalone or defined in a package) protects the data retrieved by the query from an integrity perspective. This comes as a direct consequence of the default definer rights execution of the same.

The best practices involved are:

- Validate procedure parameters for the right content and context. As an example, an atypical value for a VARCHAR2 parameter is a SQL statement itself or one involving SQL keywords related to data manipulations or data control. Another pattern can be a string of wild-card characters or non-alphanumeric characters.
- Execute user-initiated SQL-intensive transactions using stored-procedure-based API calls that are grouped by specific functions.

Enforce FGAC on the Data Transmission Itself

This ensures that the database and related network access protocol is secured independent of the location of the database and the database itself. An example of this is encryption/policy enforcement on the data in transit and/or the messages themselves.

The key indicator here is bi-directional audit logging of the network/ messaging events (i.e., from the database server to the client application and vice versa).

- Separate out production databases and their access from development and test environments.
- Leverage Oracle11g-specific database security and data protection features as far as possible and only to the extent required. By using Oracle11g native and managed drivers for JDBC and ODBC for the data access, some of these features are inherently available to the solution.
- Disable access to all unnecessary database objects in the production environment, including Oracle-supplied built-in packages such as DBMS_SQL, UTL_TCP, DBMS_XMLGEN, and the like. These have been "silent threats" in the experiences of various solution implementations.

All the code accelerators discussed in this section function as the database-application layer analog to achieve "push-button," one-touch (click-and-go) functionality at the presentation layer.

6.12.4   Design Pattern for a Typical Code Accelerator

A business-context-specific policy/logic can be declaratively and/or programmatically incorporated at the database and/or application level using custom stored functions, user-defined operators, and the like. They can be called from SQL and/or the embedded programming language using the language-specific API, still maintaining Oracle nativity, compile-time and run-time dynamism, and reusability. This performs an event like enabling interactive user controls and tracking/trapping/notification/handling process activity or processing a business-function, data-set and/or data-object, information delivery, or a combination of these. The key focus points are:

■ A variety of query types, especially those that are criteria-bound and time-bound, are more critical in nature, mandating the use of optimal data structures that leverage Oracle DB–specific functionality in their processing logic to enable consistent and continuous data access/updates. In addition to using bind variables, queries can be parameterized to enable reuse and also prevent illogical queries being dynamically generated.

■ Running embedded language–based stored procedures from within Oracle11g poses another challenge. The language design needs to synchronize with the DB design. This boils down to the fact that "best-practice" code design for one high-performing embedded-language may not be necessarily be the best-practice code design for another embedded language when executed inside Oracle11g or in the application. Care should taken to achieve seamless interoperability so that compilation and execution performance are not affected, thereby increasing the chances for portability of the application/code.

Oracle11g has great code optimization features for Java, .NET, .PHP, and HTML/XML code running inside the DB. A best practice is to use these features and write high-performing code with built-in "seamless-streamed" processing routines for the embedded language involved, so that it executes as closely as possible to an Oracle-specific SQL/PL/SQL stored procedure. By being both seamless and streamed, it provides a coherent (or consistently phased) code-design pattern for a freeflow execution of the code, thereby maintaining a freeflow process for data management and information dissemination.

This enables pragmatics similar to the "divide-and-conquer" approach by having specific code accelerators at each individual Tier while at the same time streamlining all of these for a coherent and consistent execution.

At the database Tier, use Oracle11g native database functionality, such as enhanced programming language specific features, as well as the inherent database features to achieve efficient database functioning and application-contextual data/information accuracy, reliability, and efficiency.

The key indicator is to build a design that when implemented has minimal impact on the database and application functioning and at the same requires no or (minimal changes) to the data management processes involved. Oracle11g and its cross-language compatible native capabilities are the "best fit" to be leveraged to get such a result.

Oracle11g's SOA functionality can be leveraged to build a Data Services engine that can incorporate the above-stated event and logic processing and expose them via services for a more pervasive and enhanced usability and reusability.

- At the application layer, programming language–specific code layers can be designed to augment the default functionality provided by Oracle11g. An "intelligent" code design is to use the Oracle11g IMDB cache on the application Tier and write connectivity/accessibility code to enable faster access/updates to data at the end-user level. Oracle11g automatically takes care of the synchronization and coordination of the in-memory cache and the underlying database.
- A unified information structure can be designed and implemented using a code enhancer similar to the Data Services engine (mentioned above), using the Data Services engine as one of its components, and managing seamless coordination across the database, application-cache, and presentation Tiers.
- For existing Oracle11g-based applications:
  - Use Oracle Database Vault and multilabel security to ensure data protection at the database and application levels.
  - Use Oracle Audit Vault to monitor end-to-end data, process activity, audit, and log the results. This application helps in

fraud and anomaly detection and remediation. Oracle Total Recall acts as a failover rollback mechanism in case of any security breaches. And all of these are built directly into the Oracle11g database kernel and can be simply enabled to activate the functionality.

■ Embedded languages like PL/SQL, C/C++, Java, C#, and PHP can use the respective programmatic extensions to IMDB cache and thus leverage the benefits of IMDB cache with little or no application code changes.

■ The so-designed code accelerator can leverage:

■ Oracle JRockit JVM for Java/J2EE-based solutions to accelerate Java-only applications running against Oracle11g. This provides direct integration of internal as well as external server-side specific Java class libraries with Oracle11g. The generic JDBC driver can be used to access non-Oracle data sources via JDBC callouts in conjunction with the Oracle SAX and DOM parsers.

■ Oracle Weblogic Server for Web-based solutions to accelerate RIA applications running on the Web.

■ Oracle ADF (Faces) for a unified, collaborative, and interoperative application/solution development framework that is cross-embedded-programming-language-enabled (Java, .NET, PHP, Web Services, etc.).

■ Specialized data types, such as XML Types, Large Objects, and the like should be optimized to ensure that the respective elements in the type lineage are accurate. As an example, when using XMLType, Oracle validates that both its element type and the XMLNodeType are in sync. This enables efficient processing based on the data type.

Publish data/information to the embedded-language environment using an Oracle-native API corresponding to the language in context to leverage the programmatic features of the same. This can be done by using an object structure or an XML structure at the application program level to make the content "transient" and a (bidirectional) flow the from DB to the application. This is part of the information unification process.

The best practices for object-relational mapping, using LINQ framework with XML and using polymorphic associations, were discussed in detail in Chapter 5 on Data Structure Management, in the sections on Best Practices for using Objects, LINQ to Objects, and LINQ to SQL.

Summary

This chapter described the best practices for data management in terms of end-to-end functionality from the design and coding pragmatics standpoint. Beginning by outlining a best-fit design strategy for data management in an embedded programming language implementation, it moved to next-level topics such as the data access layer involving connectivity and interaction of the application code with the Oracle DB, the role of metadata in data/content consolidation, and the recommended best practices for Oracle in the ADO.NET space. Subsequent sections dealt with the best practices for data retrieval, manipulation, validation, and protection of data integrity—all of which are quintessential to data management.

This chapter also highlighted how to manage XML and unstructured content for a best degree of fit in the embedded-language solution and the how the use of XML and XML-based Data Services can seamlessly unify the disparate, huge, and multiformat data and content into a single unified information structure that is efficient, business-savvy, and user-friendly for interactivity, responsiveness, and intelligent decision making.

The next chapter delves into Application Management best practices, focusing on the application and presentation Tiers of the solution in terms of Web 2.0-enablement, Ajaxification, the introduction of dynamic visualization interfaces into the solution, and coordination with the database Tier for optimal interoperability and interprocess communication.

Chapter 7

Best Practices for Application Management

In This Chapter

- Code accelerators for rapid application development and management: Design and coding aspects
- Best practices for application Web interaction: receiving, routing, responding, redirecting, rendering, linking
- Best practices for application integrity
- Best practices for application consistency
- Best practices for security beyond user authentication: End-to-end application security
- Best fit for Oracle in the ASP.NET framework
- Best practices for templates: Use or eliminate?
- Best practices beyond HTML:Auto-generate dynamic visual content, Web Services, and mobile applications
- Best practices for creative reporting

7.1   Introduction

Application management can be broadly categorized into application development and application management. The former is all about design, development, deployment, optimization, and customization. The latter comprises administration, monitoring, auditing, and optimization of the deployed and customized solution. This in turn involves the key processes and methodologies of simplification, standardization, streamlining, virtualization, and automation from concepts to customization to management, without IT intervention. The degree of automation determines how rapid the application development can be and how self-manageable the solution can be after deployment without IT intervention. *To achieve a higher degree of automation, the efficiency of the design and coding practices followed is a key indicator, but the effective and seamless interprocess coordination and synchronization of business-IT task flows, processes, services, and events is also a major contributing factor.* Though the development cannot be 100 percent automated, given the fact that there is no one solution that fits all, it is possible to generate an application in at least of the following two ways:

- Using Oracle11g IDE and runtime platforms in the form of RAD (Rapid Application Development) tools like Oracle APEX (for generating code as well as the solution right in-database using PL/SQL, PHP, etc.), Oracle JDeveloper11g (for Java-based application development acceleration using Oracle ADF), and the like.
- Using custom code accelerators that consist of componentized modules, act as executable containers, and are reusable as desired

Automating application management also can adopt the above two methods, but the former method gives less control/flexibility over the latter in terms of self-service and manageability. However, there is a significant degree of overlap in application development and application management, and the best practices for one both supplement and complement those that of the other.

The sections that follow describe the best practices for application management end to end, and how and to what extent the intermediate tasks can be accelerated and automated.

Figure 7.1 depicts a best-fit solution integration design in a real-world application management scenario.

Figure 7.1   Best-fit solution integration design as an application management best practice.

7.2 Code Accelerators for Rapid Application Development: Design and Coding Aspects

Accelerating an application solution is not limited to choosing the best optimization strategies; it involves determining its performance impact on the operational, financial, and technical processes to which it is tailored. The key drivers for design and development in this respect are:

- The need for an accelerated (or totally new) solution
- The identification and assessment of what's in place vs. what's going to be in place
- Whether to integrate or not to integrate (with existing solutions in-place or otherwise)
- How the accelerated solution can have a business and competitive edge
- Whether altering the deployment method alone can accelerate the operational efficiency (i.e., should we move from on-premise to true-hosted or cloud-based deployment?)

However, the best practices for rapid application development pertain to the optimal time-to-deliver strategies in terms of development of the required solution and getting it up-and-running—without discounting on efficiency and business functionality. The key drivers in this respect are:

- A solution based on an architecture that is as flexible as possible to avoid redesign or recoding of some or all of its components
- A solution that can be used, reused, and unused as needed, while remaining active at the same time
- How quickly the application solution can be autogenerated (with as minimal developer coding as possible), and the best-of-the-latest tools, processes, and methodologies that can be used to result in a best-fit solution that meets business needs
- How well the acceleration performance can be quantified in terms of code and application generation, as well as from its manageability perspective—the code being generated must be generic in terms of its portability and/or conversion to another similar embedded programming language

This means the code should deliver an embedded-language neutral application programming interface (API) or some sort of declarative metacode that can be used to reuse the generated code by converting it into another embedded language, based on the technology standards for the same (e.g., JDBC, ODBC, .NET, Open Source—PHP, Python, OLEDB, etc.)

The design and coding of code/solution accelerators are governed by a set of primary practices that need to be addressed in order for their efficient implementation in a new solution being developed or in existing solution that needs to be extended or replaced.

Figure 7.2 illustrates the baselines involved in application management.

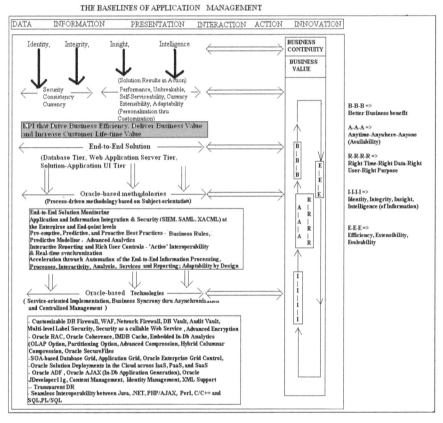

Figure 7.2   Baselines of application management..

Efficient application management requires application acceleration in addition to the under-the-hood standard management methodologies. Application acceleration can be achieved by implementing a multitude of methodologies such as:

- Providing self-configuration management through context-aware automation—the automated execution of preconfigured / dynamically (on-the-fly) generated configuration settings or key-value pairs
- Providing an architecture-by-design that enables extensibility, adaptability through self-service functions, data/content consolidation, dynamism in terms of hot-pluggable new business processes, data/content mash-up from any additional/new data source(s) as well as mix-and-merge dynamic mash-up of application components to create seamlessly embedded custom components via interactive controls at runtime, and building on user/customer experience (this clones the mechanism of dynamic business process management (BPM), service-oriented architecture (SOA), and cross-functional collaboration - to use the solution design to *auto-adapt* to dynamic context-aware needs and *auto-optimize* the same design to evolve into a superior one that can fit in the change and deliver the required results)
- Optimizing efficiency (performance through tuning and unbreakability through troubleshooting and multilevel/remote access and security). *Oracle11g enables pre-emptive performance diagnostics of in-efficient SQL by way of dynamically created baselines as the data is modified, which is also context relevant. This augmented by notification of thresholds is akin to a DB-embedded "deep-dive monitor that starts, sets, and stops on-the-fly"*
- Enabling a customer experience similar to a desktop-oriented deployment, immaterial of whether the application-solution is being accessed remotely, wirelessly, on-demand, hosted, or on-premise, using a tiered solution architecture design or otherwise (e.g., application streaming, virtual desktop implementation or VDI, etc.)
- Accelerating deployment via seamless, unified communications framework–based application delivery using click-and-go Web Services, application delivery software appliances, and the like
- Increasing automation and portability while decreasing lock-in in terms of multiplatform, cross-technology interoperability, collaboration, and information currency—getting access to current data "as it is created"—and continuous availability
- Increasing the business value and subsequently decreasing the "time-to-deliver-this-value" by using code accelerators that transform data/info based on descriptive analytics using online analytical

processing (OLAP) analytics and data mining (exploratory data analysis that identifies business patterns/variables) into business rules that serve as potential input to advanced "predictive analytics" and their optimization to arrive at actionable decisions

- Providing SOA-based real-time application/data integration using Web Services and initiated using triggering events, as opposed to conventional extract, transform, and load (ETL)/open-source/custom integration; that results in an extended/enhanced service-oriented and event-driven acceleration
- Providing End-to-end infrastructure and application monitoring in on-premise, on-demand, and hybrid deployments
- Correlating multiple performance result sets based on context-specific variables into a single, coherent view to arrive at a new application acceleration policy
- Accelerating through storage optimization (e.g., storage grid, columnar compression, SSD, D RAM flash storage, etc.), resulting in solution-centric optimized storage across database, application, UI Tiers, and operational, administration/management, user interaction dimensions
- Accelerating through managed file transfer—bidirectional monitoring and analyses of moving data/messages as they move intrasolution and intersolution
- Securing remote, wireless access across all touch points; the Oracle11g Enterprise Single Sign-On (SSO) functionality can be embedded into the solution design to ensure secure anytime-anywhere-anyone (A-A-A) access within the enterprise. The SSO authentication must be adhere to strong identity and access management policies that includes password strength validation augmented by context-aware role and policy based access credentials verification
- Enhancing the search capabilities within and beyond the enterprise by way of personalized search capsules—code accelerators targeted toward context-specific searches using optimized indexing, faceted navigation, ranked scoring, intelligent filtering (by applying the search filter before the tokenization process), tagged-search capabilities, odd-duplicates detection, and the like

7.2.1   Code Accelerator Design Pragmatics

Here's a breakdown of the same in terms of a best-fit scenario for business operational efficiency as well as architectural efficiency:

- *Oracle-DB native compatibility*—The code included in the accelerator must have Oracle-native compatibility in addition to the native embedded-language compatibility. This is an essential design practice that goes a long way in ensuring the compile-time and run-time performance of the code; and also reduces the complexity in modification of the same down the line.

  The rules of thumb for code accelerator design in this regard are:

1. *Let SQL do all the (implicit) data management that it can.* Make PL/SQL the first choice to write custom code, as it integrates seamlessly with SQL for in-memory processing and access as well as read-only, random access in Oracle11g. All of the embedded programming languages have an Oracle-native API for the data access layer that can call the SQL-PL/SQL–based stored code modules for augmenting the computation in the application Tier.

2. Use custom code to accelerate nondata-based or ineffective data–based processing, such as object-based I/O between the embedded programming code and the database objects. Typical examples include Iteration, Object Set processing, Web Services that fall outside the range of Database Services (such as those for rendering, complex aggregation, summarization, or consolidation in the Application/UI Tiers, like mash-ups based on output of content queries, nonquery-based unstructured data etc.)

3. SQL in combination with PL/SQL can also be used in code accelerators to optimize/automate database-based information processes like efficient data integration using virtual (in-memory) data views, content queries on unstructured/semistructured data (e.g., XML structures, binary documents, visual content, and the like stored in the database), caching (at the DB, application, and client Tiers) of database objects, cross-domain query caching and cross-query result set caching, in-memory (dynamic) replication of data, and so on. Oracle11g supports SQL-based access that allows XQuery and XSQL queries on XML data/content.

A good real-world use case for a SQL-PL/SQL–based code accelerator is to automate the refactoring multipliers that drive optimal code execution based on the result set size, cache size, response time as predicted by a baseline execution plan, the number of query statements cached, the type of the SQL operation being requested (DML or DQL), and the nature of execution (e.g., streamed, federated, in parallel, serial, and so on).

- *Auto-adaptability for efficient execution*—The code should be auto refactorable to adapt to changing business needs, optimization, and scalability. This means that no recoding is necessary to accelerate the solution efficiency. Efficiency can be achieved via a combination of techniques such as dynamic generation of code within code at runtime, pipelined execution (akin to vertical compute parallelism), parallelization, and componentized code modules that enable vector processing based on multiple inputs (scalar, set-based, and even processes) using the same single packet of code. Oracle PL/SQL and the related embedded programming languages all support coding in this manner, both in-database and in the application.
- *Acceleration via modular design or partitioning across Oracle11g database Tier, (Web) Application Server Tier, and end-point UI (i.e. Web browser, mobile device, etc.)*—This means that the design of such a code accelerator adheres to the rule "there is no one code design that fits all the Tiers end-to-end."
- *Test-driven development and implementation*—Evolving in computing efficiency as well as resource utilization, by going through cycles of testing, each iteration resulting in an increased performance gain, without any compilation and /or execution overheads. This can be implemented by a collaborative testing platform that enables side-by-side troubleshooting for technical and functional accuracy. Such a platform is practically realizable by using Oracle's Real Application Testing methodology that enables dynamic cuts of online production/pre-archived business data, and instant replication of the same in a test environment. This can be used to test the application-solution "as it is being developed" and using "live data", augmented by one-on-one feedback from the business team who can see the data model in place based on visual diagnostics of the data source,

flow, and result of the corresponding business process. The input from this feedback can be used to correct the inefficiency and/or re-engineer the data model (if needed). *Oracle APEX is a good integrated-development-cum-test-environment that can be used to implement this practice. It even enables one-click push-and-pop of the solution-in-test to-and-from the database as the testing process iterates*

It's all about fixing the (code) design first rather than fixing the code. Eliminate hard-coding of SQL inside the application code and implement all SQL-PL/SQL code using embedded language–specific callable API and/or in-DB stored procedures. Combining in-database processing with Oracle's multi-threaded execution gives the dual key benefits of high performance and efficient management of test results as each instance of the solution runs its own thread or process space , thereby, isolating the test sessions

---

Pre-emptive performance testing—This improves quality in applications and thus creates an efficient application delivery platform (solution in terms of application, business services, information-on-demand, and self-service intelligence). The key indicator to automate this is using dynamic code testing and solution white box testing. *A pragmatic approach to doing this is to do a Proof-of-Performance benchmarking against the existing standard industry-specific benchmarks – for similar solution attributes and parameters, that are as close as possible to the one being tested. Again Oracle's Real Application Testing can aid in this process.*

Code performance acceleration by way of dynamic code testing has the invaluable benefit of "Code is Gold" justification, for it involves writing code to test the efficiency of code.

- *Choosing between workflow scheduling and process automation (goes beyond job scheduling)*—Enhance job scheduling and management (via process automation), provide memory pooling (by enabling threads to coordinate access to shared data), provide database connectivity (via declarative and object-based API), and implement easy control and configuration of application behavior (orchestration). Use code accelerators for recreating resource pooling, job scheduling, and process automation as well as for reliability, availability, security (RAS) for Oracle embedded programming (abbreviated as OEP for the purposes of this book) applications running out-of-box in commodity-oriented (appliance-based), virtual, or cloud environments.

- *Using a business-centric solution model following an Architect-Accelerate-Automate methodology*—Architect the solution in terms of business models, services, and architectural design (data and application components, technology and deployment platforms, and integration methodologies) to optimize the following:
  - Business-centricity is the practice of business-centric and solution-specific business and IT process segmentation, prioritization, and automation using business-process to IT- process mappings. These mappings can be optimized for efficiency using code accelerators for a better, easier, faster design, implementation, deployment, and customization—all of which have a direct impact on operational efficiency.
  - Provide users with Web access to collaborative content (e.g., workflows, documents, shareable content from Social Networking sites, etc.) as well as to transactional content (operational business transactions–based information, such as summarized or aggregated transactions partitioned by business variables etc.). Oracle11g WebCenter Suite enables the near real-time content extraction and delivery from collaborative Web sites such as LinkedIn, Digital Libraries etc. – to the solution platform. Existing Oracle-based solutions can leverage this functionality by integrating the extra piece for collaborative content sharing. For a design-from-the-start, the best practice is to leverage SOA-based operational integration techniques.

A real-world use case of improved content analytics in action is based on entity extraction, concept clustering, text mining, Web mining, and the like to help discover insight-driven hidden patterns and collections of content from large-size binary textual information (documents, e-mail messages, CRM/online forum comments, blogs, microblogs, etc.) and can be efficient in finding "searchable" content based on keywords to detect anomalies and outliers in the data profiling process, which isolates the invalid/bad data. This improves data quality, which in turn improves the data extraction, eventually resulting in a closed-loop circuit for source data integration—the basis for the solution information processing.

■ Use Oracle data integration (a combination of data federation, CDC, and streaming replication) of operational data in real time, as well as analytical (historical) data, to enable information synchronization. Here's a recommended rules set:

1. Use change data capture (CDC) and replication as part of the ETL mechanism or by itself to consolidate multiple sources of data into the Oracle database, the data-source for the solution. This applies to both online transaction processing (OLTP) and OLAP environments, as well as for operational business intelligence needs. The replication can also be done using an Oracle Streams based methodology.

2. Use data federation as an information delivery mechanism that creates a consolidated view of the source data, either for further processing or for presentation to the users. The "information delivery" process can use the streaming mechanism, in real-time or right-time, using any of the technologies that Oracle supports for the same: execution via pipeline chaining, data visualization, SOA-based information delivery via Data Services, virtualization, and on-demand (hosted) deployments such as "pure" hosted delivery, or SaaS cloud computing models.

3. The key is that in data federation, no copy is made of the source/processed data; there is only an abstraction of multiple fragments of (disparate) data (be it source data or harnessed data) for the purposes of customer-centric data isolation—but based on a centralized repository or otherwise.

A code accelerator can be used to implement a custom-designed data integration framework in situations where most of the source data involves homogenous data sources (i.e. Oracle-to-Oracle and/or external file–based). This framework can use any of the methodologies (ETL-CDC, replication, federation, streaming, and the like).

■ The ability to integrate data and content on the fly via a unified, Web-accessible database of information.

■ *Web-flow based create, read, update, delete (CRUD) operations*—The key indicator is *transactional integrity and high performance.* Code accelerators can be used to drive peak performance in Oracle and integrated (non-Oracle) application environments, primarily in terms of throughput (number of transactions/unit), speed, and workload.

The key design criteria in this respect are information-on-demand CRUD operations based on distributed and/or replicated data, transaction aborting, and trigger rollback. A trigger can refer to an event or process.

Oracle11g's database grid, along with its shared-nothing, high-ratio compression–enabled data storage grid, enables subsecond performance in terms of throughput and scalability.

A code accelerator comes in handy to accelerate the transactional integrity of concurrent transactions on distributed data by providing a layer of "virtual ACID-compliant transactions" using in-memory partial transaction partitioning by way of seemingly a-synchronous replication and currency of changed data, on the fly, that ensures a pseudo-two-phase commit, resulting in fast response times for Web-based queries that are highly latency-sensitive. The transaction is ultimately rolled back if the two-phase commit fails, and the requestor is subsequently alerted. As an example, business operations transacted via high-demand Web sites that are mission-critical, e.g. creation and derivation of data that is time-bound, in an integrated online application for "as-is" and on-the-fly requests, on an ultra-urgent basis, are realizable in subseconds for the resulting information because they are inserted concurrently and synchronized in real-time, as two disparate transactions. The subtle difference here is the one between "request successfully submitted" and "request successfully approved." Oracle11g alos supports extending this methodology for Web Services based transactional integrity.

- *Data virtualization*—This is a key design consideration for improving application-solution performance, be it physical infrastructure consolidation into a virtual (software-based) machine (VM) to leverage the benefits of vertical (scale-up) and horizontal (scale-out) scalability, or A-A-A accessibility via live application streaming (on-demand and just what's needed) from a pre-implemented single virtual machine view or image of the end-to-end solution, or just a VDI that virtualizes the application and database Tiers only (i.e., just software) . However, the reliability–high availability–security in virtual environments affects the performance of the same.

In the case of high-volume OLTP solutions, it takes prudence to ensure that in-memory replication and application state are one-on-one. This boils down to the fact that a disaster recovery mechanism is required to automatically load-balance and enable transparent failover of VM solutions without losing the transaction or the application state. A recommended design best practice for such a mechanism is to have a physical-to-virtual machine consolidation capacity ratio of 3:4, given an optimal consolidation density. Application performance in virtualized environments depends on the impact of virtualized applications on business processes, access rights, security, and transactional integrity. The functionality required to effectively manage virtual environments is also of critical importance.

Oracle11g enables all of this by way of the application grid, database grid, and real application clusters. Data virtualization, alongside replication, using application, storage, and database grids also contributes towards effective disaster recovery.

The choice between data virtualization and replication is analogous to the one between data federation and replication. Data virtualization is a better solution for information unification than physical data consolidation in solutions that need real-time data integration across multiple data sources, as it responds efficiently to rapidly changing data syncing. Another use case is in systems that run on-demand and need to scale in and scale out as data grows and user base increases. It has the potential to integrate any type of data deemed as business-critical and needs to be synchronized. Data replication, on the other hand, is a good choice in distributed computing environments, and is often employed to replicate data in-memory for ultra-fast access and response to heavy traffic site requests.

- *Security*—The secure socket layer (SSL) mechanism provides a substantial level of security for the Web solution by protecting the URL-level data interaction against possible hacking. It works in conjunction with HTTP for data-in-transit. SSL-based security is a good jumpstart mechanism for guarding against emerging threats like phishing, malware, cybercrime, and the like. This can be supplemented with database firewall and solution-level firewall in addition to the network firewall, real-time diagnostics of all data and actions end-to-end, *and in-lined data protection and prevention policies.*

The key indicator here is to ensure continued security end-to-end.

- *Web application delivery and access management*—This involves deploying the solution in on-premise (within the enterprise) and on-demand (i.e., hosted or out-of-enterprise) environments, with the proper user authentication and access privileges for the same. The key indicators in this respect are:
  - Web application delivery can be accelerated using custom-coded or compatible out-of-box application delivery installers that are OS-, technology- and deployment platform–agnostic, or can be more specific to each customer deployment. These must be click-and-install automation oriented and provide transparency, (near) zero downtime, and efficient interoperability irrespective of the deployment platform.
  - Effective and strengthened end-to-end security for data, processes, and privileged identity and access management. This includes access governance and audit, bidirectional traffic monitoring on the network, and database firewall, Web application firewall, and network firewall.
  - Conforming to governance, risk, and compliance audits can be implemented as Identity-as-a-Service and Security-as-a-Service in Web-enabled environments.
  - Transitioning from unstructured silos to a streamlined seamless integrated enterprise solution within and beyond the enterprise.
- Using Web application delivery mechanisms to achieve optimal scalability-in terms of pre-allocated resources, data, and user base, as well as unpredictable on-demand provisioning of the same-by way of Software-as-a-Service (SaaS), Platform-as-a-Service (PaaS), and Infrastructure-as-a-Service (IaaS).
  - *Using Mobility-as-a-Service for mobile web application delivery*—This has the advantages of continuous availability even in case of network failures, end-user device independence, right-time/real-time syncing of information, and local end-device authentication.

- *Timely access to quality information* is critical to business success. However, building the necessary foundation can seem a daunting task to IT organizations faced with more project requests, an increasing number of data sources, growing data volumes, and evolving systems.

- *Protecting mission-critical data and PII (personally identifiable information)*—This involves determining "critical" data hotspots and the segregation of mission-critical data and PII across customer/ end-user domains, business domains, and end-to-end access touch points to protect the data from being compromised in terms of potential data leakages, privileged user abuse, and external vulnerabilities like threats, hacking, and the like.

- *Self-service adaptability*—This allows for dynamic user interactivity; superior customer experience: easy, effective, and efficient extensibility to future add-on functionality; transparent integration with external applications; and a collaborative unified view of information across the enterprise.

- *Solution efficiency*—High performance by design, using an optimal architecture, and interactive Web 2.0 GUI to deliver a personalized Web presentation dashboard, A-A-A availability, and improved analytics that are context-aware by design. Oracle11g Advanced Analytics enables all this by way of "live" interoperability between the application output and offline Microsoft Excel–based spreadmarts. In addition, it provides high availability, disaster recovery, and data protection to the finest granularity levels of industry-standard requirements.

Recognize that disaster recovery goes beyond backup, archival, and recovery. Current trends in technology, such as virtualization and its use in implementing a virtual desktop; data de-duplication as an alternative to data backup; and multinode-based server, database, and application clustering, coupled with transparent failover for high-availability and the like, add to the durability, viability, and business continuity of the solution.

7.3   Best Practices for Application Web Interaction: Receiving, Routing, Responding, Redirecting, Rendering, Linking

Here's a recommended list of the practices for the same that are top line:

- Enable single-click URL navigation.
- Introduce self-service functionality in the UI by way of Ajax-based/dynamic-code driven components that enable user-controlled publishing of information/results, integrated search capabilities that deliver personal-enabled results, and the like.
- Simulate IntelliSense for user controls, similar to the SQL IntelliSense enablers like "redlining errors," "auto-hyphenating end-of-line words," "outline statements," and "auto-casing or camel-casing." This is also a good use case for building a template of these customized controls that can be reused for user interaction with the Web interface.
- Provide context-aware rendering of query results dynamically; this is *personalization by way of customization.*

  Users can define their own queries; the inherent query execution can be optimized and their results personalized based on user-specific or customer-specific run-time criteria. Here's a bulleted list of recommended practices for the same:

  - Provide interactive GUI-based controls that enable the user to define queries based on multiple run-time criteria that can be specified using business domain–friendly language. These input query specifications can be converted transparently into an optimized query using a code accelerator that employs static and/or dynamic SQL.
  - Auto-insert "close tags," "attributes quotes," "namespace declarations," and "other markup—comments or specialized tags" that are generated on the fly.
  - Auto-parse text, including XML-based text from Oracle character large object (CLOB) columns using flexible mappings and transformations, and process it at a granular line-by-line level or at XML Schema attributes/DTD (Document Type Definition) levels.
  - Auto-cache and auto-download DTDs and XML Schemas to accelerate XML generation for XML-based reports or output.

- Auto-capture XML execution statistics and visually present them for quick-resolution diagnostics and performance optimization—*especially for content delivery in XML format.* This must include elapsed execution time, database name, login name, host server name, count of rows affected (both reads and writes), type of server-based connection used to process the content (e.g., multithreaded and connection pool–enabled, dedicated server, or the like) in addition to the DB-specific run-time statistics such as the data I/O involved, CPU cycles consumed, latch/lock information including that on waits, log-based audit trails captured during the online monitoring process, and the like.
- Enable query execution parameters at run-time by auto-setting the same (e.g., query execution time-out, the number of rows to process before this timeout occurs, *ANSI SQL-92 Query Execution indicators*, dynamic fixing of the upper limit for the size of CLOB and NCLOB (National Character Large Object) data if it helps in efficiency, etc.) *This also helps in ranked scoring of the query performance.*

Note that NCLOB data is stored inside the Oracle database in Unicode format, allowing a maximum byte limit of 128 terabytes as of Oracle11g and upto 4GB pre-Oracle11g. It is needed to deliver the data in a National-language specific character set. NCLOB provides a unified input-output format that is Unicode-compliant, of all CLOB-based content regardless of the National language (character set) involved. Oracle takes care of the to-and-from implicit conversions as of Oracle10g. Pre-Oracle10g, use the conversion function TO_CLOB and TO_NCLOB to get the same results.

- Auto-display results from multiple queries, or queries against multiple databases based on efficient auto-merging using virtual federated views created and consumed on the fly—for example, to handle ad-hoc queries.
- Auto-prefix or -suffix the DB server name, converted into business semantics–mapped text, thereby avoiding the prefixing of the DB login name to the results to protect privacy of

the user. This can be implemented at the database level, using client identifiers via PL/SQL API such as DBMS_APPLICATION_INFO to capture the user-specific information, or at the application level by using Java or .NET based client identifiers or IDs; augmented by custom PL/SQL, Java, or .NET code.

- Enable context-aware user interface grouping, segregation and rendering of the same, based on *dynamically generated domain-specific templates* that enable enhanced interaction and near real-time response to user-requested actions.
- The receive-route-respond-redirect workflow is of primary importance in Oracle-based Web Solutions that transact/operate in real-time on data that is time-variant or location-variant. From a Web-enabled interaction standpoint this means the following:

1. The user request is submitted to the Web Server (using the Web-based UI),

2. The authentication, authorization, and user input credentials are validated for accuracy

3. The request is delegated, including redirection to the appropriate client-to-server process that handles the request.

4. The request (e.g., a query against the database or the Web Server) is processed.

5. The results of the processed request are verified (a second round of validation) for accuracy.

6. The output is redirected to the appropriate user client process for any further processing on the client-side.

7. The results are delivered to the UI in the appropriate manner.

8. The results are enabled to be published online. This promotes collaboration and sharing of information within and beyond the enterprise, preserving the integrity, consistency, and security of the information, by enabling access to the right data to the right user at the right time. As an example, context-specific information can be published to online portals, Wiki pages, shareable .pdf files, or shared workspaces.

Oracle11g, in combination with Oracle SOA Suite, Oracle Weblogic Server, Oracle WebCenterSuite, and the Oracle ADF-based application design, can be used in combination with the grid computing methodology (at any/all solution Tier/s) to architect a SOA-based Web Service for click-and-go implementation—build, orchestrate (the workflow), integrate, coordinate, collaborate, automate, deploy, expand (scale on-demand), extend (add functionality on-demand), and adapt (self-service to evolve and innovate by using and improving on the outputs in a cyclic fashion). Rapid application development tools like Oracle JDeveloper11g, Oracle Eclipse Platform using SpringSource, Oracle APEX, and Oracle SQL Developer Data Modeler can aid in extreme application development process.

This is a huge operational efficiency and collaboration plus; at the same time; it enables the solution to penetrate more deeply into the usability landscape, across distributed locations and time-dependent requirements, with the flexibility to stretch or shear horizontally or vertically. And all of this comes with the most needed business benefit—*that of continuous consistency and persistency of results, reliability, availability, security, and self-manageability.*

7.3.1   Personalized A-La-Carte of Customer/End-User Service Requests: A Real-World Use Case of Application Web Interaction

- Implement a domain-specific persistent store of online solution services that are a no-miss to the application user in terms of relevance. Web Services in this scenario encompass a master list of supported application-specific services from which the user can pick. This can be implemented by a repository-based store in Oracle database or a persistent in-memory store in the application Tier, and can be invoked by deploying it as an Information Service callable on-demand from the Web UI.

- Implement interactive drag-and-drop controls for the user to pick the services of choice. Using a code accelerator the grouping, segregation, and rendering of the selected choices can be done in real-time, as the drag-and-drop is happening. This can be done using Oracle-supported Java-based, .NET-based, and PHP/AJAX/Javascript/Perl–based functionality and deployed as persistent objects, in-database objects, or in-memory objects. The consistency and interoperability can be done using an Oracle ADF–based or Oracle Coherence–based custom code accelerator.

Note that the management of these objects is facilitated by the inherent dynamic memory allocation/de-allocation and purging capabilities of Java/.NET frameworks.

■ Implement a Service Requests Enabler to auto-capture each user service request as an event and encapsulate them into a composite-process module (with its own workflow), which is then executed dynamically to arrive at the results. The design pattern for such an Enabler can be based on a custom-created User-Service-Requests-Pick-List Integration Web Service on the fly using federation to consolidate each individual service request.

■ Stream the obtained results by using maplets that synchronize the event-action-result on an individual service–request level. The same custom-generated Integration Web Service can be used to include this step and its automation as well. More pervasive results can be rendered as Custom Information Visualizations.

The orchestration of the end-to-end process flow is handled by various Oracle-based engines at the database, application, and presentation layers in conjunction with SOA-based framework of Java, and .NET based Web Services.

The final results can be deployed as another Web Service itself—one that can be used to perform tracking and analysis of customer experience trends in a shared manner to enable grouping them into "Most Frequently Requested" and "Highest Rated" categories. Taking a step further, this can be standardized into a Service Requests Template based on the user context and domain involved.

7.4   Best Practices for Application Integrity

Application integrity is all about ensuring correctness and validity of the application functionality per business needs in terms of data, processes including events, interfaces, and their orchestration—and maintaining this state, irrespective of how the application is used, who uses it, and where it is deployed, and immaterial of how the underlying data/information, business/IT processes, and metrics are changed, added, and/or removed, on-demand or otherwise. This ultimately boils down to data integrity, in terms of validity of data, information flow, and consolidation of disparate content into a unified view; process integrity, in terms of synchronizing business processes with IT processes, either using workflows or process automation; and interprocess and intercomponent coordination and communication that are application context–aware and happen in an organized manner.

Chapter 6 addressed the issue of data integrity and the best practices to be implemented for the same. This section discusses the best practices to implement application integrity end-to-end (i.e., across the overall solution).

The KPI for application management from an integrity and consistency standpoint is to implement the same for optimal efficiency (both solution efficiency and business-operational efficiency) alongside flexibility, in a seamless and transparent manner.

Here's a recommended list of the practices for the same that are top line:

- *Auto-generate code*—Use code to generate new code that can encapsulate, automate, and/or accelerate solution-specific application components to implement changing business processes and demands.
- *Read and write data variables dynamically*—This is required as part of auto-generation of code and can be used to enhance the accuracy of relevant business metrics being delivered as KPI, especially involving change as a result of user interaction.
- *Use a common information integrity framework*—Maintain a continuous and consistent state of integrity of the entire data/information lifecycle, starting from source-data quality to the unified information delivered to the end-user. This includes Web transactional integrity as well.

7.4.1   A Design Pattern for a Common Information Integrity Framework at the End-to-End Solution Level

- Implement in-database or in-memory business rules processing that map to contextual business attributes and processes for increased validity and accuracy of the end-to-end data and its flow. *This is an absolute requirement for processing unstructured content for search, query, and modification purposes.* This can be done by an intelligent coupling of federation and replication based on the data volume, the complexity of the analytics, and the user-request based data/content integration involved.

- Provide dynamic and efficient information delivery via real-time data federation and in-memory replication, using the database cache for example, to speed up the processing involved, and optimizing for read-only access, in-memory access, and random I/O (direct cache-based or secondary storage access bypassing the disk). Oracle11g's application-centric SSD and Flash cache–based secondary storage, coupled with solution acceleration mechanisms like Oracle RAC clustering at the database level (via Oracle DB Grid) and the application level (via Oracle Application Grid) and Oracle Data Guard or Active Data Guard provide what Oracle calls "Maximum Availability Architecture."

- Use Oracle Secure Files (or the Database File System) to incorporate efficient and effective managed I/O of offline file-based data by applying inline DB optimizations in a simulated manner.

- Implement a code accelerator to enable long-term data archival for both offline and online (active) data, including archival of logs (all mission-critical solution activity and audit logs). This can be done by a set of automated code-modules that correspond to multiple business processes and are executed in a streamed, pipelined, and/or parallelized fashion, eliminating redundant processing and storage. Using memory-centric storage and processing eliminates the wear and tear of disk or Flash-based storage, as this is based on D RAM (high performance gains with less storage space).

- Automate querying and the auditing of queries; this involves dynamic execution of queries—both generating queries on the fly based on ad hoc user requests, and executing in-place queries on the fly (especially, for auditing them). The key differentiator here is to implement an "intelligent query generator" that employs a combination mechanism of data and data flow pattern detection and the user-request action to generate a "context-aware" query that outputs optimal results in terms of data/content relevance, execution plan, response time, and resource utilization. Oracle11g has a number of methods to achieve this: for example, automatic SQL Tuning based on SQL plan baselines, capturing the active session history, the most recently introduced multiplan baselines for a single query (in Oracle11gR2), and the like.

- Share data seamlessly between Oracle and the host environments, with no "intermediate" stacking involved.

- Use REF CURSORs over custom code, an intelligent choice in the embedded programming scenario. Using REF CURSORs provides for dynamic sharing of scalar data and set-based information between the various in-solution components, as well as with other integrated solutions. This is because a single REF CURSOR variable can be defined to cater to multiple queries constructed on the fly (the benefits of dynamic SQL) and the fetching and further processing of the results from the query can be done on the client side in a client platform–centric manner (i.e., by using the embedded language context, deployment platform, etc.) as well as in a custom-centric manner (as needed by the client).
- Globalize data and code; application components; and the entire solution itself. A best practice is to implement this as Software-as-a-Service by itself or by combining Infrastructure-as-a-Service and/or Platform-as-a-Service.
- Localize data and privatize code, application components, and the entire solution itself.
- Use an Oracle database stored package for data integrity.
- Use callbacks to validate data-in, data-out.
- Use callbacks to validate application Web flow.
- Use callbacks for alerting/messaging.
- Perform interactive validations; acceptance and confirmations should be based on required and/or re-entered user input.
- Virtualize at the application level; this is the best bet for state-full Web-solution integrity, better adaptability, and "live" application streaming.

Virtualization enables dynamic control of the degree of flexibility that can be introduced into the solution, based on business IT demands. The solution doesn't necessarily have to be cloud-deployed.

- Evolve the application through innovative and actionable intelligence, one business metric at a time. Quantify the qualitative measurement and performance metrics of corresponding business metrics and build on the same to evolve the solution in terms of more "intelligent" business metrics that exhibit actionable performance and accountable business efficiency.

7.5 Best Practices for Application Consistency

The case for application consistency is made by the key business driver that the solution must enable "a unified business view of the customer"—and the customer can be a business or consumer/end user. This in turn makes the IT case for application consistency that is driven by:

- Streamlined management across solution Tiers that align with business domains/hierarchies
- Automation of the workflow vis-à-vis business processes, which in turn simplifies change management of the solution with respect to future-proofing
- Flexible integration services that enable interoperability with other systems spanning multiple lines of business and multiple use-case scenarios (transactional/operational, analytical, on-demand, predictive and descriptive business intelligence, etc.)
- Autosynchronization and state-full capabilities for data-in-transit and data-at-rest, as well as the Web application representational state

In a nutshell, application consistency mandates the need for active application processes that run in real-time, all the time, and asynchronously to ensure a transparent consistent state of the end-to-end application that provides the right data to the right user at the right time.

Here's a recommended list of the practices for the same that are top line:

- Implement cross-transactional consistency in Web-based DML operations using distributed in-memory data replication and a "virtual" two-phase commit mechanism. *A key design indicator for this is to synchronize replication and commit operations that can be implemented using policy-based imperatives to manage various commit points.*
- Minimize the creation of IT processes by reusing the in-place design to "generate" derived processes for extended business needs that can be componentized at an individual level or in combination—a huge performance gainer in large-scale solutions.

- Handle multiple user requests using optimistic locking at the Web server level that eventually cascades downstream to the database server level
- Use solution accelerators that can be exposed by using SOA-based services to enable multitenancy of Data Services calls, Web Services calls, and Java Services calls, using (code) design to derive and drive newer, accelerated, or optimized (code) design.
- Implement robust synchronization between in-place solution components and post-deployment component extensions by way of continuous, automated Web application monitoring end to end and analysis of the delta for any functionality, or security discrepancies.
- Provide on-demand custom rolling of the solution based on selective choice and integration of solution components. This can be implemented via a "virtual solution implementation" (akin to virtual desktop implementation, or VDI), using live federation and streaming of the same orchestrated by a virtualized and/or managed grid console.
- Effectively manage the solution in on-demand deployments by extending the same in terms of adding hot-pluggable components/ Web Services.
- Effectively monitor the solution in on-demand/hosted/cloud deployments, especially tracking user sessions, whether they are end point–based or enduser–based.
- Ensure trusted security in the hosted environment; this is beyond the control of enterprise IT.
- Manage solutions that involve transformational technologies, such as virtualization, cloud computing, and data center consolidation, especially when a single solution employs the use of multiple such technologies. This can be achieved by transforming business IT processes/workflow into callable Web Services, using the standard-ization-simplification-synchronization-virtualization-automation technology imperatives.

7.5.1 Multitenancy of Data Services Calls, Web Services Calls, and Java Services Calls

Web Services refer to solution-centric application modules, hardware, software, or a combination of both that can be accessed over the Internet using a Web browser via SSL. These services are delivered by using a design based on virtualization and grid computing. Virtualization enables fanning of multiple "virtual" images of a single physical machine (server, database, storage) combined with the application solution, using service-oriented architecture. Each "virtual" image is a complete end-to-end solution instance by itself (and can leverage the full functionality of the original parent solution). The management and synchronization between the physical and virtual machines is done by using virtualization software, known as VMware, that sits between the application solution physical machine and the multiple virtual images. Grid computing enables on-the-fly capacity, resources, and application-module expansion/contraction in an on-demand fashion.

Encapsulating business services into a single module that can be delivered as a Web Service provides for multitenancy of the application solution—that is, a single physical instance of the solution can be partitioned into one or more virtual user-centric instances of the same, dynamically. Each Web Service can be accessed by using a callable API that can be embedded in other applications, or via a Web-based interface such as a browser. Data Services calls and Java Services calls are special cases of Web Services calls that are specific to data/content unification and delivery and are Web Services–implemented using Java or J2EE technology, respectively.

The greatest benefit of delivering business services as Web Services in the embedded programming scenario is that they are implementation language agnostic. This means that a business process implemented using one embedded programming language such as C# (based on .NET) can be deployed and accessed by applications built using non-C# based languages such as Java, C/C++, PHP, and the like on multiple platforms that support browser-based callbacks in addition to Windows.

Here's a design pattern for implementing application consistency for data and content using virtualization technology:

1. Integrate the data/content from multiple data sources using data consolidation techniques like federation and decouple this from the solution into one single virtualized content layer. The unification of data can be done in-database, and a Virtualized Content Layer can be created using Oracle-based virtualization methodologies like the Database/Application Grid.

2. The unified content layer can reside in a persistent in-memory database cache or a separate "true" global virtual image that sits between the application solution and the database. The former option enables coupling of the unified content to the application

as a persistent cache that autosyncs with any changes happening on the fly. The latter option enables more pervasive access by means of real-time streaming of requested content from the single virtual image, as opposed to from the Oracle database.

The KPI here are as follows:

- Application consistency, in terms of delivering data/content, is derived implicitly and the virtualization involved enables A-A-A accessibility to any needed data source–based information. This can be done in real-time and automated as a business process into the solution workflow, as well. From data creation/loading to storage to integration to secure access across multiple users, multiple domains, and multiple platforms, it provides a seamless delivery of information and at the same time an accelerated performance through efficient data storage, access, and inter- and intraprocess management.
- Evolving this design by applying to each individual application involved in the overall solution enables application consistency in terms of syncing the data/content, workflows, and messaging to improve the productivity and efficiency in multi-application integration scenarios.
- A consistent state of solution availability for business continuity provides a flexible and transparent mechanism for server, database, and storage management; online and (near) real-time backup and recovery and automatic failover for disaster recovery; and dynamic scale-in and scale-out in terms of capacity, resources, and user base.

The key indicator for multitenancy is that neither the business solutions team nor the customer's IT team need to worry about the administration of the physical and virtual environments involved.

Figure 7.3 presents a design architecture for implementing application solution consistency.

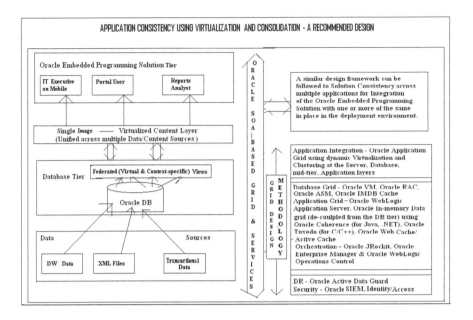

Figure 7.3   A design-architecture for application consistency..

7.5.2   A Real-World Scenario that Demonstrates the Use of These Best Practices for Implementation

Application solution performance acceleration is required to ensure a consistent performance curve of the solution in context. Performance can degrade due to variability in the workload (such as data volume growth, resources utilization reaching the maximum limit, etc.), changing deployment platforms (from on-premise to on-demand, from stand-alone to an integrated/embedded environment, etc.), or scalability (increased number of users, etc.). These conditions ultimately leads to poor response times and a dramatic slowdown of the operational processes end to end in terms of IT impact. The corresponding business impacts can bring about inferior customer experience, which directly lowers business value in terms of revenue and productivity.

In such cases, both the solution design and the solution usage of the design need to be optimized. This can be done using one or more of the following steps:

1.   Review the configuration/initialization/instantiation parameters for the end-to-end solution to fill/fix/set performance-related imperatives such as resource allocation and cache sizing, and

enable/disable default set values that have minimal impact at run-time like debug-mode and the like. This also includes those related the end-point client platform, such as necessary plug-ins, browser incompatibilities, etc. *All of these can be grouped together into a template categorized by the solution context and the execution platform and stored in a common-format template for re-use (such as XML-based templates).*

2. Optimize the data flow, the data integration flow, the business process flow, and the user input–based action-response processes.

3. Correlate all the data sources involved and the interdependencies between the various solution components, including the integration scenarios involved

4. Provide deep-dive diagnosis and resolution in terms of isolating emergent problems based monitoring logs and immediately resolving those problems to prevent further escalation.

5. Analyze the end-to-end application solution response time(s) across various "live" user sessions. This enables a correlation between varying workloads and overall response times to determine the point(s)-of-least-response. Using visualization, this data can be retrofitted into a *performance pipeline* that comprises other time-based analyses derived from other business imperatives, such as domain-specific functionality vs. solution-component performance; comparison with previously released application performance results involving the same variables for analysis; and the like.

6. Fix invalidated objects on the database side and eliminate idle/hung processes not directly associated with the run-time execution at the database/application levels.

7.6   Best Practices for Security Beyond User Authentication: End-to-End Application Security

User authentication is the first step in ensuring valid user entry into an Oracle-based Web-enabled embedded programming solution. To implement an increased level of security to handle all kinds of threats and attacks—not just at the database level, but across the end-to-end solution—the security infrastructure design needs to be as robust and rigid as possible. This in turn involves tightly securing the network, application, and the database Tiers for any kind of vulnerabilities. Security of the solution extends beyond user authentication, creating a whole new world of Web application security, access, and identity management.

The KPI for solution security is one that differentiates between a security breach (which occurs as a result of in-the-solution code) and a risk (or vulnerability) threat or attack (which occurs as a result of out-of-solution misuse to break the code and opens the doors for unexpected/emerging security lapses). Design a framework based on the severity of the each of them, mapping their direct impact on the business sensitivity of the solution in context, prioritizing the resolution and risk mitigation processes to be implemented, and leveraging this information to provide analysis, resolution, and mitigation to ensure a continuous end-to-end security.

Here a list of Key Security Indicators to focus on while designing and developing a Web-based solution security, access, and identity management framework:

- Focus on "all issues that matter most" from the customer-centric point of view, rather than from the IT standpoint.
- Supplement business activity monitoring (BAM) with database and network activity monitoring. BAM is less capable (and sometimes incapable) of detecting lapses in-database code like SQL Injection [S-a-a-S] Security.
- Capture user session activity by tracking and tracing each and every active user session, irrespective of the type of user (on-premise, on-demand, end-point device, etc.)
- Base the security design on the corporate as well as regulatory governance, risk, and compliance policies, including policies for access and identity compliance.
- Introduce false positives and false negatives based on the business functionality and use of the Web solution by using code accelerators that preintegrate with the security business rules for preventive testing.
- Increase the level of confidence in the integrity of the delivered solution, by doing an assessment and analysis of potential threats as a result of the architectural design, deployment platforms, and integration requirements involved. This raises a key security problem to be addressed—securing the data, content, and information flow between the database all the way through to the Web

application, including interaction with other applications, Web Services, and external mash-up content at run-time. This applies to both to both data in-transit and data-at-rest.

The typical remediation measures are designing reusable test plans that can be automated using reusable code accelerators and integrated into the process flow to autodetect and fix similar vulnerabilities dynamically.

- The reliability and efficiency of application code in terms of unbreakability, abuse, and execution efficiency is a key indicator. In addition to peer code reviews, perform both white-box testing and black-box testing in the build/test phases, accompanied by analysis of the cause-effect-resolution results of the same; finally culminating in the white-listing and black-listing of the solution components. All of this can be encapsulated in a code accelerator for security and automated.

- For mobile/end-point/on-demand hosted/cloud-based user access, lock in the end-to-end (run-time infrastructure and application solution) configuration settings—including the security settings, too, as these are specific to the particular end-point-device/end-user in context—into a reusable configuration file or end-point Web Services capsule that is autodeployed and set/executed at the end-user/end-device system start-up. This freezes the particular user/device security till a new update of the same is installed, based on changed roles. Hence, no other end-user/end-point, including the privileged user, can gain access to this. This further accelerates the process of application white-listing and black-listing security practices detailed above.

  This approach can be used for on-premise deployment platforms, too.

Remember that all of the above focus factors are interlinked and share common ground. The key point to be noted is to use the design of the security framework to detect and derive the cause and effect of errors, threats, and attacks; and to use the same design to arrive at an optimized remediation/resolution best practice that can be transformed into a new or improved security policy (one that aligns with the so-called "feedback-loop" strategy) and seamlessly integrated into the overall end-to-end solution security process.

Inlining application security into business IT solution design via process automation is probably one of the best practices for security end-to-end, especially when the solution in context is custom-built as a new application. It can be achieved by architecting the design for security and its management at the solution design phase (as opposed to doing it after the build phase, as is generally the case) and by integrating it with the respective IT processes (vis-à-vis business processes), so that IT security becomes part of the arteries of the end-to-end solution. The benefits derived are twofold:

1. It is easier to fix the design of the process where a particular violation occurred and sync it with the code and the overall Web workflow than to identify the same at the testing phase and redo the work completely (including code changes) to fix it.

2. It eliminates the need to develop repeatable security fixes that are needed for effective and efficient security to be in place.

To implement this strategy in practice, a code accelerator can be used to enable application-aware and policy-aware code design and implementation, which can be automated and integrated into the overall process workflow. Any additional rules needed can be plugged into the appropriate code accelerator by adding new code or an entirely separate code accelerator. These extra rules will surface during the iterative test-driven development and deployment before delivering the solution to the production environment.

Any latency in time-to-delivery caused by this approach can be definitely undermined compared to the costs required to fix issues in the deployment and post-production stages, which of course can be very large.

For a solution based on embedded programming languages, just designing with in-built security policies is not enough. To implement the design for effective use, the associated code must be efficient on par with the design. This in turn depends on the language-specific coding run-time deployment platforms – to account for security lapses due to bad coding practices and level of security supported (or rather limited) by the run-time platform.

Introduce static code testing and dynamic code testing, which are crucial to identifying both code flaws as well as code vulnerabilities. Static or "white box" testing enables the detection of semantic errors and other code discrepancies that are inherent to the solution, including those that impact execution performance. The best way to put static code testing in practice is to use an Oracle-based integrated development environment (IDE) (e.g., Oracle JDeveloper, Oracle APEX, Oracle Developer Tools for .NET, etc.) that has in-built "radar detectors" that scan for code errors and alert on an "as-is" basis during the testing while developing. Another intuitive way is to turn on database-level code optimization parameters and enable the same at the language-specific level, augmenting these with custom code accelerators that scan for code flaws.

A recommended best practice is to always enable the code optimization parameters at the DB as well as the language-specific levels during the develop-test phases that go hand-in-hand and/or in iterations.

On the other hand, dynamic code testing, or "black box" testing, is a best practice for radar-detection of solution vulnerabilities such as hacking, attacks, and emerging threats like privilege manipulation and escalation, SQL Injection, and cyber-threats. The easiest way to implemente this is by simulated hacking or penetrating testing that is manually done in a "fire-drill" type code. However, the recommended best practice is to use a code accelerator that adopts a pre-emptive design using code to generate "published" code on the fly that in turn breaks the (subscribed) solution-code in all possible ways, automated and streamlined into the end-to-end-workflow. This comes in very handy for scanning "out-of-solution" attacks (i.e., those that result from user interaction/exploitation and expose vulnerabilities in the code).

Dynamic code testing needs to be augmented with an overall solution activity monitoring module that comprises database activity monitoring and database firewall; Web application monitoring and Web application firewall; and network activity monitoring and network firewall. By doing this, threat risk assessment and back-tracing of the source code that caused it can be analyzed so that the right remediation measures can be taken. *This is part of the application -solution white-listing and black-listing, in terms of isolating its components into "go-ahead" and "no-go" categories. This addresses issues that are most often not detectable by traditional firewalls and antivirus software.*

Oracle versions 10gR2 and beyond provide for self-manageability, auto-detection, and fixing of security errors and business-logic vulnerabilities, to a certain extent. Oracle Real Application Testing allows testing on a snapshot of the "live" application in production (even in RAC-based infrastructures), and the Oracle Application Testing Suite11g can be used to perform both static and dynamic code testing.

Java as an embedded programming language is a good choice for both Java and nonJava–based applications, as it has a very high level of security built into its architecture. The code accelerator can be made language-neutral by converting it into a Java Stored Procedure that can be exposed using generic API (e.g., ODBC) for use in nonJava environments, or as a Web Service that can be invoked from the client end point.

This does not mean that Java is the only choice for secure code. All it means is that Java is a very good choice. Other embedded-language interfaces, such as .NET-based C# and J#, C/C++, PHP/Ajax, Python, and Perl can follow their supported code securing features and expose them via a language-neutral API/Service. Their transparent interoperability is the key here.

A best practice implementation scenario is to use static and dynamic code testing augmented by end-to-end solution monitoring, vulnerability analysis, and back-tracing the application code source of the traps/lapses and their fixing methods.

Last but not least, backup the end-to-end security policies in place. This can be archived not only for restore operations, but also for duplication/replication of the same in similar demanding situations by consolidating them into a reusable hot-pluggable template.

7.6.1   Real-World Use Cases for Implementing Web Security Policies

The set of best-practice policies outlined earlier for securing a Web application can also be put into action for building a case of real-world business implementations. Two such use cases are described in the sections that follow.

Custom Security Extender for User Identity

In a nutshell, this is the management of inactive users or rather User IDs. Simple as it might seem, in enterprise-based or remotely deployed environments it is a major bottleneck to track the "rearview" status and history of all users who are no longer authorized to use the application solution. This means freezing these user accounts, but that only prevents future access. Here are the steps for a design pattern for implementing a security extender for inactive users that dilutes all user activity that occurred until the point the user ID is disabled:

1. Create a subdata model that extracts the user activity of all inactive users from the global user activity monitoring log/repository. The end-to-end activity monitoring of enterprise user base (both within and remote) must be already in place as part of the overall security and activity monitoring module. This module runs both asynchronously and continuously.

2. Register this extracted subset log of inactive users as an "active event" that stores point-in-time flashback activity and is the working set for processing involved.

3. Analyze and deliver this event, including the analysis synopsis, as a Callable Web Service that is SOA-based and therefore is adaptable and flexible enough to be scaled on-demand.

4. Build a secondary monitoring accelerator that automates steps 1 to 3 based on continuity, asynchronous execution, and real-time capture of the primary monitoring module to track inactive users and their activity as each user ID is disabled (i.e., in real-time). To implement this, either stream-based processing or message-oriented processing can be used. The former approach is more efficient, as it involves no or minimal parsing.

The key indicator here is the SOA-based reusable design, which enables seamless deployment, execution, and analyses across business, customer, and user domains. This means there is no need to spin a different security extender (in other words, a different silo) for each domain that is a candidate for such an implementation.

In fact, a best practice for implementing security in a Web-based environment, is to deploy it as a callable, reusable, extendable, adaptable Web Service that works across all Oracle-based embedded language solutions. This approach eliminates the need to re-engineer the existing design and involves refactoring (if needed) at a minimal level (in terms of time-to-implement and changes-to-implement).

Custom Security Extender Preventive Protection

This use case focuses on using (past) threats and breaches to prevent (future) threats and breaches. In other words, this involves capitalizing on previously detected information leakages and vulnerabilities and their remediation measures by reusing their resolution policies as pre-emptive security policies and wiring them into the overall security architecture.

The design pattern for such an implementation is similar to that of the use case for security extender for user identity (as described in the previous subsection) except that the following factors need to be taken into consideration:

- The key indicator here involves capitalizing on previous customer experience. If the solution is yet to be deployed in production, the previous customer experience refers to one derived based on a similar postproduction solution tailored toward a business domain of similar relevance and context. Otherwise, it refers to the customer/monitoring experience of the current solution running in production, and improving on the same.
- This can be treated as a special case of *reality mining* in which the focus is on the customer experience rather than on the IT/technology experience in terms of security intrusions and leakages, their cause and effect, and resolution-prevention-assessment-assurance.

Leverage the people, processes, and technology loopholes and their fixes to prevent future loopholes.

7.7   Best Fit for Oracle in the ASP.NET Framework

The first and foremost KPI for using Oracle in an ASP.NET environment is its ability to align and synchronize ASP.NET framework-based efficiency imperatives with Oracle SQL-PL/SQL–based efficiency imperatives by implicitly enabling them through the ODAC, ODP.NET Managed Data Provider, and Oracle ADF. This greatly increases performance by leveraging the right Oracle-compliant data access provider for faster access, optimized resource utilization, and reduced disk I/O.

The Oracle ADF is fully compliant with the ASP.NET Framework and enriches it by way of enhanced Web Page features and controls like dynamic page sectioning, faceted highlighting, multipart posting of content streams like binary .pdf files, and the like.

Here's a list of key role players to keep in mind:

- .NET GUI objects called in an ASP.NET Page can gain access to a non-Oracle based Web Application Server (sitting on top of Oracle) via in-memory distributed cache or Oracle Coherence, thus enabling a .NET consumer and an external Web Server provider to communicate to each other. (This is an SOA-based Web Services mechanism,)
- Architecture can be designed and developed that converts an existing ASP.NET application in-DB to generate a PL/SQL-based Web 2.0 application that is readily deployable. The Key Design Indicators are:
  - Unified data/info view based on subject orientation and integration of information— that is, volatile for OLTP and Operational OLAP/business intelligence (BI), nonvolatile for OLAP, time-variant, A-A-A, right time-right user-right data-right job.
  - Process-oriented through automation for business operational efficiency
  - Service-oriented through Web Services for user/UI interaction and delivery (remotely, mobile devices)
  - Scalable and fast application generation within the DB level
- Dynamic query generation using any permutation and combination of ad hoc variables (including both data attributes and filter/search criteria) enables a higher degree of data and application visibility in terms of who is querying what data. This increased visibility aids in the end-to-end application monitoring process.
  - Faster execution of date-based range queries submitted via the ASP.NET page.
  - Caching of most-frequent search conditions used at the page level and binding them to relevant request-based queries. This can be done by tagging these using labels and applying inclusion/exclusion criteria before constructing the final query, replacing HTML-based expressions using smart filtering of char/text expressions before tokenization, and the like.
  - Dynamically cluster the top n searches into a "Favorite Searches" list using URL-enabled rendering. Merge mutually exclusive searches into an *Other Searches"* list rendered as URL

links. This can be an intermittent task that lasts only for the particular session or it can be cached to be reused on every Web page session initiation.

- Oracle can be used as a backend database to a Web-based ASP.NET application, thereby leveraging its unparalleled functionality in terms of efficiency, scalability, availability, security, and multitenancy for information and solution delivery and customization. This can prove to be a best-fit approach to arrive at a faster, flexible, and extensible enterprise-wide integration of existing ASP.NET solutions in both on-premise and on-demand deployments.

- The centralized and persistent management of user authentication and authorization is gained by consolidating user privileges into a role-based policy-driven repository that allows for a business-driven privileges assignment and at the same time preventie privilege escalation and data loss. This means that the ASP.NET access lists can now be made persistent and more fine-grained, ensuring the viability of the solution to a stronger degree. So page indirection, redirection, and subsection rendering can be based on user roles that are assigned on the fly by a flipflop change in the database.

- A dynamic mapping mechanism based on access control lists can be put in place using a code accelerator that abstracts any hard-coded user roles in the ASP.NET application code in the Oracle DB, thus providing for multilevel security for user privileges protection, including those for privileged users.

- ASP.NET container independence exposes the ASP.NET application as a Web Service autogenerated in the Oracle database, which can enable solution acceleration by isolating the application-code-layer from the user-deployment platform environment. This approach allows for distributed application replication in terms of usability and adoption simply via a Web browser—across disparate functional domains, avoiding multiple deployments of the solution every time.

- The state of the Web page can be persistently cached and synced in real-time with the visual content that is being displayed/modified during user interaction. Even the user context state can be stored as a callable entity in the database, and just re-rendered by default every time the page is opened or the same is auto-refreshed on page invocation. The key indicator here is to capture the statistics of the cache, which can be done using enable flags in configuration files that are dynamically set and reset

---

Modularization is the key to application stability and acceleration! And there's no need for REFRESH-keying of the page to enable the changes on the fly.

- Digital signing of the page output uses a context-specific auto-generated signature before an export operation initiated by the user. The digital signature can be a unique ID that is autocreated using hashing on key business attributes
- Page portability and dynamic template generation uses asynchronous transformation into XML format that includes the tagged as well multi flex attributes in the Schema.XML.
- Live drag-and-drop customization of page-based content dynamically derives data and URL-enables it for detailed drilldown using *context-specific templates* (implemented using JSP-based, ASP.NET based, or scripting-language based code).
- Implement navigation controls for multipage reports, such as progress bars for page-to-page scrolling, single-click scrolling, mouse-based scrolling, random scrolling to an input page number, and the like.
- Export the report output in such a way that it can be reused by other business models/applications via import. This can be done by exporting into a common XML format that is suitable to fit into any industry-standards based solution or a custom .pdf format.
- Implement auto-triggered events such as auto-complete, auto-navigate, key-stroke/single-character-based auto-filtering, drag-and-drop, point-and-click and one-click functionality
- Proactively measure loading, refresh, request, and response metrics at the Web page level as well as individual page-component level. This can be implemented using ASP.NET specific code-snippets or codelets that are activated using timed events. Oracle ADF also supports coding of this type of design patterns. This aids in improving the page request-response velocity or, in other words, the ability to accelerated page rendering and bidirectional Web interaction.

A real-world use case of this is to determine which actions are latency-neutral and thus do not require instant, subsecond, or submillisecond response to an interactive action.

7.8 Best Practices for Templates: Use or Eliminate?

The use of templates as a method for standardizing best practices for reusability has been outlined in earlier sections during discussion of code accelerator design, application integrity, consistency, Web interaction, and security. These all make a strong case for the use of template-based solution design and development. Templates are designed using static content (they can include code too) and placeholders that allow for run-time content to be dynamically embedded in the appropriate places to create the required solution output. This is automated by using template-friendly configuration files, XML-based dynamic code embedding, and the like.

Here's a list of recommended use-case scenarios for use of templates to accelerate the design and development of the application solution:

- As pointed out in the earlier section, a code design template can be created to encapsulate the design implementation for converting an ASP.NET application in-DB to generate a PL/SQL-based Web 2.0 application that is readily deployable. This templatecan be extended/customized for reuse in additional such implementations. Even the underlying metadata design can be flattened into an XML-based (hierarchy) file template.

- Just as a Master Data Management (MDM) implementation gives a 360-degree view of customer-centric, context-specific data/content, a Master Application Management (MAM) implementation can provide a seamless integrated view of the embedded programming solution and the various in-place, external applications by means of a unified metadata definition of the business process and services master data involved, business-critical master data relevant to the overall consolidation, and the data/content and integration task flow services aligned with the business processes. The architecture, as well as the code tied to it, can be generated into a MAM template that can be reused or refactored for further improvement. Such a template can incorporate both the design pattern and the code base; it can be file-based (XML template),

SOA-based (callable Web Service template), or pure API based (callable API template). This increases the time-to-value while minimizing the resources and risks of a new design and implementation—without affecting the stability of existing applications.

- Use a visualization template that incorporates visual content with placeholders for embedding dynamic content, as in the case of template-based report generation

7.9   Best Practices Beyond HTML: Auto-generate Dynamic Visual Content, Web Services, and Mobile Applications

Visual analysis, callable Web Services, and mobilization of applications are emerging as the next-generation user-oriented methodologies for faster and more accurate analyses, under-the-hood seamless integration and collaboration, and A-A-A accessibility and availability. The implementation of these methodologies extends beyond the normal capability and usability of HTML/XML, which encompasses a varied spectrum of accelerated markup languages such as XACML (eXtended Access Control Markup Language) to implement security for XML messages-in-transit; WML (Wireless Markup Language), which is the analogue of HTML for mobile applications deployment platforms; and the like.

The sections that follow highlight some recommended best practices for the same.

7.9.1   Auto-generate Dynamic Visual Content

- *Centralized point-of-control, shared point-of-processing-and-storage, and distributed point-of-access, farsighted point-of-application-visibility*—These are the uncompromising benefits of the combination of data/content visualization, SOA-based Web Services, and mobile platforms for application deployments, which is a high-end business accelerator by way of a superior customer experience that enables both customer retention and acquisition.

The best business benefit that can be derived from visual content is its ability to enable data-as-input to turn into data-as-asset by way of transforming it into data-as-unified-information and evolving into data-as-decisions-in-action.

A real-world use case of this can be for on-the-fly information/ report distribution to heterogeneous applications such as external dashboards, messaging systems, Web portals, and even Excel spreadsheets. Here's a typical usability pattern of the same:

- Consolidate business-context data from heterogeneous sources and formats into a single seamless view that can be transformed into a 3D-visual display showing the correlated business variables and the corresponding quantitative values, which can be extrapolated by the business user on the fly to arrive at qualitative markers in the same display.

- Propagate this business-enhanced display in real-time to a BI dashboard of another operational system or an Excel spreadsheet which can be used by a data steward/CIO "as-is" for corporate decision making. This dynamic data interoperability can be implemented by means of a code accelerator that functions as a "live" (i.e., as the application is running) data integration add-on or service.

- Auto-refresh both the visual display in the solution UI and the "live" output in the dashboard/Excel as changes are made in either place, and implement the ability to make these changes persistent in the Oracle database, if required.

- Perform all of the analysis/processing in-memory and in an integrated fashion. This accelerates the processing and execution efficiency of the dynamic flow of the content stream(s).

The key design indicator here is that the user has the control to navigate, drilldown, exchange, or generate new content in any manner that best fits the need in context, analyze, and perform metrics-based measurements.

- *Visual alerting*—This can be used for deadlock exceptions that mandate user relogin to the solution or otherwise.

As a real-world use case, the application can be forced into a "modal" state during high-severity error occurrence, with visual alert message prompts requiring interactive user response/acknowledgement.

- *Visual content–based searching*—This involves the transformation of text-based visual content, such as scanned image files comprising text or 3D .pdf files, into multipart regular text documents. This can be done by generating dynamic code at run-time that in turn generates snapshots of text-searchable document files, based on user-specified search criteria. The source visual content can still be stored in the Oracle database and accessed on demand. *This also serves as a use case for application templates, as the underlying code design pattern can be auto-converted into a standard template for text-based search in visual content.*

- *Visual interaction*—This can involve any combination of user-controlled action-response, including Flash-based interactivity or visualization of information presented. Recommended scenarios are:
  - For mash-up of internal (or in-solution)/external video content, derive custom-specific visualizations that enable real-time interaction, such as knob controls, progress bars, speedometer/odometer simulated controls, and the like.
  - Evolve 2D graphs and charts to corresponding 3D visualizations that render the relevant details in a much sharper manner. This can help with 3D analysis of transactions or events as they happen in real-time by capturing these events using process/workflow automation and auto-generating 3D visual images dynamically on the fly. Examples are early detection of flaws/fraud based on the transactions, as-is analysis of user-session activity, and the like.

Here's a code design pattern for the same:

1. Dynamically capture the associated transactions/processes as they are getting executed, and auto-transform each of them into 3D visualizations, processed in-database or in-memory using Ajaxification, PHP, C# and WPF API, Java API, C/C++ API, etc. along with SQL-PL/SQL.

2. Integrate the resulting 3D image/video output with the data details of the transactions/user-interaction events seamlessly, using a code accelerator designed for content integration. (Multiple design patterns for the same have been detailed in Chapters 4 and 6.)

3. Expose the consolidated 3D content and data to the presentation interface via a seamless and tagged representation using specific Web Services or dashboards, downloadable reports via URL links, and the like.

   - Double-click on report-specific business attributes for hierarchical, drilldown, and/or drill-across thresholds.

- Mouse-over bubble tips provide business-savvy help and recommendations, abstracting the technicality involved from the user.

- Merge statistical data, historical trend data, and predictive analysis–based projections and proposals in one visual view-let, using color coding– and line art–based patterns (e.g., using different colors in combination with bold-font lines, regular-font lines, dotted lines, etc. to represent each of these categories).

- Enable visual analysis–based troubleshooting for online problem tracking and resolution (e.g. auto-converting monitored database, user session, or business process activity on the fly) for real-time diagnosis as the solution is being used. This is essential for pre-emptive and proactive diagnostics and troubleshooting—especially for optimization—that drives the business continuity of the solution, eliminating downtime incurred in maintenance operations. Another very important use of this skill is to capture and analyze the self-tuning capabilities implemented in the solution for relevant process-flow performance and possible improvements of the same.

- Remember that tracing/monitoring is done online; problem-solution analysis and resolution measures are done offline and subsequently introduced during the solution offline phase.

- *User-controlled Flash-based navigation*—This can involve a directory-structured dashboard sectioning/subsectioning based on runtime criteria. This can be implemented by dynamic generation of visual subpages that auto-profiles, auto-classifies, and auto-clusters randomly user-selected objects into context-specific visual substrata. This derived set of outputs can be organized into a hierarchical visual tree-based structure or a directory-based user-centric content structure. The Oracle ADF, with its inherent Java-based, .NET-based, Javascript, and XML functionality for *asynchronous* processing, execution, and control can enabled Flash-based GUI-object rendering and seamless interoperability. Again, this can be done in-DB, in-memory, or archived as a Web Service, or *even standardized as a template.*

7.9.2 Web Services

Implementing best practices as Web Services based on SOA enables multi-tenancy of business services by way of deploying and running a single instance of the application solution on a dedicated server, and enabling multiple clients (or users) to access the solution using copies (or images) of the server-based application solution instance. This is done using virtual partitioning of the single server instance.

Web Services enable seamless deployment and use of the solution in on-demand (true-hosted or cloud-based), on-premise, and hybrid plat-forms. Access control and management can be done via a centralized visual control (e.g., Oracle Enterprise Grid Control) or programmatic API. The latter involves callable Web Services.

Here's a list of best practices for using Web Services in real-world solution implementations:

- Information loss prevention and security via Data Services, either API–based or exposed as Web Services.
- Reusable business operational processes exposed as Web Services that enable subject-oriented business-domain functionality captured in a service-oriented capsule and accessed over a Web UI. This is different from the business IT solution workflow, although it too can be exposed using Integration Services that automate the same for multitenancy and shared-computing.
- Dynamic data transformation on the fly and real-time reporting based on it, to generate personalized/ad hoc reports based on inter-active user-controlled data/content changes.
- Accessibility of the solution on-demand across user end-points such as mobile devices/platforms and those that are remotely accessed—with all the enterprise functionality still enabled.

The KPI here is a Web Services–based implementation that allows to use the existing IT infrastructure to augment/extend the solution with custom Web-based reporting that is OS-, technology-, and touchpoint-agnostic at the same time.

7.9.3   Mobilizing Applications

The Oracle-supported methodologies of application grid, virtualization, and cloud computing broaden the pervasiveness of the embedded programming solution beyond on-premise and wired networks to non-enterprise/wireless/mobile platforms. The best-fit deployment methodology for such application mobilization is by using Web Services that are both centralized (in terms of management, synchronization, and control) and distributed (in terms of access/usability) at the same time. Here's a list of best practices for mobilizing application solutions in real-world solution implementations:

- Design and develop a code accelerator for online and offline archiving of end-device information. This can be done using a unified metadata design and metaprogramming code design tailored to capture a copy of context-specific end-device information (online and offline) as it is created or altered; and syncing and streamlining the same through automation.
- The mobile solution efficiency in terms of customer experience and use on the end-point mobile platform must be on par with a similar desktop-based experience. This means that information can be accessed, modified, and synchronized in a high-performance (with the minimal latency possible), interoperable, and user-interactive manner, without compromising on the flexibility, high-availability, and security of the solution.

  The use of a consolidated virtual image of the end-to-end solution followed by live application streaming of multiple images based on it, that are one-on-one with each mobile end device's deployment requirements is a best-fit pragmatic approach to implement such a strategy. This in turn provides the flexibility to plug-and-unplug mobile users on demand, all through a centralized control.

The KPI is to enable translucent caching and management of the cache to facilitate high-performing computation on the mobile end device.

Oracle11g Enterprise Manager Grid Console supported by a custom application grid (via virtualization) that combines in-db, in-memory, processing and integrated workflow-based event processing with Oracle RAC-based clustering enables an out-of-box implementation of the same.

- Use Web Services to deploy the solution as a Mobile Software-as-a-Service. This approach enables the primary issue of security and information protection and usability, continuous monitoring, and context awareness to be implemented implicitly, because it is built into the solution to be deployed. However, the key indicators here are the following:
  - Ensure that this in-built functionality is end-point device–agnostic. This means that the Oracle-enabled data/content encryption and user access are turned on by default and this state is preserved on each and every mobile device the solution is running. Also, ensure that the point-of-contact aligns with the point-of-control, confirming that the end-point device is traceable during the application monitoring process, while it is active.
  - Implement local authentication at the individual device level, but controlled by a SoD (segregation of duties)–based authorization
  - The solution network space either includes only those devices that comply with this Mobile SaaS or the network is layered in with a Security-as-a-Service appliance or gateway to take care of Web Service security if the solution is used in external cloud- and/or true-hosted environments.
  - Auto-disable end-user controls specific to the application solution context when the user logs off the same. This can include those in an equivalent desktop experience, like cookies, offline content, wireless-centric features such as Bluetooth, Internet access through wi-fi to get onto the network, and the like.

This approach enables effective realization of QoS (Quality of Service) by ensuring that the right content is available to the right user on the right end device.

7.10   Best Practices for Creative Reporting

Creative reporting is all about turning data into information and presenting it in a manner that enables the users (no matter who the users are) to apply their analytical insight and stewardship expertise to derive or discover results that support decision-making and to implement these results in ways that drive business efficiency, both operationally and competitively. What is so "creative" about this? The results that support decision making evolve the data into "intelligent information" and implement that information to drive business efficiency, both operationally and competitively, thus making it "actionable"—this justifies the creativity involved.

This approach depends on the following key indicators, which are part of the application management process:

- Web-enablement and provisioning for on-demand access (A-A-A)
- Ability to link historical data with operational data, in real-time, at the right time, and all the time, before presenting it to the user
- Dynamic presentation interface, in terms of on-the-fly analysis, data visualization, live interaction (via instant action-response capability), and self-service functionality, that is better-faster-easier to use
- Cloning point-in-time and flashback query functionality on the reporting side; this means capturing the report execution context "as-is," including the user-driven controls and the report output (i.e. when the report was run at a given point in time). This can be either cached or archived (the latter option is recommended) to enable context-specific, user-centric report viewing and analysis based on an "as-of" snapshot of archived report output.

Here's a list of best practices from the design and information presentation perspectives:

- *Robust data integration mechanisms*—These support information processing and integration from disparate/multiple data sources to create a unified view of domain-specific data that can be isolated by user/customer, but still consolidated into a centralized "information" store. Chapter 6 on Data Management highlighted many design and development best practices for the same (e.g., real-time federation via dynamic virtual views, streaming, in-memory data replication of operational data as well as data at rest, leveraging SOA– and SaaS–based computing, etc.) The fine points to be noted in regard to report output are:
  - Incorrect representation of NULL/empty values in the report output (though the corresponding values in the database are

valid). As an example, decoding a gender field in a report that is stored as 0s and 1s for "Male" and "Female" values respectively, and leaving it NULL or empty for all other cases, in a report that involves aggregation by gender can result in incorrect COUNT values for each gender value grouping. Remember that in many application solutions involving embedded programming, the values NULL and/or empty can be considered valid for all outlier values of the particular column in context.

- Synchronization between dissimilar source and target data types for columns representing the same business attribute. This is a very important and in fact a necessary practice to be implemented, which can be done by use of meta-data definitions aligning with the target database types, (that is mostly, Oracle11g, but can be any custom-format type) or meta-programming (e.g., for data visualizations) in the report presentation

---

Key design indicators include the elimination of intermediate data containers and metadata repositories, and middle-Tier data access components, as well as the use of data virtualization to complement physical data replication and consolidation. This is a smart choice for operational data integration bypassing the database/data warehouse as required for operational and continuous BI, as well as for correlating complex event processing (CEP) results across disparate solution Tiers like virtual deployment platforms and the physical environment, etc.

- *Direct information input from operational data*—Implement operational business intelligence by giving the end user the ability to access data/content directly from the operational systems, bypassing the database/data warehouse/data mart Tier in the solution in context. The application/presentation interface must provide this flexibility, using operational data integration processes that are secure, continuous, event-driven, and automated. One way to implement this is to use data virtualization.
- *Content mash-up at run-time*—This involves collating external as well as on-screen/in-place content into a single seamless merge in the report on the fly (by way of user interactivity such a click-and-go, drag-and-drop, knob-based controls, or a list of values select/multiselect). It is recommended that the content to be mashed-up

be URL addressable. This includes mash-up of multiple UI segments on an on-demand and user-driven basis. A typical example is embedding a custom analytic 3D scoreboard as an add-on business component, in an existing Visual Report.

- *Information/content creation/transformation/re-presentation from the presented information*—Plug-and-play capability for the user to do this built into the reporting dashboard.
- *360-degree analysis of information*—This includes drilldown, drill-across, and hierarchical analysis. Of particular importance is drill-across reporting involving silos, for example, when reporting across platforms such as on-premise and on-demand applications. The Oracle-based embedded programming solution might need to access external data sources like those that are public/private/hybrid cloud-based or other legacy systems. The key design indicators to achieve this are:
    - Build a business analytics appliance that can be embedded into the Oracle-based solution on-demand and is both customer-centric and data-driven. This can be implemented using real-time data federation into dynamic virtual views and subsequent streaming, and integrated into the solution workflow as a SOA-based service component that can be processed in-database or in-memory. In-database analytics enable more efficient processing, as they reduce the context switching between the embedded programming language environment and the SQL-PL/SQL engine, especially when invoked in a real-time fashion. The same procedure can be followed for integration into the workflow using an analytic integration SOA-component.
    - Deliver the above constructed module as a database Web Service in the form of SaaS so that it is both SaaS enabled and SaaS enabling. *SaaS enabling is the functionality required here that supports on-the-fly integration of the same based on the drill-across scenario in context.*
    - The SOA component analytics appliance can also be transparently cached in-memory and/or replicated as needed to enable the cross application drill-across reporting.
- *Rich data visualization*—This is provided in terms of enhanced controls for user-interactivity and visual analysis.

A real-world use case of this is the ability to provide control to the user to build personalized customized or subreports in an interactive manner, as well as viewing in-database stored content, such as .pdf documents, as Flash-transformed images. Oracle ADF Faces Ajax components and the seamless interoperability of Oracle, Java, and .NET technologies enable this to be practically implementable by means of a code accelerator that employs process-driven SOA and REST Web Services to create a dynamic .pdf view-let that can be used and reused, and at the same time is highly scalable.

- *Information presentation in pixel-perfect, picture-perfect formatted reports*—These reports should adhere to business-friendly terminology.
- *Active (live) and interactive reporting*—These enable customization of data-based report columns to dynamically derive report fields and URL-enable them for click-and-go navigation, thus enabling the user to explore the information in detail using *context-specific templates* (implemented using JSP-based, ASP.NET-based, or scripting-language based code, and delivered as a JSP report template file, ASP.NET template file, or custom-scripted file), or a single custom-field derived from another report, multiple data-based columns. To extend a step further, these report-only derived columns can be used as Oracle table-based column stores and presented in multiple formats.
- *Implementation of navigation controls*—These are a necessity for multipage reports, such as progress bars for page-to-page scrolling, single-click scrolling, mouse-based scrolling, random scrolling to an input page number, and the like.
- *Ability to export the report output to be reusable by other business models/applications via import*—This can be done by exporting into a common XML format that is suitable to fit into any industry standards–based solution or a custom PDF format. *A real-world use case of this is to auto-email the report securely to a user-specified e-mail group list, followed by an custom alert notification of the same – this must include return receipt confirmation by the user involved. A best practice to implement this is to in-line the corresponding code component as part of the overall reporting workflow. It can be further extended as a customized service component the execution of which can be automated and reused as needed.*

- *Auto-triggered events*—Auto-complete, auto-navigate, key-stroke/single-character-based auto-filtering, drag-and-drop, point-and-click and one-click functionality.

- *Implementing keyboard-less and mouse-less navigation*—Make these independent of each other.

- *Implement end-to-end workflow reporting*—This reporting should be based on business activity, user session activity, IT process activity and interactivity across database, application, and UI automation and monitoring. This helps not only in troubleshooting and optimization from an IT solution perspective, but can help in re-engineering the underlying workflow into a high-level logical business IT process (visual) model for business benefit as well.

- *Self-service kiosk simulation*—Use touchscreen (one touch) and voice-activated interaction, on-the-fly download capability in multiple formats (that are industry-compliant and user-friendly), click-and-go report sectioning, bursting, and distribution (including e-mailing and messaging, publishing and sharing).

- *Report execution optimization*—This involves improving run-time performance of reports (including content-based reports) by refactoring at the report-level only—that is, without modifying other Tiers of the solution architecture, such as the underlying database structure/data model, the application architecture (including virtual views, cached in-memory federated data-sets, etc.) and without affecting report functionality. Oracle Reports 11g, as well as the Reports Interface in Oracle ADF and the custom-generated Dashboard Reports in Oracle APEX, Ajaxification, ODP Tools for .NET, and/or Oracle JDeveloper11g, along with custom PHP and Perl scripting, provide the flexibility needed to separate the UI-based reports components from the DB and the application Tiers. *This is a direct derivation from the best practice outlined in Chapter 3, which emphasized a design based on isolation of the DB-Tier from the application and UI layers of the Oracle embedded programming solution.* Oracle provides various mechanisms to tune the in-report SQL and custom-code logic by using dynamic cursor variables as opposed to opening multiple cursors; packaging queries based on data relevance as opposed to sectioning by query-complexity; using modularized functions to return deterministic results and encapsulate all of them isolated by business functionality into a package at the report level; using cursor expressions in report SQL statements, especially when combining independent result sets; and de-normalizing queries at the report level to gain speed by reducing joins.

- *Dynamic data-set manipulation in the report output*—That is, in the live output. This involves creating/modifying/removing "live" snapshots of the report output based on user interaction and input controls. This is a special case of the "live" data integration stated in the section "Best Practices beyond HTML," earlier in this chapter.

- *Report embedding*—Oracle11g enables the embedding of reports that are URL-addressable, on-the-fly, as well as providing URL-link output for drilldown or click-and-go functionality. Additionally, JSP-based reports can be used to generate reports based on external templates like Excel-based templates and the like.

- *In-database report generation*—Leverage the capabilities of in-database report generation using componentization and execution of SQL-enabled embedded-language code that is precompiled and stored in-database. The individual components can be written in any embedded language, but since the logic is encapsulated in a SQL-enabled Oracle DB function, the solution in context can use the necessary components for reporting specific to the embedded language involved, and dynamically manage their selection and integration using an automation service that orchestrates the same in a context-aware call-binding. The automation service itself can be coded using dynamically generated rules, cached persistently in the application Tier or disk-I/O free storage, whose data model is a "virtual" metadata definition of the report meta-definitions.

- *Row-level and column-level security policies*—Implement these at the Oracle database level, thereby avoiding additional custom logic to allow display of the right data to the right user.

- *Generation of context-specific computation functions*— Use a code accelerator to generate these functions on-the-fly. They can be used to perform real-time or "as-is" analysis based on the report output—that is, the result set from multi-valued, query-based, or SQL-based databases. This process basically involves code generating code and obfuscating it into a binary format; it can be implemented using C#, Java, C/C++, PHP, or Perl code that dynamically creates macro-like functions that can be in-lined and executed. A unified reporting metadata schema can be designed to derive a common, consistent, coherent view of the disparate data and standardize it into a report-based template repository that can be imported as needed.

- *Use a code accelerator for dynamic XML formatting at run-time.*
  - Auto-format mixed (mash-up) content on the fly.
  - Auto-reformat "pasted" content on the fly and auto-format on the completion of end tag.

  This can be implemented by using the interoperability features of Oracle and Java, .NET, C/C++, PHP, and the like. Three examples of doing this are:

  1. By using a Java stored or .NET stored procedure that compiles and stores the custom Java or .NET code in the Oracle11g database. This stored procedure can be converted into a Database-based Web Service that can be invoked by any consumer of the same. Or the Oracle stored procedure can be invoked by the standard API specific to Java, .NET, C/C++, PHP, and the like.

  2. By using a common invocation model that enables calls to code-based objects to/from Java and .NET. This is suitable for prebuilt code modules that enhance the dynamic XML formatting.

  3. By using the Oracle ADF to create a unified code module that can be exposed via reusable Web Services to the client environment.

- Use a code accelerator to accommodate time-variant constraints into report input and execution, thereby providing a highly flexible user-controlled reporting environment. This gives the user the ability to run reports using all relevant permutations and combinations of business context–specific variables, such as value-by-relevance, timestamp, sliding windows, and so on, including report output distribution and bursting parameters.

- For reports based on ranking, such as top *n* results, driven by business attributes, especially those that change at run-time, ensure consistency of the top *n* rank order across hierarchies in the report data, i.e., for both drill-across, drilldown, and drill-up. Note that preserving the rank in case of drill-across is also important, as these reports can involve overlapping data that spans multiple business contexts, but driven by the same business attributes.

- Avoid dynamic SQL in report queries. Use lexical-based queries for direct SQL and SQL embedded in Java, .NET, C/C++, or PHP languages. Oracle11g provides the flexibility of using this by means of API for each of these languages.

Summary

This chapter described the best practices for application management in terms of end-to-end functionality from the application solution design and the corresponding code design pragmatics standpoints. Starting with design strategies for code accelerators for a rapid embedded programming language implementation, it detailed the best practices related to application integrity, consistency, application Web interaction, end-to-end application security and identity management, and Web application access beyond HTML in terms of dynamic visualization, Web Services, and Mobility-as-a-Service. It also explored the best fit for Oracle in the ASP.NET framework and the recommended practices and use cases for integrating ASP.NET applications with Oracle. Finally, it touched upon the best practices for Web-based reporting and the limitless capabilities of the same. Throughout the chapter, emphasis is laid on aspects such as how the solution can be accelerated using advanced Oracle-based functionality, and methodologies as well as presentation of real-world use-cases of some of the recommended best practices were discussed. The next chapter deals with evolving the best practices for data structure, data, and application management into application development frameworks that demonstrate the tried-tested-true quality-of-excellence of these best practices for best-fit real-world implementations.

Chapter 8

Application Development Frameworks

In This Chapter

- Application development framework: A pragmatic "best-possible" solution
    - For a transactional solution
    - For a reporting and analysis solution
- Master error management framework
- Performance tuning framework
- Debugging framework

8.1 Introduction

Application development frameworks provide for a standard template for implementing a particular task. Examples of PL/SQL tasks that call for such templates include error logging and performing ETL (extract, transform, load) operations using PL/SQL. The framework provides both the design and code development features that can be used to implement the task in the best possible manner suitable for the application requirements (such as business or functional requirements that the application is targeted to) and criteria (such as functional and technical feature/product–specific factors that need to be taken into consideration while implementing the business rules as per the application requirements) in question. The sections that follow discuss frameworks for four different tasks that are frequently implemented in most PL/SQL applications—error logging, DML auditing, ETL, and performance tuning.

8.2   Application Development Framework: A Pragmatic "Best-Possible" Solution

Rapid application development, as the name implies, is all about achieving the better business benefit by way of a least time-to-deliver application solution that addresses the needs of a rich Web presence, usability, and intelligence coupled with the flexibility to enhance/extend/adapt to on-demand changes in business, and optimize on the business results to evolve/innovate into a better customer-centric business solution. The corresponding imperatives on the development and deployment of technologies and methodologies to arrive at such a solution are multifold, irrespective of its business-centric use—transactional, analytical, or a combination of both:

- A customer-focused solution that is business process–driven and services-oriented, to ensure seamless and transparent collaboration between business operations and IT operations across the enterprise
- A standards-based solution that enables a flexible architecture capable of self-optimization, self-manageability, and self-serviceable user interactivity, thereby providing consistent business operations and information management across the enterprise
- A unified view of the user experience and business results, based on a centralized and correlated analysis of business and technology specific attributes that contributed to the same

The key indicator for implementing such a framework is the rapid prototyping of the so-designed application solution architecture as a demonstrated business use case, and its provisioning as a click-and-go application development infrastructure service by way of Web Services and automation for fast, secure, efficient, and cost-effective application development and deployment. Using Oracle ADF for the design methodology, along with Oracle APEX, Oracle JDeveloper, or Oracle Developer Tools for .NET for the corresponding integrated development and runtime platforms, a personalized customer-centric application development framework (ADF) for an Oracle-based embedded programming solution can be put into practice. For the purposes of this book, this custom framework is abbreviated as OEP-ADF.

OEP-ADF extends beyond the traditional virtualization and implementation technology trends to encompass:

• A software-oriented design consisting of application infrastructure and application deployment that are loosely coupled and automated.
• New policies/rules/KPIs (key performance indicators) that can be crafted from the performance, diagnostics, and advanced analytics–based analysis of the solution and embedded into the solution design as custom optimizer services, custom business processes, and customer-centric KPIs and streamlined via workflow-based integration. Oracle Business Rules can be used to derive and optimize the business rules, and Oracle Advanced Analytics can be used for the KPIs.

The OEP-ADF can be used as a model-based design that, when implemented, automatically generates a customer-centric OEP solution, including auto-generation of the embedded code based on a specific set of input and business-domain variables.

The frameworks described focus on the following key indicators, applicable to both transactional as well as reporting and analysis solutions:
- The need for a customer-centric solution
- Changing trends in customer-centric dynamics

Why a "Customer-Centric" Solution?

To reprise the famous quote, "no two snowflakes are the same." This quote has its analogs in the context of customer-centric solutions:
- No two customers are the same
- No two end-users are the same
- No two business solutions are the same

Changing Trends in Customer-Centric Dynamics

- Context specificity drives content specificity
- Customer is different from (end) user
- Customer experience is different from (end) user experience
- Consistency of the information exposed to the customer/end user takes precedence over consistence of functionality; this is a key indicator of choice for the specific *solution infrastructure*—database (DB), online transaction processing (OLTP), data warehousing

(DW), Business Intellgence (BI) tools, rich user interface, and the like—and *solution architecture* (the customer-centric design of the IT solution)

- The business value of a solution is better decided based on ROC (return on customer) vis-a-vis CLV (Customer Lifecycle Value) than on ROI (return on investment) and/or TCO (total cost of ownership). Ultimately results are the only returns that matter most, and from a business standpoint, a better-business-benefit (B-B-B) from the IT solution is the only required and recognized value – the B-B-B is the bottom line of the end-to-end implementation of the solution. This means the business impact of the solution (not the IT impact) measures the ROI. This approach goes beyond custom implementation; it depends upon the leveraging of customer experience and the user experience to enable the solution to evolve beyond intelligence.

8.2.1 For a Transactional Solution

The framework described focuses on the following key indicators specific to a transactional solution:

- Key business indicators of transactional solution architecture
- Key IT indicators of transactional solution architecture
- Key implementation indicators
- Key prize-for-the-price indicators

Key Business Indicators of Transactional Solution Architecture

- A high level of user-input data/content and user interactivity— available anywhere, at anytime, by anyone (A-A-A)—that is dynamic and transactional in nature, such as rich Internet applications (RIAs)based on Web 2.0 and Flash-based technologies RIAs are also termed as Rich Information Applications, depending the domain-specific context in which they are deployed and used.
- Business continuity through enterprise-wide reliability, availability, security (RAS)
- Coherency and consistency of information and business results across the distributed enterprise
- Efficiency, scalability, and share-ability of the transactional content across the enterprise

Key IT Indicators of Transactional Solution Architecture

- Management of dynamically growing data, especially when the rate of such growth cannot be predetermined due to high transactional and query throughput
- Horizontal (scale-in) and vertical (scale-out) scaling of the underlying database infrastructure to accommodate data growth on-demand; this can be addressed by using a combination of database clustering and database grid computing using data virtualization
- Coherency and consistency of information and business results across the distributed enterprise
- Continuous and on-demand database connectivity as the user base increases
- Efficiency, scalability, and unified view of the transactional content across the enterprise
- Intelligent database contention resolution and cache coherency management

Key Implementation Indicators

- Standardization
- *Optimistic locking*—Oracle11g enables multiversion concurrency control of transactions by eliminating transactional data contention and thereby minimizing locking; this prevents read operations from interfering with DML (Data Manipulation Language) write operations and increases the performance of transactional Web applications.
- *Synchronization (and streamlining)*—Implement distributed caching and coherency control in the database Tier for data-intensive applications. Note that the cache invalidation and synchronization (maintaining a coherent state of frequently changing data) are done in the database Tier (using, for example, Oracle in-memory database, or IMDB, cache), with the data itself cached on the application Tier and/or separate distributed cache (data) servers.
- *Database/data virtualization, partitioning, and clustering*—Oracle Real Application Clustering (RAC) allows the primary application database to be partitioned into multiple physical servers. This horizontal scale-out of database instances (each containing a subset of the overall dataset) enables the transactional bandwidth to be shared across multiple physical servers, thus reducing insert/ update/delete processing latency in high-volume transaction

workloads. Partitioning is the horizontal slicing of data by a group of columns that are most needed by the business application for querying. Data virtualization involves creating dynamic federated views of spanned partitions based on runtime criteria and returning a consolidated view of the same. Oracle11g enables this by way of cross-database joins and creates federated views of the same in the IMDB cache. The Oracle Database Grid technology combined with Oracle RAC allows for dynamic provisioning of the physical and database/data servers/instances required for the same.

- *Automation*—The self-tuning capabilities of Oracle database allow for dynamic setting and execution of database parameters, depending on the user and transaction workloads, especially in mixed payload environments—such as auto-selection from multiple execution plans, auto-enable optimizer hints for I/O intensive queries, and implicit data compression to enable ultrafast random I/O—as well as auto-tuning the underlying database structures based on dynamic profiling of application-solution workloads.

- *Connection pooling and caching at the database Tier*—Multiple user connections can be set to be auto-cached and managed dynamically in the database as opposed to the application/data access layer. This optimizes SQL queries across database instances and clusters.

- *Dynamic load testing at the database and application levels*— Oracle Real Application Testing, along with the Oracle Application Testing Suite, enables as-is stress testing of a live production environment, in case of performance degradation due to data and/or workload growth. This in turn minimizes downtime by enabling troubleshooting for the same without having to take the solution offline.

Key Prize-for-the-Price Indicators

- A customer-centric transactional solution based on commonality, comprehensiveness, concurrency, and coherency, defined by industry-recognized standards
- Efficiency in terms of high throughput and optimized data access
- Transactional continuity in terms of:
    - Business continuity (reliability, availability, security)
    - Continuous event processing
    - User-driven interactivity

- Self-adaptability by enabling the database to auto-tune, and thereby evolve and innovate for better operational efficiency
- Scaling the Oracle DB and Web infrastructure for Web 2.0 technologies:
  - Delivers scalability and performance for Web and enterprise computing for Web 2.0 using Oracle11g database
  - Deploys a highly reliable solution combining scalable servers, next-generation storage, and networking technologies with Oracle11g DB, Oracle11g Fusion Middleware, Oracle RAC, Oracle IMDB Cache, Oracle Database and Application Grids, Oracle Coherence, Oracle WebLogic Suite, Oracle Service-Oriented Architecture (SOA) Suite, and Oracle WebCenter Suite
  - Processes transactions and queries at least two to three times faster with the pretested architecture, best practices, and performance results from Oracle Coherence running on Sun servers, and the Oracle-Sun Database Machine (Exadata V2) and Oracle-HP Database Machine (Exadata V1).

8.2.2   For a Reporting and Analysis Solution

A reporting and analysis solution enables analysis and presentation of unified business domain–specific information that can serve as input for advanced analysis (by business analysts, data stewards, corporate officers, etc.) and reporting. Simply put, this is a data warehousing (DW) and business intelligence (BI) solution that uses the Oracle DB as a data warehouse for data-in-store (both historical and continuously changing) and/or a BI tool for accelerated analytics and decision support. This subsection outlines the best-practice pragmatics for an A-A-A architecture for a customer-centric Oracle-based reporting and analysis solution.

The framework described focuses on the following key indicators specific to a reporting and analysis solution:

Key business indicators of DW-BI solution architecture

- Key IT indicators of DW-BI solution architecture
- User perception of data, data access and data integration
- Architectural design best-fit practice for Oracle11g-based DW-BI solution for A-A-A
- Key implementation indicators
- Key prize-for-the-price indicators

- Key Business Indicators of DW-BI Solution Architecture
- *A-A-A accessibility*—Providing the right answer to any user, any query, any time; in this case, the right answer is the one that can lead to actionable decisions
- *Business continuity*—Enterprise-wide reliability, availability, security (RAS)
- "Behind the wheel" control for business users of the BI solution:
  - Understand the customer's/user's position—Choice and design of the solution should be "organic" in that their key criteria must be based on the users' perception of data—how the users and analysts peruse, reason, and use the data by turning it into information based on fact-based analysis.
  - One size doesn't fit all anymore—Today, there is more than one ALL. Solution usability extends beyond current industry demands and requires *intelligent solution adaptability* that is as "current," comprehensive, and consistent as possible, even long down the road. Irrespective of changes in the business goals, industry trends, technology, and customer base, the solution must be able not only to cope with change, but also to leverage it to optimal advantage.
- *Self-service BI*—The solution must offer self-service interactivity and responsiveness, with minimal IT intervention. This implies that the solution must provide unprecedented flexibility in terms of unbounded and instantaneous "analyze-and-derive" action-response capability. Prebuilt key performance indicators (KPIs) do not always facilitate this, as not all KPI-based reasoning promotes new areas of discovery—e.g., for improvement, trends, and the like.
- Share-ability of information and business results across the distributed enterprise.
- *Information assurance, in addition to information security*—This must be provided for both data and users, anywhere, at anytime, by anyone, in terms of risk assessment and mitigation and quality assurance.

Key IT Indicators of DW-BI Solution Architecture

- *A-A-A accessibility*—This requires both real-time and right-time accessibility (instantaneous and continuous, yet intermittent and persistent).

There must be a unified data centralization framework—a unified data integration framework at the source data level as well as at the data/content delivery stage—providing unified information presentation from the standpoint of A-A-A accessibility without compromising on efficiency and productivity. This framework should have the ability for SOA enablement as well as having SOA-enabling capability by way of Data Services that is embeddable in any existing SOA-based services and/or on-premise platforms.

The foundation for such a solution calls for a seamless workflow that is event-based and is in line with the infrastructure management, capable of real-time and on-demand data services, application services, and portability. This implies the following:

- *How the data flow is coordinated and synchronized depends on how the code is written*—There is a ripple effect; the security of data also depends on security of code. and this in turn propagates to the security of sensitive and customer-specific data throughout the end-to-end solution, both internally and externally: protection against unauthorized user access (and insider threats) for both static data and data in-transit, protection against data breaches, data loss prevention, and robust database, user, and network activity monitoring and audit-logging of the same (bidirectionally). Oracle11g's pre-integrated Advanced Encryption and Masking, Secure Backup, and Advanced Security; Oracle Database Vault and Label Security; and Oracle Configuration Management for Security, Audit Vault, and Total Recall provide a "defense-in-depth" methodology to achieve bulletproof security of data, end-to-end.

- *Optimal performance indicators are based on the specifics of the data: who, where, why, when, how*—The performance indicators are in terms of ability to handle high-volume data flows: instant response to query requests based on temporal effects in data; flattening unstructured content and merging it with external content; real-time availability; high-throughput in the case of transactional data updates; and the like. These indicators in turn ensure that information is available at the right time at the right place for the right user. Oracle11g database's high-performance and high-availability features of group policy invocation, column-based fine-grained access control, fine-grained dependency control, transactional data consistency cross-databases, and implicit design and self-tuning capabilities can accelerate and automate data management and optimization. The best practice is to design the data flow in sync with the business process flow so that they not only align in terms of IT processes but also provide business agility, eliminating the need for IT intervention in the long run—and leaving some scope for extensibility and innovation. These features add up to an ideal data infrastructure flow up to the end-user presentation layer for data availability and access.

Oracle11g provides some of the greatest and largest technologies, such as like enterprise data integration, dynamic data provisioning, and dynamic Data Services based on SOA Web Services that provide both agility and mobility of information within the enterprise and beyond, as well as in-memory data replication and processing for ultra-high performance.

- *Interactive search capabilities on all kinds of data/content*—Using declarative, direct SQL-based full-text or regular expression–based searches yields meaningful results with the least response time. This functionality can be implemented using personalized search enablers exposed via Web Services, as a callable application programming interface (API), or a combination of both

The key indicators are the business drivers significant to the solution:

- *Separate the DW and BI layers to help minimize/eliminate silos in the solution architecture, such as middle-Tiers and metadata layers*—Let the DB do as much of this work as possible. Use IMDB cache to eliminate a middle-Tier for distributed data federation (on-premise and on-demand). Use in-memory data replication (of both operational data and historical data); this distributed grid can be stitched in-memory to the application/solution layer. In Oracle11g, flatten online analytical processing (OLAP) cube-based data into ROLAP cubes (Relational OLAP) cubes which follow a Star-schema design model), still preserving the "intelligent refresh" of the same. This allows the real-time and batch data changes to trickle down to the ROLAP cubes on the fly.

- *Combine accessibility (right data at the right time to the right user) and availability (RAS) via a unified connectivity and integration framework*—The framework should comprise comprehensive management and control over connectivity; all solution touchpoints (including end-user devices); ansecurity within and beyond the enterprise (Web-based SOA-appliance secure gateways, local policy enforcement, and access control). Here's a list of key design indicators for the same:

    - In perspective of the separation of DW and BI layers, data access (DA) and data integration (DI) are two symmetrically different processes. DI promotes DA.

    - The key to efficient data access is using the right data access connectors/adapters. This gives a huge benefit, as the challenges posed by complex data for both DA and DI are eased; unstructured data requires data quality too.

    - Incorporate operational BI to enable direct access of (source-system) data to the BI solution, bypassing the data warehouse (DW).

    - Operational DI is not necessarily real-time, but allows the right data to be available any time , keeping the DW "current" for A-A-A.

  RAS end-to-end

    - Introduce virtual data federation by creating context-aware federated data views based on a virtual metadata dictionary created via an "abstraction layer" (i.e., a single view) and then federated downstream into Oracle11g.

    - Create on-the-fly joins based on different data subsets to populate this federated data view.

    - Introduce Shared Services using SOA-based deployments (driving business agility and continuity using SOA connectivity and integration); these have the ability to share agnostically across multiple domains.

    - Augment role-based access control and fine-grained access control with context-based identity and access management. The roles allocation and separation are based on content-aware/solution-aware policies that are federated based on context-specific attributes/domains. This gives a more tightly coupled security design in that:

- Role-based access control is more static in nature whereas context-based access control is more dynamic in nature
- This design is implemented using SOA-based security. Oracle ESB as well as Oracle Identity Management solutions now support XACML (eXtended Access Control Markup Language) for handling XML-threats (e.g., XSS, XSRF, etc.) and are also Security Information and Event Management (SIEM) and Security Assertion Markup Language (SAML) compliant. The combination of XACML, SIEM, and SAML ensures stronger Web Services Security, including Web perimeter security.
- This solution enables delegated authentication coupled with local authorization. This is especially important for end-point security (e.g., end-device security for mobile and external Web Services–based deployments).

User Perception of Data, Data Access, and Data Integration

- Interactivity is self service–enabled via controls.
- The language and semantics are business-savvy.
- The presentation is user-friendly, with high-definition data visualization and easy navigation.
- The results are integrated into a single view that is context-specific and time-sensitive.
- Actionable, in that it turns data into informative decisions that can be put into action and beyond. The actionable customer/user BI insight is leveraged to evolve/create new BI analytics (that promote the BI efficiency), reaching beyond the IT solution lifecycle to encompass the customer lifecycle.
- Data access (DA) and data integration (DI) are two different tasks:
  - DI lays the foundation for data access; both contribute to the acceleration of BI informatics.
  - DI promotes interoperability of data between disparate databases, applications, hosted data services, and the like.
  - DA is all about data availability in a unified manner that is consistent, comprehensive, coherent across all business domains, and context-specific to boot.
  - Data Services and Data Integration Services are two separate tasks:

- DI Services are about processes that trigger a DI task based on events.
- DI Services are used to streamline a (new) DI process into a DI workflow.
- Data Services are primarily related to data access (either data in-place or data that has been transformed, derived, aggregated, or merged from new and/or existing data).

Both Data Services and Data Integration Services can be exposed as Web Services based on SOA. Both can serve as providers and consumers of Web Services using SOAP, WSDL, XML, and the like.

Figure 8.1 depicts the high-level view of data integration and the users' perception of data and information. Figure 8.2 depicts the architectural design for a best-practice DW and BI solution implementation.

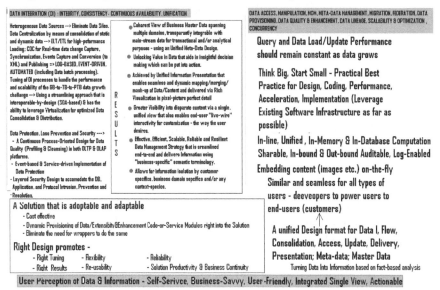

Figure 8.1   High-level view of data integration and user perception of data.

Key Implementation Indicators

- Standardization
- Synchronization (and Streamlining)

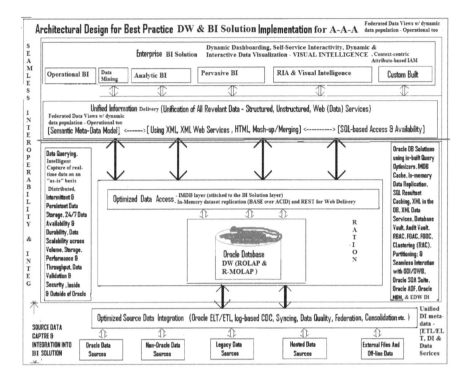

Figure 8.2   Architectural design for a best-practice DW and BI solution implementation.

- Virtualization (enabling real-time streaming of the BI solution across all solution touchpoints, from on-premise users, to beyond-the-enterprise access via remote access application delivery, to end-point devices)
- Automation
- Elimination of solution silos, such as metadata layers, middle-Tiers. and the like

Keep an eye on predefined KPIs in out-of-the-box solutions. They don't permit discovery of new analytical metrics.

Key Prize-for-the-Price Indicators

- A customer-centric reporting solution based on commonality, comprehensiveness, and coherency, and defined by industry-recognized standards
- Efficiency, in terms of high performance and non-breakability
- Continuous BI, in terms of:

- Business continuity (reliability, availability, security or RAS)
- Continuous event processing
- Self service driven
- (Sort of self-) adaptable, because the solution is able to evolve and innovate; the harvested customer experience is leveraged to dynamically create new business analytics that enable businesses to make farsighted, actionable decisions
- Powerful predictive analytics; Predictive analytics models are built via enhanced data mining models that leverage the self-adaptability of the solution and facilitate customer-centricity, such as customer target models with more sophisticated decision-making capabilities
- Hybrid solution model: DW and BI layer separation enables the leveraging of a hybrid solution model; such as using an open source BI solution for reporting and analysis that is seamlessly integrated with the Oracle11g DW solution

8.3   Master Error Management Framework

8.3.1   Error-Logging Framework

The error-logging framework refers to logging of SQL and/or PL/SQL errors occurring during program execution, as well as customary application-specific error messages. Here, *logging* refers to capturing the following information about each error:

- An identifier pertaining to the code block where the error occurred
- The actual error code and error message
- The line number where the error occurred, including the error execution stack (the sequence of program steps that led to the error)

Error logging in this manner is not only useful for tracking runtime errors, but also helps tremendously in later debugging, as well as code correction. Error logging should be a must for all applications running interactively, such as OLTP applications. In batch mode, error logging can be enabled for programs that do incremental batch updates and disabled for those performing one-time massive loads. While you are logging errors, be sure to consider the following factors:

- The type of error being logged; is it a critical error, a warning, or an informational message?
- Oracle SQL or PL/SQL errors or application-specific errors (i.e., errors raised due to exceptions in embedded language programming code)
- Execution of same program multiple times, for example, in multiple sessions or by multiple programs in a single session

Taking these factors into consideration, you can control error logging by using a control table; it can be implemented using the two database tables. The control table can have a column to enable/disable error logging, and the implementation tables can be designed as an error information logging table and lookup table. The error information logging table can have additional columns to accommodate the information about the application and program being captured. A PL/SQL package provides the API for the implementation logic.

Here's the framework for such an implementation:

1. Error logging information is recorded in two database tables.

2. PL/SQL package API is used to program the logging process.

3. Error logging can be enabled/disabled using an audit control table. This is done at the application and/or current program levels. This table will always have a row for each application with current_program_name set to a single space.

4. Additional rows with valid current program names define the granularity of enabling/disabling; these rows take precedence over the single row with a blank current program name.

5. Each program is error-logged if error logging is turned on.

6. Application contexts can be used instead of a control table if the number of applications or modules needing error logging is not large. This makes control more secure and tightly integrated. An application context is session-concerning information stored in secure data cache in UGA (User Global Area also termed Program Global Area) (or SGA which is the System Global Area); it can be used to incorporate access-control mechanisms. A context is specified as a set of *attribute, value* pairs that can be defined, set, and accessed using an associated package. They are used to ensure that every data transaction is logged correctly, to turn

DML auditing/error logging off or on, and to implement fine-grained security by using application attributes to control what data users can access.

7. Each application can have its own context with its own attributes. In each case, setting the application context attributes on a case-by-case need basis can enable some level of fine-grained security in your application. For example, a library application can have a library context defined with an attribute called privileged_user whose value can be set to Yes for a specific group of users accessing the application. This value is set transparently once such a user logs in. This is secure because it is session-specific, is owned by SYS, and can only be set by the PL/SQL package associated with the context. This method is more secure and more tightly controlled than using packages. Also, multiple contexts, each specific to an application, can be created.

Here's the design of the data structures:

- *Error-logging information table (ERROR_LOG table)*—This table holds key information like application name, calling program name, current program name, unique session code, block identifier name, message type, error code, error text and description, a key information column that captures the information about the transaction that caused the error, and miscellaneous comment columns
- *Lookup table (CUSTOM_ERROR_MESSAGES table)*—This table contains application specific messages. Its key information includes the message number, message text, and message type, such as informational, warning, or critical error.

Listing 8.1 shows the code for this process.

Listing 8.1   *Creating data structures for error-logging framework.*

```
DROP TABLE ERROR_LOG;
CREATE TABLE ERROR_LOG
(
EL_ID NUMBER NOT NULL
CONSTRAINT PK_ERROR_LOG PRIMARY KEY,
APPLICATION_NAME VARCHAR2(100) NOT NULL,
CURRENT_PROGRAM_NAME VARCHAR2(100) NOT NULL,
CALLING_PROGRAM_NAME VARCHAR2(100) NULL,
```

```
UNIQUE_SESSION_CODE VARCHAR2(100) NOT NULL,
BLOCK_NAME VARCHAR2(100) NULL,
DESCRIPTION VARCHAR2(2000) NULL,
MESSAGE_NO NUMBER,
MESSAGE_TYPE VARCHAR2(10) NOT NULL,
MESSAGE_DESC VARCHAR2(4000) NOT NULL,
KEY_INFO VARCHAR2(2000) NULL,
COMMENTS1 VARCHAR2(2000) NULL,
COMMENTS2 VARCHAR2(2000) NULL,
COMMENTS3 VARCHAR2(2000) NULL,
COMMENTS4 VARCHAR2(2000) NULL,
COMMENTS5 VARCHAR2(2000) NULL,
DATE_CREATED DATE NOT NULL,
USER_CREATED VARCHAR2(30) NOT NULL
)
/
ALTER TABLE error_log ADD CONSTRAINT FK_ERROR_LOG
FOREIGN KEY MESSAGE_NO REFERENCES
CUSTOM_ERROR_MESSAGES(MESSAGE_NO);
CREATE TABLE CUSTOM_ERROR_MESSAGES
(
MESSAGE_NO NUMBER NOT NULL,
MESSAGE_TEXT VARCHAR2(2000 CHAR) NOT NULL,
MESSAGE_TYPE VARCHAR2(10 CHAR) NOT NULL,
DATE_CREATED DATE NOT NULL,
USER_CREATED VARCHAR2(30) NOT NULL
)
/
DROP TABLE audit_control;
CREATE TABLE audit_control
(APPLICATION_NAME VARCHAR2(100) NOT NULL,
CURRENT_PROGRAM_NAME VARCHAR2(100) NOT NULL,
RETENTION_PERIOD NUMBER NOT NULL,
ERROR_LOGGING_ON VARCHAR2(1) DEFAULT 'Y' NOT NULL
CHECK (ERROR_LOGGING_ON IN ('Y','N'))
)
/
ALTER TABLE audit_control ADD CONSTRAINT
PK_AUDIT_CONTROL
```

```
PRIMARY KEY (APPLICATION_NAME,
CURRENT_PROGRAM_NAME);
DROP SEQUENCE seq_el_id;
CREATE SEQUENCE seq_el_id MINVALUE 1;
```

The design of the package application programming interface (API) for the error-logging framework consists of public constants for the completion status and three procedures, as described here for the pkg_log_error package:

- Public constants for the message type—M for informational message, E for error message, and W for warning message
- Procedures such as log_error_info—This logs any Oracle Server/ PL/SQL errors
- Function get_message_text—This retrieves the message text for a given message number and type

Listing 8.2 shows the code for this process.

Listing 8.2   *Package API of error logging framework.*

```
CREATE OR REPLACE PACKAGE pkg_log_error
AS
-- Public Message Types
C_ERROR CONSTANT CHAR := 'E';
C_WARNING CONSTANT CHAR := 'W';
C_INFORMATION CONSTANT CHAR := 'I';

PROCEDURE log_error_info(
p_application_name IN
error_log.application_name%TYPE,
p_curr_program_name IN
error_log.current_program_name%TYPE,
p_calling_program_name IN
error_log.calling_program_name%TYPE,
p_block_name IN error_log.block_name%TYPE,
p_description IN error_log.description%TYPE,
p_msg_no IN error_log.message_no%TYPE,
p_msg_type IN error_log.message_type%TYPE,
p_msg_desc IN error_log.message_desc%TYPE,
```

```
    p_key_info IN error_log.key_info%TYPE DEFAULT
    NULL,
    p_comments1 IN error_log.comments1%TYPE DEFAULT NULL,
    p_comments2 IN error_log.comments2%TYPE DEFAULT NULL,
    p_comments3 IN error_log.comments3%TYPE DEFAULT NULL,
    p_comments4 IN error_log.comments4%TYPE DEFAULT NULL,
    p_comments5 IN error_log.comments5%TYPE DEFAULT NULL
    );

    FUNCTION get_message_text (p_message_no IN NUMBER,
    p_message_type IN VARCHAR2) RETURN NUMBER;

    END;
    /

    CREATE OR REPLACE PACKAGE BODY pkg_log_error
    AS

    FUNCTION get_message_text (p_message_no NUMBER,
    p_message_type IN VARCHAR2)
    RETURN VARCHAR2
    IS
    v_message_text
    custom_error_messages.MESSAGE_TEXT%TYPE;
    BEGIN
    SELECT message_text
    INTO v_message_text
    FROM custom_error_messages
    WHERE message_no = p_message_no
    AND message_type = p_message_type;
    RETURN (v_message_text);
    EXCEPTION
    WHEN others THEN
    RETURN(NULL);
    END get_message_text;
    PROCEDURE log_error_info(
    p_application_name
    IN error_log.application_name%TYPE,
    p_curr_program_name
```

```
IN error_log.current_program_name%TYPE,
p_calling_program_name
IN error_log.calling_program_name%TYPE,
p_block_name
IN error_log.block_name%TYPE,
p_description
IN error_log.description%TYPE,
p_msg_no
IN error_log.message_no%TYPE,
p_msg_type
IN error_log.message_type%TYPE,
p_msg_desc
IN error_log.message_desc%TYPE,
p_key_info
IN error_log.key_info%TYPE DEFAULT NULL,
p_comments1
IN error_log.comments1%TYPE DEFAULT NULL,
p_comments2
IN error_log.comments2%TYPE DEFAULT NULL,
p_comments3
IN error_log.comments3%TYPE DEFAULT NULL,
p_comments4
IN error_log.comments4%TYPE DEFAULT NULL,
p_comments5
IN error_log.comments5%TYPE DEFAULT NULL
)
IS
PRAGMA AUTONOMOUS_TRANSACTION;
v_el_id error_log.el_id%TYPE;
v_error_logging_on
audit_control.error_logging_on%TYPE;
BEGIN
BEGIN
SELECT error_logging_on
INTO v_error_logging_on
WHERE application_name = p_app_name
AND current_program_name = p_curr_prog_name;
EXCEPTION
WHEN NO_DATA_FOUND THEN
```

```
BEGIN
SELECT error_logging_on
INTO v_error_logging_on
FROM audit_control
WHERE application_name = p_app_name;
EXCEPTION
WHEN NO_DATA_FOUND THEN
NULL;
-- RAISE_APPLICATION_ERROR(
-- -20002,'Error Logging not set up for
-- application ' ||p_app_name);
WHEN OTHERS THEN
NULL;
-- RAISE_APPLICATION_ERROR(
-- -20003,'ERR getting setup info for
-- application ' ||p_app_name||': '||SQLERRM);
END;
WHEN OTHERS THEN
NULL;
-- RAISE_APPLICATION_ERROR(
-- -20001, 'Error Logging not set up for '||
-- ||'(application, current program) ('||
-- p_app_name||', '
-- ||p_curr_prog_name||')'||SQLERRM);
END;
IF v_error_logging_on = 'Y' THEN
SELECT seq_el_id.nextval
INTO v_el_id
FROM DUAL;
INSERT INTO error_log(el_id, application_name,
current_program_name, calling_program_name,
unique_session_code,
block_name, description, message_no, message_type,
message_desc,
key_info, comments1, comments2, comments3, comments4,
comments5,
date_created, user_created)
VALUES (v_el_id, p_application_name,
p_curr_program_name,
```

```
p_calling_program_name, SYS_CONTEXT('USERENV ',
'OS_USER'),
p_block_name, p_description, p_msg_no, p_msg_type,
p_msg_desc,
p_key_info, p_comments1, p_comments2, p_comments3,
p_comments4,
p_comments5, SYSDATE, USER);
COMMIT;
END IF;
EXCEPTION
WHEN OTHERS THEN
NULL;
END log_error_info;

END pkg_log_error;
/
```

Note how the unique session ID is derived from the OS_USER attribute of the system context USERENV.

Calling Program

The calling program invokes a call to log_error_info to log the error information based on the control parameter error_logging_on. Listing 8.3 shows the code for a sample calling program using the error-logging framework.

Listing 8.3   *Skeleton code for calling program using the error-logging framework.*

```
CREATE OR REPLACE PROCEDURE proc_test_error_logging(
ip_input_source IN VARCHAR2
)
IS
v_status NUMBER := 0;
v_app_name VARCHAR2(100) := 'PLSQL';
v_curr_prog_name VARCHAR2(100) :=
'PROC_TEST_ERROR_LOGGING';
BEGIN
BEGIN
-- Insert1
INSERT INTO ......
EXCEPTION
```

```
WHEN OTHERS THEN
v_status := 1;
pkg_log_error.log_error_info(v_app_name,
v_curr_prog_name, NULL,
'Insert1', NULL, NULL, pkg_log_error.c_error,
SQLCODE, SQLERRM,
ip_input_source);
END;
BEGIN
-- Update1
UPDATE......
EXCEPTION
WHEN OTHERS THEN
v_status := 1;
pkg_log_error.log_error_info(v_app_name,
v_curr_prog_name, NULL,
'Update1', NULL, NULL, pkg_log_error.c_error,
SQLCODE, SQLERRM,
ip_input_source);
END;
BEGIN
-- Delete1
DELETE......
EXCEPTION
WHEN OTHERS THEN
v_status := 1;
pkg_log_error.log_error_info(v_app_name,
v_curr_prog_name, NULL,
'Delete1', NULL, NULL, pkg_log_error.c_error,
SQLCODE, SQLERRM,
ip_input_source);
END;
EXCEPTION
WHEN OTHERS THEN
ROLLBACK;
pkg_log_error.log_error_info(v_app_name,
v_curr_prog_name, NULL,
'Proc Test Error Logging', NULL, NULL,
pkg_log_error.c_error,
```

```
SQLCODE, SQLERRM, ip_input_source);
RAISE;
END proc_test_error_logging;
/
```

The pkg_log_error package can be further improved to include specif-ics for common predefined PL/SQL exceptions and non-predefined Oracle errors by defining public constants for them. Examples include NO_DATA_FOUND and TOO_MANY_ROWS exceptions. Also, cus-tomized exceptions can be defined for associating specific error codes with them so that they can be more meaningfully captured. Secondly, the calling program had a RAISE in the final WHEN OTHERS exception handler. This kind of behavior is application specific and can be treated accordingly. For example, an additional parameter can be defined for the log_error_info procedure that directs whether to raise the exception again.

8.3.2   DML Auditing Framework

The DML auditing framework refers to auditing of DML statements (INSERT, UPDATE, and DELETE statements) being executed within PL/SQL stored subprograms.

Here, *auditing* refers to capturing the following information about the execution or result of execution of each DML statement:

- An identifier about the statement itself
- The number of rows affected by the statement
- The success or failure of the statement; this again is a special case of error logging and is captured by using the error-logging framework

Auditing DML statements in this manner is useful in applications that run a multitude of transactions using programs having numerous INSERT, UPDATE, and DELETE statements. The criteria for DML auditing in such situations depends on the following factors:

- The number of DML statements being executed in a single pro-gram
- The same program being executed multiple times—for example, in multiple sessions or by multiple programs in a single session
- Whether to audit DML also depends on where the application is running. If the application is mission-critical and is running in

production in high-priority mode, the failure of every DML needs to be trapped. In this case, DML auditing needs to be enabled. On the other hand, if the application is running in batch mode involving massive bulk loads, each DML operation need not be tracked and DML auditing can be disabled

Taking these factors into consideration, you can control DML auditing by using a similar control table and implement it using the two similar database tables as in the error logging framework. The control table can have a column to enable/disable DML auditing, the master table can have the same structure as used in the error-logging framework, and the detail table can have additional columns to accommodate the DML statistics. The package API changes accordingly to accommodate the DML auditing framework.

Here's the framework for such an implementation:

- Audit and error logging information recorded in two database tables
- PL/SQL package API used to program the logging process
- Auditing, error logging, and DML auditing enabling/disabling done using the audit control table
  This is done at the application and/or current program levels. This table will always have a row for each application with current_program_name set to a single space. Additional rows with valid current program names define the granularity of enabling/disabling, and these rows take precedence over the single row with a blank current program name.
- Each program is audited if at least one DML statement is present and DML auditing is on, regardless of the number of rows affected by the DML
- Application contexts can be used instead of a control table if the number of applications or modules needing DML auditing is not large; this makes control more secure and tightly integrated

Here's the design of the data structures:
- *Audit master (AUDIT_MASTER table)*—The key information here includes the application name, calling program name, current program name, unique session code, start and end timestamps, completion status, information identified by a unique ID, and miscellaneous comment columns.

- *Audit detail (AUDIT_DETAIL table)*—The key information here includes block identifier name, description, number of records inserted, updated, and/or deleted, columns that are part of primary and foreign keys, and miscellaneous comment columns to record PK/FK/comment information of DML records. These records are identified by a load detail ID that points to an audit master record. Listing 8.4 shows the code for this process.

Listing 8.4   *Creating data structures for DML auditing framework.*

```
DROP TABLE AUDIT_MASTER;
CREATE TABLE AUDIT_MASTER
(
AM_ID NUMBER NOT NULL
CONSTRAINT PK_AUDIT_MASTER PRIMARY KEY,
APPLICATION_NAME VARCHAR2(100) NOT NULL,
CURRENT_PROGRAM_NAME VARCHAR2(100) NOT NULL,
CALLING_PROGRAM_NAME VARCHAR2(100) NULL,
START_TIMESTAMP TIMESTAMP NOT NULL,
END_TIMESTAMP TIMESTAMP NULL,
COMPLETION_STATUS VARCHAR2(100) NULL,
UNIQUE_SESSION_CODE VARCHAR2(100) NOT NULL,
COMMENTS1 VARCHAR2(2000) NULL,
COMMENTS2 VARCHAR2(2000) NULL,
COMMENTS3 VARCHAR2(2000) NULL,
COMMENTS4 VARCHAR2(2000) NULL,
COMMENTS5 VARCHAR2(2000) NULL,
DATE_CREATED DATE NOT NULL,
USER_CREATED VARCHAR2(30) NOT NULL
)
/
DROP TABLE AUDIT_DETAIL;
CREATE TABLE AUDIT_DETAIL
(
AD_ID NUMBER NOT NULL
CONSTRAINT PK_AUDIT_DETAIL PRIMARY KEY,
AM_ID NUMBER NOT NULL,
BLOCK_NAME VARCHAR2(100) NOT NULL,
DESCRIPTION VARCHAR2(2000) NULL,
```

```
    RECS_INSERTED NUMBER NULL,
    RECS_UPDATED NUMBER NULL,
    RECS_DELETED NUMBER NULL,
    RECS_ERRORED NUMBER NULL,
    PK_FK_INFO VARCHAR2(2000) NULL,
    COMMENTS1 VARCHAR2(2000) NULL,
    COMMENTS2 VARCHAR2(2000) NULL,
    COMMENTS3 VARCHAR2(2000) NULL,
    COMMENTS4 VARCHAR2(2000) NULL,
    COMMENTS5 VARCHAR2(2000) NULL,
    DATE_CREATED DATE NOT NULL,
    USER_CREATED VARCHAR2(30) NOT NULL
    )
    /
    ALTER TABLE audit_detail ADD CONSTRAINT
    FK1_AUDIT_DETAIL FOREIGN KEY AM_ID
    REFERENCES AUDIT_MASTER(AM_ID);
    DROP TABLE audit_control;
    CREATE TABLE audit_control
    (APPLICATION_NAME VARCHAR2(100) NOT NULL,
    CURRENT_PROGRAM_NAME VARCHAR2(100) NOT NULL,
    RETENTION_PERIOD NUMBER NOT NULL,
    DML_AUDIT_ON VARCHAR2(1) DEFAULT 'Y' NOT NULL
    CHECK (DML_AUDIT_ON IN ('Y','N'))
    )
    /
    ALTER TABLE audit_control ADD CONSTRAINT
    PK_AUDIT_CONTROL
    PRIMARY KEY (APPLICATION_NAME,
    CURRENT_PROGRAM_NAME);
    DROP SEQUENCE seq_am_id;
    CREATE SEQUENCE seq_am_id MINVALUE 1;
    DROP SEQUENCE seq_ad_id;
    CREATE SEQUENCE seq_ad_id MINVALUE 1;
```

The design of the package API for the DML auditing framework consists of public constants for the completion status and three procedures, as described here for the pkg_audit package:

- Public constants
  - Message types, such as M for informational message, E for error message, and W for warning message
  - Final status, such as SUCCESS, SUCCESS WITH EXCEPTIONS, or FAILED
  - Statement type, such as DML or ERR
- Procedures
  - Initialize—The very first statement after BEGIN for every calling program. It records the app name, the program name(s), and the kick-off time. Also returns DML audit control parameters (dml_audit_on and error_logging_on).
  - Log_audit_info—This logs the Oracle Server/PL/SQL error or DML statement identifier message, along with the audit statistics of the DML.
  - Finalize—The last statement before END, this updates the completion time and final status.

Listing 8.5 shows the code for this package API

Listing 8.5   *Package API of DML auditing framework.*

```
CREATE OR REPLACE PACKAGE pkg_audit
AS
-- Public Status Constants
c_success CONSTANT VARCHAR2(100) := 'SUCCESS';
c_success_with_exceptions CONSTANT VARCHAR2(100)
:= 'SUCCESS WITH EXCEPTIONS';
c_failed CONSTANT VARCHAR2(100) := 'FAILED';

PROCEDURE initialize(
p_dml_audit_on OUT
audit_control.dml_audit_on%TYPE,
p_am_id OUT
audit_master.am_id%TYPE,
p_app_name IN
audit_master.application_name%TYPE,
p_curr_prog_name IN
audit_master.current_program_name%TYPE,
p_calling_prog_name IN
audit_master.calling_program_name%TYPE
```

```
DEFAULT NULL
);

PROCEDURE log_audit_info(
p_dml_audit_on IN
audit_control.dml_audit_on%TYPE,
p_am_id IN
audit_master.am_id%TYPE,
p_block_name IN
audit_detail.block_name%TYPE,
p_description IN
audit_detail.description%TYPE,
p_recs_inserted IN
audit_detail.recs_inserted%TYPE DEFAULT 0,
p_recs_updated IN
audit_detail.recs_updated%TYPE DEFAULT 0,
p_recs_deleted IN
audit_detail.recs_deleted%TYPE DEFAULT 0,
p_recs_errored IN
audit_detail.recs_errored%TYPE DEFAULT NULL,
p_pk_fk_info IN
audit_detail.pk_fk_info%TYPE DEFAULT NULL,
p_comments1 IN
audit_detail.comments1%TYPE DEFAULT NULL,
p_comments2 IN
audit_detail.comments2%TYPE DEFAULT NULL,
p_comments3 IN
audit_detail.comments3%TYPE DEFAULT NULL,
p_comments4 IN
audit_detail.comments4%TYPE DEFAULT NULL,
p_comments5 IN
audit_detail.comments5%TYPE DEFAULT NULL
);
PROCEDURE finalize(
p_dml_audit_on IN
audit_control.dml_audit_on%TYPE,
p_am_id IN
audit_master.am_id%TYPE,
p_comp_status IN
```

```
audit_master.completion_status%TYPE
);

END pkg_audit;
/

CREATE OR REPLACE PACKAGE BODY pkg_audit
AS

PROCEDURE initialize(
p_dml_audit_on OUT
audit_control.dml_audit_on%TYPE,
p_am_id OUT
audit_master.am_id%TYPE,
p_app_name IN
audit_master.application_name%TYPE,
p_curr_prog_name IN
audit_master.current_program_name%TYPE,
p_calling_prog_name IN
audit_master.calling_program_name%TYPE
DEFAULT NULL
)
IS
PRAGMA AUTONOMOUS_TRANSACTION;
v_dml_audit_on audit_control.dml_audit_on%TYPE;
BEGIN
BEGIN
SELECT dml_audit_on
INTO v_dml_audit_on
WHERE application_name = p_app_name
AND current_program_name = p_curr_prog_name;
p_dml_audit_on := v_dml_audit_on;
EXCEPTION
WHEN NO_DATA_FOUND THEN
BEGIN
SELECT dml_audit_on
INTO v_dml_audit_on
FROM audit_control
WHERE application_name = p_app_name;
```

```
p_dml_audit_on := v_dml_audit_on;
EXCEPTION
WHEN NO_DATA_FOUND THEN
RAISE_APPLICATION_ERROR(
-20002,'Auditing parameters not set up for '
||'application '||p_app_name);
WHEN OTHERS THEN
RAISE_APPLICATION_ERROR(
-20003,'ERR getting auditing parameters for '
||'application '||p_app_name||': '||SQLERRM);
END;
WHEN OTHERS THEN
RAISE_APPLICATION_ERROR(
-20001,'Auditing parameters not set up for '
||(application, current program) ('||
p_app_name||', '||p_curr_prog_name||')'||SQLERRM);
END;
IF v_dml_audit_on = 'Y' THEN
SELECT seq_am_id.nextval
INTO p_am_id
FROM DUAL;
INSERT INTO audit_master(am_id, application_name,
current_program_name, calling_program_name,
unique_session_code,
start_timestamp, date_created, user_created)
VALUES (p_am_id, p_app_name, p_curr_prog_name,
p_calling_prog_name,SYS_CONTEXT('USERENV ',
'OS_USER'),
SYSTIMESTAMP, SYSDATE, USER);
COMMIT;
END IF;
EXCEPTION
WHEN OTHERS THEN
p_am_id := to_number(to_char(SYSDATE,
'yyyymmddhh24miss'));
END initialize;

PROCEDURE log_audit_info(
p_dml_audit_on
```

```
IN audit_control.dml_audit_on%TYPE,
p_am_id
IN audit_master.am_id%TYPE,
p_block_name
IN audit_detail.block_name%TYPE,
p_description
IN audit_detail.description%TYPE,
p_recs_inserted
IN audit_detail.recs_inserted%TYPE DEFAULT 0,
p_recs_updated
IN audit_detail.recs_updated%TYPE DEFAULT 0,
p_recs_deleted
IN audit_detail.recs_deleted%TYPE DEFAULT 0,
p_recs_errored
IN audit_detail.recs_errored%TYPE DEFAULT NULL,
p_pk_fk_info
IN audit_detail.pk_fk_info%TYPE DEFAULT NULL,
p_comments1
IN audit_detail.comments1%TYPE DEFAULT NULL,
p_comments2
IN audit_detail.comments2%TYPE DEFAULT NULL,
p_comments3
IN audit_detail.comments3%TYPE DEFAULT NULL,
p_comments4
IN audit_detail.comments4%TYPE DEFAULT NULL,
p_comments5
IN audit_detail.comments5%TYPE DEFAULT NULL
)
IS
PRAGMA AUTONOMOUS_TRANSACTION;
v_ad_id audit_detail.ad_id%TYPE;
BEGIN
IF p_dml_audit_on = 'Y' THEN
SELECT seq_ad_id.nextval
INTO v_ad_id
FROM DUAL;
INSERT INTO audit_detail(ad_id, am_id, block_name,
description, recs_inserted, recs_updated,
recs_deleted, recs_errored, pk_fk_info, comments1,
```

```
            comments2, comments3, comments4, comments5,
            date_created, user_created)
            VALUES (v_ad_id, p_am_id, p_block_name,
            p_description,
            p_recs_inserted, p_recs_updated, p_recs_deleted,
            p_recs_errored, p_pk_fk_info, p_comments1,
            p_comments2, p_comments3, p_comments4,
            p_comments5, SYSDATE, USER);
            COMMIT;
            END IF;
            EXCEPTION
            WHEN OTHERS THEN
            NULL;
            END log_audit_info;

            PROCEDURE finalize(
            p_dml_audit_on IN audit_control.dml_audit_on%TYPE,
            p_am_id IN audit_master.am_id%TYPE,
            p_comp_status IN audit_master.completion_status%TYPE
            )
            IS
            PRAGMA AUTONOMOUS_TRANSACTION;
            BEGIN
            IF p_dml_audit_on = 'Y' THEN
            UPDATE audit_master
            SET completion_status = p_comp_status,
            end_timestamp = SYSTIMESTAMP
            WHERE am_id = p_am_id;
            COMMIT;
            END IF;
            EXCEPTION
            WHEN OTHERS THEN
            NULL;
            END finalize;

            END pkg_audit;
            /
```

Note how the unique session ID is derived from the OS_USER attribute of the system context USERENV.

Calling Program

The calling program invokes calls to the packaged procedures pkg_audit.initialize(), pkg_audit.log_audit_info(), and pkg_audit.finalize() to store the audit information based on the control parameter dml_audit_on. The initialize procedure outputs the value of this control parameter, which is used by the other two procedure calls.

Listing 8.6 shows the sample calling program code using the DML auditing framework.

Listing 8.6   *Calling program that uses the DML auditing framework.*

```
CREATE OR REPLACE PROCEDURE proc_test_audit(
ip_input_source IN VARCHAR2
)
IS
v_am_id NUMBER;
v_status NUMBER := 0;
v_recs_count NUMBER := 0;
v_recs_inserted NUMBER := 0;
v_recs_updated NUMBER := 0;
v_recs_deleted NUMBER := 0;
v_recs_errored NUMBER;
v_desc VARCHAR2(4000);
v_success_status VARCHAR2(100);
v_dml_audit_on VARCHAR2(1);
v_app_name VARCHAR2(100) := 'PLSQL';
v_curr_prog_name VARCHAR2(100) := 'PROC_TEST_AUDIT';
BEGIN
-- call initialize
pkg_audit.initialize(v_dml_audit_on, v_am_id,
v_app_name,
v_curr_prog_name);
BEGIN
-- Insert1
INSERT......
v_recs_inserted := SQL%ROWCOUNT;
```

```
v_desc := v_recs_inserted || ' for insert1';
pkg_audit.log_audit_info(v_dml_audit_on, v_am_id,
'Insert1', v_desc, v_recs_inserted);
EXCEPTION
WHEN OTHERS THEN
v_status := 1;
END;

BEGIN
--Update1
UPDATE......
v_recs_inserted := 0;
v_recs_updated := SQL%ROWCOUNT;
v_desc := v_recs_updated||' for update1';
pkg_audit.log_audit_info(v_dml_audit_on, v_am_id,
'Update1', v_desc, v_recs_inserted, v_recs_updated);
EXCEPTION
WHEN OTHERS THEN
v_status := 1;
END;

BEGIN
-- Delete1
DELETE......
v_recs_inserted := 0;
v_recs_updated := 0;
v_recs_deleted := SQL%ROWCOUNT;
v_desc := v_recs_deleted || ' for delete1';
pkg_audit.log_audit_info(v_dml_audit_on, v_am_id,
' Delete1', v_desc, v_recs_inserted,
v_recs_updated, v_recs_deleted);
EXCEPTION
WHEN OTHERS THEN
v_status := 1;
END;

IF v_status = 0 THEN
v_success_status := pkg_audit.c_success;
ELSIF v_status = 1 THEN
```

```
v_success_status :=
pkg_audit.c_success_with_exceptions;
ELSE
v_success_status := NULL;
END IF;


pkg_audit.finalize(v_dml_audit_on, v_am_id,
v_success_status);

EXCEPTION WHEN OTHERS THEN
  ROLLBACK;
  RAISE;
END;
/
```

The error-logging framework can be combined with the DML auditing framework to provide a robust and sophisticated audit and error logging framework. For example, the pkg_log_error.log_error_info procedure can be called in each of the exception handlers for the proc_test_audit procedure. This provides for a complete auditing and error-logging solution.

8.4   Performance Tuning Framework

Performance tuning is part and parcel of any application, and PL/SQL is no exception. After all, the bottom line of an application running in production is that it needs to perform optimally. *Optimally* primarily refers to increased output response time for input (either from the user when the application is running interactively or otherwise), based on criteria such as load (number of users and operations), network traffic, and system resources.

From an application perspective, performing tuning involves the following aspects:

1.   Monitoring and tuning Oracle DB code (includes SQL, PL/SQL, or stored program units)

2.   Monitoring and tuning of application code (i.e., embedded language code)

Monitoring involves tracking the way the application is executing, including tracking the count of steps involved and the time taken and number of executions for each step.

Tuning involves tuning the SQL and the PL/SQL. SQL constitutes a significant portion of code for PL/SQL applications that are data intensive (and most of them are). Tuning of SQL queries (this comprises not only SELECTS but also UPDATES and DELETES) most often results in increased performance.

There are several factors you need to consider while tuning SQL:

- The size of the table
- The size of the result set
- How often the table is updated
- The number of concurrent queries against the table

Tuning PL/SQL applies to both data-intensive and computationally intensive applications and depends on several factors, including:

- Data structures used
- Data management methods used
- How the application routines (mostly consisting of packages, standalone subprograms, and trigger code) are coded
- How the application code is organized

These factors (for both SQL and PL/SQL) as a whole in turn depend on the type of application environment (such as online transaction processing (OLTP), OLAP, and so on) and the resource's availability.

This section provides a performance framework in terms of SQL and PL/SQL monitoring and tuning from an application development perspective.

8.4.1   Framework for Monitoring and Tuning SQL

First, let's discuss a framework for monitoring and tuning SQL. The most common performance bottleneck of a PL/SQL application is from the embedded SQL included in it. The first step is to monitor how the SQL is running so you can determine the cause of the poor performance. Once this is determined, the next step consists of determining how to improve the performance. Oracle, as of release 10g, has provided several tools that help in monitoring and tuning SQL. The following steps provide a framework for monitoring and tuning SQL.

Monitoring the SQL

You should monitor the SQL used through tracing, SQL Tuning Advisor (as of Oracle 10g), SQL Access Advisor (as of Oracle 10g), SQL Performance Analyzer (as of Oracle 11g), Automatic Workload Repository (AWR) (as of Oracle 10g), and Automatic Database Diagnostic Monitor (ADDM). Monitoring SQL consists of capturing and analyzing the SQL for the following criteria:

- Statistics about the parse, execute, and fetch phases, including the number of reads, gets, executions, parse calls, elapsed time, CPU time, memory usage, and I/O usage for each SQL statement in a single session
- Execution plan for each SQL statement in a single session
- Identification of long-running SQL at the session or instance level
- Identification of problematic SQL at the instance level; this includes statistics about the various sessions in an instance, such as number of reads (session logical reads and physical disk reads), executions, CPU load, long-running SQL, session and system events, locked objects, waits, I/O usage, database time, resource-intensive SQL (and PL/SQL), and any locked objects.

Statistics about the parse, execute, and fetch phases can be obtained easily by using tracing. Tracing can be done using SQL Trace, which can be enabled via one of the following methods:

- The database parameter SQL_TRACE
- The packaged procedures DBMS_SESSION.set_sql_trace or DBMS_MONITOR.session_trace_enable (as of Oracle 10g); the DBMS_MONITOR package enables tracing on multiple sessions

Once tracing is enabled and the SQL runs, the performance statistics are output to a trace file on the database server that can be formatted and read using utilities like the tkprof utility. The trcsess utility (as of Oracle 10g) can be used for merging trace information from multiple trace files into a single file.

In addition to the previous statistics, the trace file also contains information about session waits.

Execution plans for each SQL statement can be obtained using EXPLAIN PLAN (that can be used at the client level) or the packaged function dbms_xplan.display (as of Oracle 9iR2). The trace file generated by SQL Trace also contains an execution plan for the SQL statement if necessary.

Long-running SQL pertains to SQL that is taking an unusually long time; this information can be obtained using dynamic performance views v$session and v$session_longops. Also, long-running SQL can be monitored asynchronously (that is, in real-time), as it is being executed using two new views, V$SQL_MONITOR and V$SQL_PLAN_MONITOR (as of Oracle 11g). Both I/O and execution statistics are recorded. The Active Session History statistics can also be used to identify the cause for the delay by obtaining a phase-by-phase breakup of SQL execution based on row-level activity information for the SQL statement in question.

Problematic SQL pertains to identifying SQL problem areas at the instance level. Dynamic performance views, AWR (queried using views), and ADDM (using an AWR snapshot and generating reports from the analyzed output) can be used to identify such problem areas. Even AWR baselines can be employed, and automatic performance statistics can be obtained for this SQL.

Improving the SQL

You can now begin to improve the SQL using the output from monitored analysis. The key elements in determining the bad performance are the reads, gets, executions, parse calls, and shareable statements, as well as the CPU time, elapsed time, execution plans, and resource-intensive SQL. Based on these elements, you can make an approach to tuning the SQL in the following ways:

1. *Analyze the execution plan.* This helps in finding any SQL not using indexes where required. Implementing the required indexing speeds the query. The execution plan also helps in determining the access paths such as the join methods used that can be improved by using hints or otherwise.

    Caching the results of SQL statements (via hints available as of Oracle 11g) also helps in speeding up queries. SQL Execution Plan baselines can be used to capture and reuse existing plans and improve these plans based on analyzed criteria.

2. *Find out if any locks exist on the database objects being used.* Also find out if any system waits are blocking resources. This can be done using dynamic performance views and AWR. Resolving

object and resource contention helps in minimizing execution time.

3. *Analyze whether already parsed SQL statements can be shared and reused* by deciding on the use of bind variables, especially when using dynamic SQL. The use of bind variables reduces instance memory in the SGA.

4. *Analyze the database initialization parameters* to determine whether they are set optimally. For example, the parameter OPEN_CURSORS, when set to a high value, is useful for soft parsing avoidance and improves runtime performance of embedded SQL in PL/SQL.

5. Determine whether object statistics are available for use by SQL execution.

Slow-running SQL can be ferreted out by analyzing the underlying tables and/or indexes. This can be done using the DBMS_STATS.GATHER_SCHEMA_STATS procedure. The cost-based optimizer uses these statistics to determine the cost of the SQL statement.

The SQL tuning process can also be configured to run automatically in Oracle 11g by automatic scheduling of SQL Tuning Advisor tasks to run at specific time periods. The Automatic Tuning Optimizer, along with the SQL Tuning Sets, Profiles, and Tuning Information Views, can provide recommendations on how to tune the SQL involved to perform optimally. *Oracle11g auto-generates SQL baselines as the data gets created/changed, which are run-time context driven and can be used to correlate with existing baselines to better detect and analyze the cause-effect relationship(s), and proceed with the fine-tuning of the same. The new baselines along with the problem-solution analyses can be saved and even re-used as a fine-tuner baseline for similar run-time contexts.*

8.4.2   Framework for Monitoring and Tuning PL/SQL

This framework has a broader scope with regard to application performance tuning and involves a considerable effort on the part of both the developer and the administrator.

Although most of PL/SQL monitoring occurs at execution time, some aspects of bad performance can be identified at compile-time. This can be done using compile-time warnings. These are warning messages generated during compile-time that notify you about potential performance-related problems during runtime.

These are applicable to stored PL/SQL program units and are named PL/SQL blocks.

A standard framework for PL/SQL monitoring and tuning is outlined here:

1. *Use compile-time warnings to identify potential runtime performance issues.* This can be done by setting the PLSQL_WARNINGS parameter or by using the DBMS_WARNING built-in package. Stored programs can be compiled with warnings enabled in a development environment, modified as per the warning messages, and then compiled in production with warnings turned off. A good example is the warning generated when a WHEN OTHERS clause does not have a RAISE or RAISE_APPLICATION_ERROR (in Oracle 11g).

2. *Monitor PL/SQL code at runtime* for the four criteria—the order of code execution, the overall execution time, the number of executions and time taken for each execution, and the resource-intensive PL/SQL in terms of memory, I/O, and CPU usage.

   ■ The order of code execution can be obtained by using PL/SQL tracing. This can be implemented using the DBMS_TRACE package. PL/SQL tracing can be enabled or disabled using the PLSQL_DEBUG parameter.
   ■ The overall execution time, the number of executions, and the time taken for each execution can be obtained using the PL/SQL profiling. This can be implemented using the DBMS_PROFILER package. Dynamic execution profiles about dependent subprograms (both called and calling) of a particular PL/SQL program can be obtained using the DBMS_HPROF package (as of Oracle 11g).
   ■ The resource-intensive PL/SQL can be obtained using AWR and ADDM.

   This provides an overall impact of badly performing PL/SQL code in an application.

3. *Audit PL/SQL program units* to capture the start time, end time, status of completion (success, failure, or abnormal termination), unique ID identifying the program unit invoker (useful in case of the same program unit being called by multiple users or multiple

times), the number of database records processed, and the key data involved. This, combined with error logging, provides for a flexible tracing of application logic that helps in monitoring PL/SQL execution.

You can audit PL/SQL program units by writing a standard auditing package along with audit control mechanisms that enable/disable auditing at the application/program level. The audit control can be done using application contexts (more fine-grained) or regular database tables. A discussion of this type of auditing has been presented in the subsection "Master Audit Management Framework" earlier in this chapter.

4. *Tune the PL/SQL code commensurate with the findings of the monitoring.* This can be done using the following approach:

- Use optimal data structures involved, such as PL/SQL cache tables
- Use optimal application program structures involved, such as packages (and pin them if necessary)
- Use other PL/SQL performance-specific features, such as NOCOPY hint, caching function result sets (as of Oracle 11g), enhanced native compilation (useful for compute-intensive programs), efficient array processing (for performing batch-DML in PL/SQL), pipelined and/or parallelized table functions, fine-grained dependency tracking (as of Oracle 11g), invoker rights (useful for writing dynamic utilities, centralization of code, and decentralization of data), and definer rights (useful for sharing SQL, database-driven application security, decentralization of code, and centralization of data).
- Use optimal application logic, such as optimizing loops and function calls, using application contexts as an alternative for bind variables in dynamic SQL, and the like.
- Use default PL/SQL code optimization based on initialization parameters such as PLSQL_OPTIMIZE_LEVEL (when set to 2, the default in Oracle 10g, it provides aggressive optimization; when set to 3, as of Oracle 11g, it provides for automatic intraunit inlining of code).

- Tune Oracle memory specific to PL/SQL execution, such as the SGA in the shared pool.

A discussion of performance-tuning PL/SQL features is found in Chapter 10 of this book.

8.5   Debugging Framework

Debugging involves tracing the source and cause of any errors that occur during runtime. Debugging differs from error-handling, which consists of trapping these errors. This section describes a framework for debugging application code.

Debugging comes into picture after the code has run and aids in troubleshooting the application. Runtime errors can occur due to exceptions raised by the Oracle Server (due to failure of SQL and/or PL/SQL code) or can be logical errors that affect the functionality of the application. Exceptions raised by the Oracle Server are more visible in the sense that they are thrown to the calling environment in the form of error messages trapped by the code and customized or in unhandled form. Logical errors are less visible because they are inherent in or dependent on the data or results from the application. Only after careful analysis can logical errors reveal a functional glitch in the application and hence in the underlying code.

Debugging and error-handling go hand in hand and, in fact, complement each other. An efficient error-handling mechanism in place enables easy, smart, and quick debugging. However, not all errors can be debugged using error-handlers alone. There are certain scenarios where the execution of the SQL-PL/SQL code and/or embedded language code needs to traced line-by-line to determine the location of an error or its cause. This is true in the case of unhandled exceptions and logical errors. In certain situations, the actual error occurring in a production system needs to be simulated in a test environment to determine the real problem. This is turn depends on the input dataset, which might vary from production to test environments, and hence the so-called simulation might not always be possible. However, simulating the test data first, per production, can help solve this problem in most cases.

Whatever the scenario, implementation of a debugging framework helps enable efficient debugging. Retaining the implemented debugging framework (along with the code for debug message logging) while deploying the code in production environments is recommended, as it ensures a fairly easy and efficient way of troubleshooting a live problem that can otherwise cause unnecessary delays in fixing it. Although it seems to affect performance, this impact will be minimal if proper care is taken in implementing the framework on an on-demand basis based on criteria, such as by individual user, application module, program, or even table level; an access-analysis interface for the debug information being stored; and periodic purging of unnecessary debug data.

The design of any debugging framework consists of the following essential tasks:

- *Putting a robust error-handling mechanism in place* (before running the application). This will serve as the base for trapping any errors.
- *Introducing debug messages as part of the code asynchronously.* This can operate on a flip-flop basis, with debug messages being logged transparently on demand.
- Testing of the application solution:
  - Reactively, to identify the cause and solution of "live" errors
  - Completely, monitoring not only the code to get the execution profile, but also end-to-end activity, and analyzing the various problem-resolution scenarios encountered for proactive and preventive troubleshooting to fix the errors and improve performance
- Resolution of the logical/server errors and optimization for enhanced efficiency.

8.5.1   Putting a Robust Error-Handling Mechanism in Place

The first step of error handling has been discussed in detail in Chapter 5 on "Best Practices for Robust Error Detection and Handling." A combination of the techniques described in this chapter provides for a rich set of error-handling routines that encompass both error trapping and error logging.

8.5.2   Introducing Debug Messages as Part of Code Asynchronously

With error-handling implemented, the second step starts the debugging process by following a similar mechanism to log any debug messages (in contrast to error messages). A debug message is simply a string of text that tags the location and position of a line or portion of code in a subprogram. It is specified just before the code snippet to which it refers. The code snippet can have a second debug message tagged to it to indicate its end point.

Likewise, a particular subprogram can be host to a number of such debug messages. Any debug logging framework can be devised to generate and log debug messages inside areas of code that are identifiable as important and/or critical. Here's a brief outline of the steps involved:

1.   Create two tables called DEBUG_LOG and CUSTOM_DEBUG_MESSAGES (similar to the ERROR_LOG and CUSTOM_ERROR_MESSAGES tables as described in the Master Message Management Framework). The second table defines a master list of all possible debug messages to be pooled together; it is optional. If the second table is omitted, the first table can serve as the central repository of all debug messages in place.

2.   You can flip-flop the logging of the debug messages by using an audit control table. The audit control table used for error logging can be modified to add another column called DEBUG_ON, which turns debugging on and off in a session on an individual application/module/program basis. Each program is debug-logged only if debugging is turned on. Application contexts can be used instead of a control table if the number of applications/ modules needing debugging is not large so that control is more secure and tightly integrated. This table can also be used to control on-demand debugging based on external criteria, such as user authentication, in addition to that at the application/subprogram level. Situations that demand that debugging be turned off include batch programs (especially when processing huge number of rows) and initial loads to ETL processes.

3.   You can implement concurrency control while logging debug messages by capturing the unique OS user of the current session, rather than the application user login or the database user login, in conjunction with the calling/called program information. This allows you to log information about users executing a program with maximum accuracy, in case the same program is being called by multiple sessions or is called multiple times in the same session. All of the embedded programming languages involved provide the ability to implement this using *CLIENT IDENTIFIER* indicators that can be used in single-sign-on (SSO) as well as secure proxy authentications.

Listing 8.7 shows the code for the table structures mentioned.

Listing 8.7   *Code for creating data structures for debug logging framework.*

```
DROP TABLE DEBUG_LOG;

CREATE TABLE DEBUG_LOG
(
DL_ID NUMBER NOT NULL
CONSTRAINT PK_DEBUG_LOG PRIMARY KEY,
APPLICATION_NAME VARCHAR2(100) NOT NULL,
CURRENT_PROGRAM_NAME VARCHAR2(100) NOT NULL,
CALLING_PROGRAM_NAME VARCHAR2(100) NULL,
UNIQUE_SESSION_CODE VARCHAR2(100) NOT NULL,
BLOCK_NAME VARCHAR2(100) NULL,
DESCRIPTION VARCHAR2(2000) NULL,
MESSAGE_NO NUMBER,
MESSAGE_TYPE VARCHAR2(10) NOT NULL,
MESSAGE_DESC VARCHAR2(4000) NOT NULL,
KEY_INFO VARCHAR2(2000) NULL,
COMMENTS1 VARCHAR2(2000) NULL,
COMMENTS2 VARCHAR2(2000) NULL,
COMMENTS3 VARCHAR2(2000) NULL,
COMMENTS4 VARCHAR2(2000) NULL,
COMMENTS5 VARCHAR2(2000) NULL,
DATE_CREATED DATE NOT NULL,
USER_CREATED VARCHAR2(30) NOT NULL
)
/

ALTER TABLE debug_log ADD CONSTRAINT FK_DEBUG_LOG
FOREIGN KEY (MESSAGE_NO) REFERENCES
CUSTOM_DEBUG_MESSAGES(MESSAGE_NO);

DROP TABLE CUSTOM_DEBUG_MESSAGES;

CREATE TABLE CUSTOM_DEBUG_MESSAGES
(
MESSAGE_NO NUMBER NOT NULL
CONSTRAINT PK_CDM PRIMARY KEY,
```

```
MESSAGE_TEXT VARCHAR2(2000 CHAR) NOT NULL,
MESSAGE_TYPE VARCHAR2(10 CHAR) NOT NULL,
DATE_CREATED DATE NOT NULL,
USER_CREATED VARCHAR2(30) NOT NULL
)
/

DROP TABLE audit_control;

CREATE TABLE audit_control
(APPLICATION_NAME VARCHAR2(100) NOT NULL,
CURRENT_PROGRAM_NAME VARCHAR2(100) NOT NULL,
RETENTION_PERIOD NUMBER NOT NULL,
DEBUG_LOGGING_ON VARCHAR2(1) DEFAULT 'Y' NOT NULL
CHECK (DEBUG_LOGGING_ON IN ('Y','N'))
)
/

ALTER TABLE audit_control ADD CONSTRAINT
PK_AUDIT_CONTROL
PRIMARY KEY (APPLICATION_NAME,
CURRENT_PROGRAM_NAME);
DROP SEQUENCE seq_dl_id;

CREATE SEQUENCE seq_dl_id MINVALUE 1;
```

4. To implement the debug-logging mechanism, you can use a simple API similar to the error-logging mechanism API code. In addition, you can add a new function to this API that generates the debug message dynamically, based on specified parameters. Listing 8.8a shows an example of such a function. Listing 8.8b shows the code for the API for the debug logging mechanism. It is implemented using a package named pkg_log_debug.

5. Code a subprogram that returns the debug message information for the main program unit being called as formatted output.

6. Purge the debug logs periodically, based on criteria such as retention period, application cut-off dates, and so forth.

Listing 8.8a   *Code for generating a debug message dynamically.*

```
FUNCTION f_gen_debug_msg(
p_application_name IN
debug_log.application_name%TYPE,
p_curr_program_name IN
debug_log.current_program_name%TYPE,
p_calling_program_name IN
debug_log.calling_program_name%TYPE,
p_block_name IN debug_log.block_name%TYPE,
p_description IN debug_log.description%TYPE,
p_msg_no IN debug_log.message_no%TYPE,
p_msg_desc IN debug_log.message_desc%TYPE,
p_key_info IN VARCHAR2 DEFAULT NULL,
p_include_header IN VARCHAR2 DEFAULT 'N')
RETURN VARCHAR2
IS
v_debug_msg VARCHAR2(2000);
FUNCTION header RETURN VARCHAR2
IS
BEGIN
RETURN('In APP: '||p_application_name||
' PROG: '||p_curr_program_name||
' Called By: '||p_calling_program_name||';');
END;
BEGIN
IF p_message_no IS NOT NULL THEN
v_debug_msg :=
pkg_log_debug.get_message_text (p_message_no);
END IF;
RETURN ((CASE WHEN p_include_header = 'Y' THEN header
ELSE NULL END)||
' This code identifies '||p_block_name||
'-'||p_description||
': '||(CASE WHEN v_debug_msg IS NOT NULL THEN
v_debug_msg
ELSE p_msg_desc END)||
'(KEY INFO: '||p_key_info||')');
END f_gen_debug_msg;
/
```

Listing 8.8b   *Package API for debug-logging framework.*

```
CREATE OR REPLACE PACKAGE pkg_log_debug
AS
-- Public Message Type
C_DEBUG CONSTANT CHAR := 'D';

FUNCTION get_message_text (p_message_no IN NUMBER,
p_message_type IN VARCHAR2 DEFAULT C_DEBUG) RETURN
VARCHAR2;

FUNCTION f_gen_debug_msg(
p_application_name IN
debug_log.application_name%TYPE,
p_curr_program_name IN
debug_log.current_program_name%TYPE,
p_calling_program_name IN
debug_log.calling_program_name%TYPE,
p_block_name IN debug_log.block_name%TYPE,
p_description IN debug_log.description%TYPE,
p_msg_no IN debug_log.message_no%TYPE,
p_msg_desc IN debug_log.message_desc%TYPE,
p_key_info IN debug_log.key_info%TYPE DEFAULT NULL,
p_include_header IN VARCHAR2 DEFAULT 'N')
RETURN VARCHAR2;

PROCEDURE log_debug_info(
p_application_name IN
debug_log.application_name%TYPE,
p_curr_program_name IN
debug_log.current_program_name%TYPE,
p_calling_program_name IN
debug_log.calling_program_name%TYPE,
p_block_name IN debug_log.block_name%TYPE,
p_description IN debug_log.description%TYPE,
p_msg_no IN debug_log.message_no%TYPE,
p_msg_type IN debug_log.message_type%TYPE,
p_msg_desc IN debug_log.message_desc%TYPE,
p_key_info IN debug_log.key_info%TYPE DEFAULT
```

```
NULL,
p_comments1 IN debug_log.comments1%TYPE DEFAULT NULL,
p_comments2 IN debug_log.comments2%TYPE DEFAULT NULL,
p_comments3 IN debug_log.comments3%TYPE DEFAULT NULL,
p_comments4 IN debug_log.comments4%TYPE DEFAULT NULL,
p_comments5 IN debug_log.comments5%TYPE DEFAULT NULL
);

END;
/

CREATE OR REPLACE PACKAGE BODY pkg_log_debug
AS

FUNCTION get_message_text (p_message_no IN NUMBER,
p_message_type IN VARCHAR2 DEFAULT C_DEBUG)
RETURN VARCHAR2
IS
v_message_text
custom_debug_messages.MESSAGE_TEXT%TYPE;
BEGIN
SELECT message_text
INTO v_message_text
FROM custom_debug_messages
WHERE message_no = p_message_no
AND message_type = p_message_type;
RETURN (v_message_text);
EXCEPTION
WHEN others THEN
RETURN(NULL);
END get_message_text;

FUNCTION f_gen_debug_msg(
p_application_name IN
debug_log.application_name%TYPE,
p_curr_program_name IN
debug_log.current_program_name%TYPE,
p_calling_program_name IN
debug_log.calling_program_name%TYPE,
p_block_name IN debug_log.block_name%TYPE,
```

```
p_description IN debug_log.description%TYPE,
p_msg_no IN debug_log.message_no%TYPE,
p_msg_desc IN debug_log.message_desc%TYPE,
p_key_info IN debug_log.key_info%TYPE DEFAULT NULL,
p_include_header IN VARCHAR2 DEFAULT 'N')
RETURN VARCHAR2
IS
v_debug_msg VARCHAR2(2000);
FUNCTION header RETURN VARCHAR2
IS
BEGIN
RETURN('In APP: '||p_application_name||
' PROG: '||p_curr_program_name||
' Called By: '||p_calling_program_name||';');
END;
BEGIN
IF p_msg_no IS NOT NULL THEN
v_debug_msg :=
pkg_log_debug.get_message_text (p_msg_no);
END IF;
RETURN ((CASE WHEN p_include_header = 'Y' THEN header
ELSE NULL END)||
' This code identifies '||p_block_name||
'-'||p_description||
': '||(CASE WHEN v_debug_msg IS NOT NULL THEN
v_debug_msg
ELSE p_msg_desc END)||
'(KEY INFO: '||p_key_info||')');
END f_gen_debug_msg;
PROCEDURE log_debug_info(
p_application_name
IN debug_log.application_name%TYPE,
p_curr_program_name
IN debug_log.current_program_name%TYPE,
p_calling_program_name
IN debug_log.calling_program_name%TYPE,
p_block_name
IN debug_log.block_name%TYPE,
p_description
```

```
IN debug_log.description%TYPE,
p_msg_no
IN debug_log.message_no%TYPE,
p_msg_type
IN debug_log.message_type%TYPE,
p_msg_desc
IN debug_log.message_desc%TYPE,
p_key_info
IN debug_log.key_info%TYPE DEFAULT NULL,
p_comments1
IN debug_log.comments1%TYPE DEFAULT NULL,
p_comments2
IN debug_log.comments2%TYPE DEFAULT NULL,
p_comments3
IN debug_log.comments3%TYPE DEFAULT NULL,
p_comments4
IN debug_log.comments4%TYPE DEFAULT NULL,
p_comments5
IN debug_log.comments5%TYPE DEFAULT NULL
)
IS
PRAGMA AUTONOMOUS_TRANSACTION;
v_dl_id debug_log.dl_id%TYPE;
v_debug_logging_on
audit_control.debug_logging_on%TYPE;
BEGIN
BEGIN
SELECT debug_logging_on
INTO v_debug_logging_on
FROM audit_control
WHERE application_name = p_application_name
AND current_program_name = p_curr_program_name;
EXCEPTION
WHEN NO_DATA_FOUND THEN
BEGIN
SELECT debug_logging_on
INTO v_debug_logging_on
FROM audit_control
WHERE application_name = p_application_name;
```

```
      EXCEPTION
      WHEN NO_DATA_FOUND THEN
      NULL;
      -- RAISE_APPLICATION_ERROR(
      -- -20002,'Debug Logging not set up for
      -- application ' ||p_application_name);
      WHEN OTHERS THEN
      NULL;
      -- RAISE_APPLICATION_ERROR(
      -- -20003,'ERR getting setup info for
      -- application ' ||p_application_name||':
      '||SQLERRM);
      END;
      WHEN OTHERS THEN
      NULL;
      -- RAISE_APPLICATION_ERROR(
      -- -20001, 'Debug Logging not set up for '||
      -- ||'(application, current program) ('||
      -- p_app_name||', '
      -- ||p_curr_program_name||')'||SQLERRM);
      END;

      IF v_debug_logging_on = 'Y' THEN
      SELECT seq_dl_id.nextval
      INTO v_dl_id
      FROM DUAL;

      INSERT INTO debug_log(dl_id, application_name,
      current_program_name, calling_program_name,
      unique_session_code,
      block_name, description, message_no, message_type,
      message_desc,
      key_info, comments1, comments2, comments3, comments4,
      comments5,
      date_created, user_created)
      VALUES (v_dl_id, p_application_name,
      p_curr_program_name,
      p_calling_program_name, SYS_CONTEXT('USERENV',
      'OS_USER'),
```

```
p_block_name, p_description, p_msg_no, p_msg_type,
p_msg_desc,
p_key_info, p_comments1, p_comments2, p_comments3,
p_comments4,
p_comments5, SYSDATE, USER);

COMMIT;

END IF;
EXCEPTION
WHEN OTHERS THEN
NULL;
END log_debug_info;

END pkg_log_debug;
/
```

The important point to be noted here is how the unique session ID is derived from the OS_USER attribute of the system context USERENV.

Listing 8.9 displays the code for a sample calling program that uses the debug-logging framework.

Listing 8.9   *Skeleton code that demonstrates the use of packaged API calls for the debug-logging framework.*

```
CREATE OR REPLACE PROCEDURE proc_test_debug_logging(
ip_input_source IN VARCHAR2
)
IS
v_status NUMBER := 0;
v_app_name VARCHAR2(100) := 'PLSQLDVLP';
v_curr_prog_name VARCHAR2(100) :=
'PROC_TEST_DEBUG_LOGGING';
BEGIN
BEGIN
-- Code Snippet1
pkg_log_debug.log_debug_info(v_app_name,
v_curr_prog_name, NULL,
'Insert1', NULL, NULL, pkg_log_debug.c_debug,
'Insert1 Begin Tag',
```

```
      ip_input_source);


      /* Application Code — embedded language code, e.g.,
      stored procedure call */


      pkg_log_debug.log_debug_info(v_app_name,
      v_curr_prog_name, NULL,
      'Insert1', NULL, NULL, pkg_log_debug.c_debug,
      'Insert1 End Tag',
      ip_input_source);


      EXCEPTION
      WHEN OTHERS THEN
      v_status := 1;
      pkg_log_error.log_error_info(v_app_name,
      v_curr_prog_name, NULL,
      'Insert1', NULL, NULL, pkg_log_error.c_error,
      SQLCODE||SQLERRM,
      ip_input_source);
      END;


      BEGIN
      -- Code Snippet2
      pkg_log_debug.log_debug_info(v_app_name,
      v_curr_prog_name, NULL,
      'Update1', NULL, NULL, pkg_log_debug.c_debug,
      'Update1 Begin Tag',
      ip_input_source);


      /* Application Code — embedded language code, e.g.,
      DML */


      pkg_log_debug.log_debug_info(v_app_name,
      v_curr_prog_name, NULL,
      'Update1', NULL, NULL, pkg_log_debug.c_debug,
      'Update1 End Tag',
      ip_input_source);
```

```
EXCEPTION
WHEN OTHERS THEN
v_status := 1;
pkg_log_error.log_error_info(v_app_name,
v_curr_prog_name, NULL,
'Update1', NULL, NULL, pkg_log_error.c_error,
SQLCODE||SQLERRM,
ip_input_source);
END;

COMMIT;

pkg_log_debug.log_debug_info(v_app_name,
v_curr_prog_name, NULL,
'End of Proc', NULL, NULL, pkg_log_debug.c_debug,
'End of Proc Tag-Successful Completion',
ip_input_source);

EXCEPTION
WHEN OTHERS THEN
ROLLBACK;
pkg_log_error.log_error_info(v_app_name,
v_curr_prog_name, NULL,
'Proc Test Debug Logging', NULL, NULL,
pkg_log_error.c_error,
SQLCODE||SQLERRM, ip_input_source);
RAISE;
END proc_test_debug_logging;
/
```

Implementing such debug message logging provides the first level of monitoring code execution by revealing the control points in the code at which the execution faltered or stopped. The third step of monitoring the code to get the dynamic execution profile augments this step by tracing the finer granular details about code execution.

In addition to using database tables in conjunction with autonomous transactions, asynchronous debug messages can be logged using file I/O, pipelined table functions, the DBMS_APPLICATION_INFO packaged routines, or using the embedded programming language functionality itself.

8.5.3   Testing of the Application Solution

This primarily involves end-to-end testing of the application and tracking the order of execution of code. You track the count, time, and execution of each individual execution unit within the program (this may be a single line or another subprogram call); the same statistics for each of the descendent subprograms of the calling subprogram and the caller and called subprogram information; and finally the resources used in executing the program. A detailed procedure for end-to-end application testing has been outlined in the subsection "Application Development Framework: A Pragmatic Best-Possible Solution" in this chapter. A detailed procedure for monitoring application code has been outlined in the subsection "Performance Tuning Framework" in this chapter, as well as in Chapters 4–7 of Part II. Of key importance is the Proof-of-Performance benchmarking as part of pre-emptive performance testing described in the section "Code Accelerators for Rapid Application Development: Design and Coding Aspects" of Chapter 7. A combination of the techniques presented there provides a rich set of tools to test and monitor the code execution profile, with breakup of SQL, PL/SQL, and application code executions.

Monitoring the end-to-end activity of the solution includes end-user activity and business process activity on the business-functionality side, and the workflow and services execution and automation on the IT side. This can be streamlined into a workflow-based automated process that comprises a firewall, auditing, and log management at the network, database and the Web application levels, using Oracle Database Vault, Oracle Audit Vault, Web Application firewall, and Oracle Total Recall.

The debugging framework presented here can be automated by constructing a *generic debug utility as part of a code library* that incorporates this framework. The design and coding steps for such a utility can be derived from those built in this debugging framework and implemented as an additional automated process in-lined into the end-to-end solution workflow.

Summary

This chapter described application development frameworks. It touched upon the pragmatics of an application development framework for a best practice transactional and reporting and analysis solution; a master error management framework;. a master auditing framework; a performance-tuning framework; and a debugging framework from the perspective of Oracle-based embedded programming application construction and development.

The next chapter deals with miscellaneous techniques that have not been covered previously in the book, but are as best a fit as the others discussed so far, in terms of architecting and implementing an Oracle-based embedded programming solution.

Chapter 9

Miscellaneous Best Practices

In This Chapter

- Simulating Oracle-based datasets: Best practices for design and coding
- Building a highly visible Web site

9.1 Simulating Oracle-Based Datasets: Best Practices for Design and Coding

This section highlights a technique of streaming result sets of data over a chain of pipelined functions that serve as in-memory staged datasets. Dataset staging is used predominantly for in-memory processing, such as applications involving online analytical processing (OLAP) that require ultra-fast processing and delivery of query results or for extract, transform, and load (ETL) processing to populate a data warehouse wherein the target database needs to be fed with data available in an external source or in a different database than the target database that uses the data. It is also employed in OLTP applications that demand rapid response times for high-volume transactions such as high-traffic Web sites—when the data in an OLTP system changes rapidly and thus necessitates near-real-time streaming and/or replication of the same.

Table functions have a tight integration with SQL and hence with the Oracle database. Table functions, used in tandem with pipelining and parallelization, provide an efficient way to do the processing, federation, and streaming of the result sets in-memory in case of OLAP applications; the extract, transform, and load processes of ETL; or the complex in-memory transactional processing and distribution of OLTP systems. This high-performance technique eliminates the need for intermediate dataset temporary tables by virtue of its streaming capabilities.

To understand where a dataset comes into the picture, let us take the example of ETL processing for populating a data warehouse. The outline of what ETL is and how it is accomplished can enable a better understanding of how a dataset stage can be simulated by means of pipelined table functions. A similar theory applies to in-memory processing in OLAP or online transaction processing (OLTP) systems.

9.1.1   The In-Memory Processing Framework

The use of PL/SQL, with its tight integration with SQL and the Oracle database and its powerful features, provides an efficient way to perform complex data processing by eliminating temporary tables and their resource/CPU utilization and performing high-performance processing directly in-memory, using a combination of SQL, PL/SQL pipelining, and parallelization.

When the source data is located in a different source database, an initial load from the source can be done, followed by a changed data load (if the source data is in an OLTP system). The ideal methods are as follows:

1. Use a single SQL statement with INSERT...SELECT in the direct path mode to populate the intermediate tables for the initial load. This is faster than writing PL/SQL.

2. Use CDC (Oracle's Change Data Capture), primarily asynchronous CDC, to populate the changing rows into the intermediate tables on a periodic basis.

In-memory processing is where most of the logic/transformation(s) processing is done. It involves the following steps:

1. Validating input data before processing as necessary

2. Performing the required processing in-memory

3. Additional post-processing as needed

If the validations or logic transformations are simple, they can be moved into SQL statements that will be used by the subsequent process. Otherwise, enhanced PL/SQL techniques like bulk array processing (bulk binds) or pipelined table functions need to be used.

Using Bulk Binds

Bulk binding involve the following steps:

1. Use BULK COLLECT with the LIMIT clause in a loop to read the source data from the intermediate tables into a PL/SQL array.

2. Read the collection elements and perform the data transformations and any other processing.

3. Use the FORALL statement to load the transformed data into the target tables.

Here's a code snippet to illustrate these steps:

```
CREATE OR REPLACE PROCEDURE p_insert(
p_src_data SYS_REFCURSOR)
IS
TYPE arr IS TABLE OF src_tab%ROWTYPE INDEX BY
BINARY_INTEGER;
arr1 arr;
BEGIN
LOOP
FETCH p_src_data BULK COLLECT INTO arr1 LIMIT 100;
EXIT WHEN arr1.COUNT = 0;
/* Perform some processing on the input rows in arr1
*/
FORALL i IN 1..arr1.COUNT
INSERT INTO target_tab VALUES arr1(i);
COMMIT;
END LOOP;
END;
/
```

Using Pipelined Table Functions

Using pipelined table functions involves the following steps:

1. Define an object type with a structure equivalent to the source data record and a collection type of this object type at the schema level.

2. Create a pipelined table function in a package that returns the collection type. This function must have an input parameter of

type REF CURSOR to have the source data pumped into it. Also, define the function with the PARALLEL_ENABLE clause.

Using a table function accomplishes the following:

- It reduces the memory bottleneck to materialize the entire set of rows returned by the function in memory.
- It increases efficiency by not waiting for the function to execute completely.
- It enables parallel processing to be used, thus further increasing speed by means of parallel query execution. This is a trade-off between the resources used to create the slave processes and the time taken to execute the function.

Here's a code snippet to illustrate pipelined table functions:

```
CREATE OR REPLACE FUNCTION f_process(p_src_data
SYS_REFCURSOR)
PIPELINED
IS
TYPE arr IS TABLE OF src_tab%ROWTYPE INDEX BY
BINARY_INTEGER;
arr1 arr;
BEGIN
LOOP
FETCH p_src_data BULK COLLECT INTO arr1 LIMIT 100;
EXIT WHEN arr1.COUNT = 0;
/* Perform some processing on the input rows in arr1
*/
FOR i IN 1..arr1.COUNT LOOP
/* Populate src_row_obj which is an element of a
collection of objects corresponding to src_tab
and defined in the database with input data read
in the array arr1*/
PIPE ROW (src_row_obj);
/* Use multiple PIPE ROW statements to fan multiple
records from a single source row */
END LOOP;
END LOOP;
```

```
RETURN;
END;
/
```

Generally, the parallel pipelined table function approach leads to an order of magnitude faster than the bulk-binding approach. However, individual results may vary with the number of input records and the database resources available. For complex processing requirements, such as fanning multiple rows for each input row, the pipelined table approach can prove beneficial, as the bulk-binding approach requires FORALL to be used multiple times.

Always use schema-level types rather than PL/SQL types when defining the collection for the table function. This provides declarative control rather than programmatic control, in addition to the ability of being stored as database row sets.

When defining the pipelined table function, always encapsulate it in a PL/SQL package. This approach isolates it from database dependencies. Even a procedure in a package can be used for the bulk-binding approach using FORALL.

Additional postprocessing primarily involves outputting the processed results to a target table or to a different calling environment, such as a data grid on a Web page or as an input parameter of type REF CURSOR to a calling embedded language routine for result set shareability. Here are the techniques involved:

If the data validation and logic transformation can be moved into SQL itself, the load is simply an INSERT...SELECT into the target table or the REF CURSOR parameter. For the former, the DML error-logging facility with the LOG ERRORS clause introduced in Oracle10g Release 2 can be used, as well as the multitable INSERT and the MERGE features. This can be done in direct path mode to bypass the buffer cache.

Here's a code snippet to illustrate this step of the load phase:

```
INSERT /*+ APPEND */ INTO target_tab
SELECT <col_list> FROM src_tab
LOG ERRORS
```

```
REJECT LIMIT UNLIMITED;
```

If the processing required mandates the use of PL/SQL logic, as with the table function approach, then using an INSERT...SELECT with a query to the table function using the TABLE operator is the optimal approach. This has to be done in direct path mode.

Here's a code snippet to illustrate this step of the load phase:

```
INSERT /*+ APPEND */ INTO target_tab
SELECT * FROM TABLE(f_etl_process(CURSOR
(SELECT * FROM src_tab)));
```

Using the FORALL statement to insert into target table is another way of accomplishing the load process. However, this method may not be optimal for complex processing situations that require multiple target records for each input record. This has been illustrated in the code for the p_insert procedure, presented earlier.

Always use direct-path inserts when performing the load process. If for any reason a direct-path insert cannot be used (for example, in cases where there may be unique constraint or index violations), resort to the bulk-binding approach using the BULK COLLECT and FORALL approach. This is faster than doing a conventional INSERT.

For complex processing requirements, use direct-path INSERT...SELECT with the parallel pipelined table function approach for doing the load process. This is probably the most efficient approach.

9.1.2   Simulating Oracle-Based Data Sets Using Transformation Pipeline Chain

This subsection outlines the use of pipelined table functions to create a transformation chain that can simulate Oracle-based in-memory datasets. Consider the example of fanning multiple records from a single input row. This can be accomplished by means of a pipeline chain that queries the source table, processes the logic/transforms on the initial data, and fans out output records for each processed input row. A simple direct-path

INSERT...SELECT can be used to load the output rows returned by the pipeline chain into the target table.

Design Methodology

1. Query the source table and pass the SELECT as the input to the first pipelined table function that does the initial logic processing or transformations.

```
f_pipelined1(CURSOR(SELECT * FROM external_tab))
```

2. Pass the output of f_pipelined1 as input to f_pipelined2 as a CURSOR expression using the TABLE operator. This second function fans the multiple output records for each input row.

```
f_pipelined2(CURSOR(SELECT * FROM TABLE
(f_pipelined1(CURSOR(SELECT * FROM external_tab)))))
```

3. Do the postprocessing load into the target table using the output of f_pipelined2 with a direct path INSERT...SELECT.

```
INSERT /*+ APPEND */ INTO target_tab
SELECT * FROM TABLE(f_pipelined2(CURSOR
(SELECT * FROM TABLE(f_pipelined1
(CURSOR(SELECT * FROM external_tab))))))
```

This is more efficient than using intermediate temporary tables and breaking the process of transformation chaining into multiple steps. This technique is implemented by way of simulating an Oracle-based dataset stage, the details of which are described in the paragraphs that follow.

Implementation

A table function is implemented by creating a function that takes the incoming data as a REF CURSOR parameter, applies processing logic to each record, and outputs the transformed record(s) as a collection via the function return value. With a pipelined table function, the streaming is done on a record-by-record basis, by applying a technique called pipelining, whereby the input dataset is processed record by record. This in turn enables asynchronous streaming of function output on a row-by-row basis, which allows for "real-time" availability. This is a benefit most often needed for OLTP and OLAP applications. Also, coding packages enables inter- and intra-sharing of datasets between applications; the use of pipelined table functions is performance-efficient in at least four cases:

- Streaming data in on a row-by-row basis rather than process it all at once
- Passing huge datasets between PL/SQL programs (when combined with bulk array processing)
- Funneling multiple output rows from a single input row; in this case, table functions are the optimal choice
- Returning the first *n* rows from an input dataset involving complex transformations that otherwise cannot use direct SQL; this makes it somewhat similar to getting the FIRST *n* ROWS in a SQL SELECT statement

Query the Source Table and Pass the Source SELECT as Input

First, query the data source table and pass the source SELECT as input to the first pipelined table function that does the initial transformations, as follows:

```
f_pipelined1(CURSOR(SELECT * FROM external_tab))
```

Here's a skeleton implementation of the f_pipelined1 function:

```
CREATE OR REPLACE FUNCTION f_pipelined1
(p_src_data SYS_REFCURSOR) RETURN src_row_obj_arr
PIPELINED
IS
TYPE src_arr IS TABLE OF src_tab%ROWTYPE
INDEX BY BINARY_INTEGER;
src_arr1 src_arr;
xfrm_arr1 src_arr;
BEGIN
LOOP
FETCH p_src_data BULK COLLECT INTO src_arr1 LIMIT 100;
EXIT WHEN src_arr1.COUNT = 0;
/* Perform some initial processing on the input
rows in src_arr1 and perform assignments to
xfrm_arr1 corresponding to the target table */
```

```
FOR i IN 1..xfrm_arr1.COUNT LOOP
/* Populate xfrm_row_obj which is an element
of a collection of objects corresponding to
src_tab and defined in the database with input
data read in the array xfrm_arr1*/
PIPE ROW (xfrm_row_obj);
END LOOP;
END LOOP;
RETURN;
END f_pipelined1;
/
```

Pass the Output of f_pipelined1 as Input to f_pipelined2

Next, pass the output of f_pipelined1 as input to f_pipelined2 as a CUR-SOR expression using the TABLE operator. This second function fans the multiple output records for each input row.

```
f_pipelined2(CURSOR(SELECT * FROM TABLE
(f_pipelined1(CURSOR(SELECT * FROM
external_tab)))))
```

Here's a skeleton implementation of the f_pipelined2 function:

```
CREATE OR REPLACE FUNCTION f_pipelined2
(p_init_xfrmd_data SYS_REFCURSOR)
RETURN tgt_row_obj_arr
PIPELINED
IS
TYPE src_arr IS TABLE OF src_tab%ROWTYPE
INDEX BY BINARY_INTEGER;
init_xfmd_arr1 src_arr;
TYPE tgt_arr IS TABLE OF target_tab%ROWTYPE
INDEX BY BINARY_INTEGER;
tgt_arr1 tgt_arr;
BEGIN
LOOP
FETCH p_init_xfrmd_data BULK COLLECT INTO
init_xfrmd_arr1 LIMIT 100;
EXIT WHEN init_xfrmd_arr1.COUNT = 0;
```

```
FOR i IN 1..init_xfrmd_arr1.COUNT LOOP
/* Perform some additional processing on the input
rows
in init_xfrmd_arr1 to split one input record into
multiple output records in the format of the target
table. Populate tgt_row_obj which is an element of a
collection of objects corresponding to target_tab
followed by a PIPE ROW statement. This leads to an
assignment as per the target table format followed by
a PIPE ROW for each such output record to be fanned
from
one source record in init_xfmd_arr1 */
-- Assign tgt_row_obj here as per the first output
-- fanned record
PIPE ROW (tgt_row_obj);
-- change some fields to get a second (different)
-- output fanned record
PIPE ROW (tgt_row_obj);
-- ...... /* Repeat this for each additional fanned
record needed */
END LOOP;
END LOOP;
RETURN;
END f_pipelined2;
/
```

Do the Post-Processing Load into the Target Table

Finally, load the target table using the output of f_pipelined2 with a direct path
INSERT...SELECT statement, as follows:

```
INSERT /*+ APPEND */ INTO target_tab
SELECT * FROM TABLE(f_pipelined2(CURSOR(SELECT * FROM
TABLE(f_pipelined1(CURSOR(SELECT * FROM
external_tab))))))
```

This is much more efficient than using a temporary (or staging) table and breaking up into multiple steps. As a result, the entire in-memory processing eliminated the use of a physical intermediate table without compromising any other functionality. Starting with the data source table for the initial querying, followed by a pipelined table function chain for all of the intermediate in-memory logic processing/transformation(s), and ending in an INSERT...SELECT in direct-path mode with ERROR LOGGING for the post-processing LOAD, this technique of dataset staging is an optimal solution for in-memory processing.

9.2   Building a Highly Visible Web Site

A visible Web site is typically a database-backed Web site that supports transactional and/or analytical capabilities and at the same time provides the breadth and depth of increased data, services, and events connectivity and improved GRC, in terms of business processes and operational efficiency, change-adaptability, and preventive and detective risk mitigation and assessment.

This in turn requires functionality that enables customer-driven interaction and response, the ability to reuse services, and the ability to proactively quantify risk and mitigate the same using end-to-end monitoring and detection of business and user activity monitoring including tracking clickstream data. The following paragraphs outline a framework for building a highly visible Web site using Oracle database as the backend and an embedded programming language solution at the application layer.

1. *Identifying the business drivers*—This consists of determining the business data, including master data, the business processes that service how the business operates with the data, and when and for what use. These translate into data, services, and events in the IT implementation domain.

2. *Identifying the IT drivers*—This consists of determining:

    - The applications and their relationship to the business processes and data—are they loosely coupled or largely coupled?
    - The various integration points in the desired solution
    - The various customer touchpoints in the desired solution
    - The level of security desired (and how much of it is in place already)—this includes runtime governance and monitoring, as well
    - The level of accessibility and collaboration—does it require a Web interface or a native interface?

- The GRC policies desired (and how much of the same are in place already)
- The degree of personalization and extension required—for example, delivering data in a consolidated and interactive manner via the Web on any endpoint device
- The level of intelligence that can be incorporated proactively (via innovative key process indicators, or KPIs) based on customer experience to enable real-time decision making—a best fit for the customer and the corresponding interaction context

3. *Implementing the Web site with visibility built into it*—Visibility must be built in from the business (and customer) as well as IT perspectives.

In the following list, the first two imperatives and the sixth imperative can be implemented by adopting the following architectural design:

- Let customer-centricity be the key design indicator for the Web site.
- Design the Web site as a 100-percent Web application using the embedded language technology in context (e.g., .NET, Java, an Oracle APEX-based solution, etc.).
- Take into account the end-to-end business scope of the solution. All users need anytime-anywhere access to all authorized data/information—but there must be a unified solution platform at the conceptual (user) level.
- Enable continuous information protection in all deployment environments.
- Implement high-volume output of results by disabling on-screen complete rendering or enabling partial page rendering with partial page refresh turned on. This can be implemented using JSON or AJAX/PHP-based code segments that can be reused for similar functionality.
- Tailor the Web site for search engine optimization. The relevance of the content to the context of the search is a pivotal design factor for the architecture of the Web site.
- Ensure business semantics of contextual information presented by using a centralized information semantics

repository that is accessed dynamically based on data/content specificity and translates the underlying information into simplified business-friendly text.

- Build fine-grained visibility by implementing interactive user-controlled data visualizations rendered on-the-fly based on user-specified variables for data selection and presentation. This accelerates the time-to-insight enabling better decision support and doing it in multiple dimensions such as derivation of new key business imperatives tailored to accelerate business growth, e.g., domain expansion, business services prioritization etc.

- Minimize the number of HTTP requests from the site.

- Optimize delivery of binary content by integrating the Web site with a content delivery network interface. Mashing up external content interactively on the fly provides increased visibility of the Web site.

- Do consider portability or conversion of the Web site, particularly offsite and onsite specific elements of the Web site that need changes during conversion, as well as the rendering, visualization, and navigation aspects of the same.

- Ensure SSL strength and visibility by syncing encrypted in-transit data policies with those of the underlying network usage. Using techniques such as session initiation protocol coupled with a proxy termination and re-initiation of the SSL Web session makes the encrypted traffic completely visible to the solution monitoring component.

Five of the IT imperatives listed above can be ranked as predominant (compared to others) to the architecture and design of the same from a visibility standpoint. These are short-listed as follows:

1. The level of security desired (and how much of it is in place already)—this includes run-time governance and monitoring too

2. The various customer touchpoints in the desired solution

3. The GRC policies desired (and how much of the same are in place already)

4. The degree of personalization and extension required—for example, delivering data in a consolidated and interactive manner via the Web on any endpoint device

5. The level of intelligence that can be incorporated proactively (via innovative KPI) based on customer experience to enable real-time decision making—a best fit for the customer and the corresponding interaction context

Short-listing the above five doesn't undermine the other IT imperatives; those are also necessary for a successful implementation of the same.

Securing the Web site is vital to providing visibility for both business and IT operations. All communication taking place between the Website (and the Web application) and the Oracle Database must be traceable and secure when online, without impacting the runtime environment. Also, all data in-store must be fully secure and immune to privileged attacks.

The key design indicator in implementing the most granular level of security is by enforcing 360-degree data security at the database Tier. This must comprise common and consistent policies for encrypting all data all the time including data-in-transit and archived data, disabling application bypass to data by privileged users using SoD-based access via an unified Administration Console (that typically is controlled by the business in context and NOT by IT), and a comprehensive end-to-end monitoring and auditing module that is fully automated.

Oracle11g enables this by means of preventive and detective measures that are fully integrated with the Oracle Database and at the same time application-code-agnostic (i.e., they do not necessitate a change in the application code if the underlying security framework is changed). The preventive measures include encryption, masking, role-based SoD, and access control; the detective measures include activity monitoring, change tracking, discovery and assessment, information protection (after it leaves the application boundaries), and secure configuration.

- The *preventive controls* are implementable by using Oracle Advanced Security for encryption, data masking and secure backup, and Oracle Database Vault and Multiple Label Security for access and identity management.

- Oracle Advanced Security with built-in transparent data encryption and cryptographic functionality (at the column, table, and table-space levels) protects all data by performing encryption and decryption in the Oracle DB itself and prevents direct DB access at the OS level. automated data masking (preserving the data integrity (PK, FK, UK etc.)) enables replication of production data in development and test platforms without de-identifying the PII and other sensitive data. Network encryption and strong authentication of data-in-traffic prevent middle-man attacks.

- Oracle Database Vault and Multiple Label Security act a powerful database firewall layers for identity and access control by providing SoD and privileged user controls, along with multitenancy of application data, multifactor access control based on rules and factors that prevent data access via application bypass.

- The *detective controls* by way of Oracle Audit Vault, Oracle Total Recall, and Oracle Configuration Management ensure that the preventive controls are working:

  - Oracle Audit Vault provides detective control mechanisms by way of automated database activity monitoring, including user session monitoring and comprehensive auditing by means of a centralized audit trail repository, alerting, generation, and attestation of out-of-box compliance reports for major GRC regulations.

  - Oracle Total Recall enables transparent and secure tracking of application data as of a certain timestamp, real-time access to as-of data using SQL, secure and efficient storage of archived data in the DB, and easy-to-use incident forensics and recovery.

  - Oracle Configuration Management ensures the end-to-end configuration and change management by enforcing context-specific configuration policies that can handle the discovery, classification, vulnerability assessment, prioritization, fixing, and analysis of the solution configuration changes at runtime and in real-time. This adds another fine-grain to the visibility of the solution by enabling reporting for change management compliance.

4. *Accelerating the solution visibility by means of SOA-based reusable services of the above implementation controls*—By tying the services (which are the implementation of the above visibility measures) to the context-specific data, individual SOA modules can be created that can be exposed as custom Web Service calls. This gives increased flexibility for personalization and extension as well as on-the-fly integration, in addition to eliminating redundancy by way of reusability.

5. *Proactive actionable intelligence that is customer-experience driven*—This is a key design imperative that stands out from the traditional business intelligence norms. It involves broadening the customer experience from a call center-->contact center-->self-service–driven approach to a multichannel, multifunctional, and multidisciplinary redefinition that:

- Builds upon the intelligent domain analytics and the customer experience (or insights) in using these analytics in a quantitative manner to rank the serviceability (or time-to-service), consistency of business value, real-time decision making, and lower TCO from a business solution requirements context—using improved and accelerated policies and factors that in turn generate improved and efficient customer intelligence analytics and higher degree of customer satisfaction.
- Provides and sustains consistency of relevance with respect to the business context of the customer/end-user, thereby creating pointers/metrics to signs of preventable business issues.

Here's a design pattern for an *Optimized Customer Intelligence Analytics Service* that explains the details from concepts to customization:

1. Create optimized analytics by deriving metrics for real-time data based on the details of the context of the customer touchpoint in addition to capturing click-stream data or the interaction navigation chain. This can answer the "why" of customer

touchpoint interaction and the reason behind the behavioral pattern of "repeat" interactions by the same customer.

2. Rank the customer experience based on quantitative scores based on multiple interaction channels—IVR, Web UI, dynamic self-serve to mobile device, etc., in addition to call center or contact center—and apply classification based on the scoring, into distinct groups of customers like high-value and low-value customers.

3. Analyze the customer experience over multiple interaction touch-points and domain-specific functions to determine consistency of business services and consistency of customer satisfaction. This results in another set of optimized metrics.

4. Incorporate these optimized key performance indicators into the solution analytics design to enable certain degree of dynamism in their implementation—by using federated analytic processing, data virtualization, etc. This creates a self-adaptable execution scenario at run-time that gets driven by variables/inputs from end-user/customer interaction action-response.

5. Centralize the same into a Web-accessible KPI-repository that can be streamed in real-time as RSS feeds and/or consolidated and shared via a Wiki page. This enables existing applications to leverage the optimized KPI using Web-enabled SQL query-based access.

6. The final result is operational decision support that is not only best fit for the customer/business constraints in context, but also one that speeds up the process by allowing real-time decision making based on real-time data inputs/feeds and can be leveraged to deliver right action for the right context at the right time—all the time.

7. Accelerate the optimized analytics by creating a separate SOA-enabled Web Services component that can be reused as an Optimized Customer Intelligence Analytics Service. This gives pervasive access in terms of its use across the solution space and beyond.

Summary

This chapter described two pivotal application development best practices, namely, simulating dataset caches in-memory for high-performance processing and the design considerations for building a highly visible Web site. It touched upon the ins and outs of the design patterns involved as well as some relevant coding aspects of the same. The next chapter deals with best practices in terms of troubleshooting embedded language solutions and embedded language–specific coding standards that can simplify, enhance, accelerate, and (at times) minimize coding of the same.

Chapter 10

Best Practices in Terms of Coding Standards and Troubleshooting

In This Chapter

- Coding standards from an Oracle11g embedded programming perspective
- Tuning SQL & PL/SQL code for optimality
- Tuning embedded language code for optimality: data structures and procedural code
- Fine-tuning solution methodology for optimality

10.1   Introduction

Every application solution makes use of data and its management in one way or the other—data that is persistent, intermittent, and/or consistent in terms of existence, accuracy, and accessibility. The business case for adoption of an Oracle-based embedded programming language solution gains strength if the solution being delivered is based on accelerated and accurate analytics that provide business agility, flexibility, visibility, continuity, and operational efficiency. To implement such a solution, the underlying solution architecture as well as the code design and intrasolution process orchestration must perform optimally from code execution to communication to collaboration to customization, including the customer/end-user interaction and experience.

The key performance indicator (KPI) here is that the results, in terms of a superior customer experience, are all that matter, which in turn drives the return on customer (ROC) and ROI.

To achieve such a practical solution, it must meet specific industry standards, include technology best practices that are a best fit for its implementation, and be as fault-tolerant as possible in terms of security, risk mitigation, and prevention. This in turn mandates the same set of standards and best practices, one-on-one, for the Oracle Database (DB) Tier, the application solution Tier, and the user interface (UI) Tier. This means that not only the choice of the technology and embedded language but also the design and coding involved must employ these best practices and standards. The rest of this chapter provides a kick-start guide in terms of a best-of-breed checklist of some of the standards and best practices to be followed in the design-to-delivery process of a best-fit Oracle-based embedded programming language solution.

10.2   Coding Standards from an Oracle11g Embedded Programming Perspective

Here's a comprehensive list of best practices for Oracle11g-based embedded language programming:

1.   Tackle integration using native support for XML Web Services.

2.   Preserve HTML formatting.

3.   Enforce server-side controls designed to accelerate site development, appropriate to the embedded-language specific technology in context, such as ASP.NET server controls for .NET-based solutions, Java Servlet/JSF/JSP controls for J2EE-based solutions, Oracle ADF Faces controls for cross-technology based solutions, PSP-based controls for PL/SQL-based solutions, PHP/Ajax-based controls for solutions using these embedded languages, and the like.

4.   Use controls such as Tools tips, Bubble help, and the like.

5.   Build drag-and-drop data binding for faster data-driven functionality.

6.   Use rich data visualizations to speed up analysis and decision making.

7.   Incorporate click-once deployment to streamline solution deployment and updates.

8.   Reduce code drastically by using new and enhanced functionality in .NET Framework 2.0 and beyond, Java/J2EE 3.0 and beyond, Oracle ADF 11g, Ajaxfication, and PHP 5.0 and above

9. Use generics support in the .NET framework to write high-performance and type-safe code

10. Use code snippets to insert and customize large blocks of template code. A recommended practice is to create visual templates using smart tags, for example.

11. Employ mobile device emulators to facilitate solution development and testing. Doing this also accelerates test-driven development (i.e., preparing and running the test cases in sync with the ongoing development process), thereby saving time and gaining accuracy during system/integration testing, Quality Assurance (QA) testing, and User Acceptance Testing (UAT) in the preproduction deployment phase.

12. Create Web applications that dynamically render to hundreds of mobile type devices.

13. Use a cross-language debugger to step through application logic across multiple Tiers of the solution.

14. Troubleshoot even the most complex code using debugger visualizations and DataTips.

15. Use dynamic code modules that detect and install missing prerequisites automatically at the time of setup.

16. Catch errors before they occur by using background compilation and code editors that provide for syntax color highlighting. Oracle enables this kind of proactive compilation by way of compile-time warnings that can be activated at the individual stored program level, at the session level, or at the instance level. This is true in the case of embedded-language stored programs too; it detects and points out code that is potentially liable for any missing logical or performance-centric loopholes.

17. Use built-in membership and personalization features to enhance your site.

18. Refactoring code restructures the code. Use the embedded programming language that best maps to the target solution environment. Use its built-in functionality to create structured code stubs.

19. Incorporate performance counters and event-logging mechanisms inline into the solution, as far as possible. These can be reusable and embeddable, but when executed, they must be fully

aligned with the application workflow (i.e., inline) and not acting as an integrated component. This means that they should be part of the solution design itself, or seamlessly embeddable into the design at any point in time.

20.   Design the Web UI to enable usability across all types of Web-enabled access points (including deployment platforms). This means using a seamless and transparent interface that is based on Web 2.0, powered by a service-orietned architecture (SOA)–based design that gives an uncompromising user experience in terms of flexibility and efficiency. Oracle provides a rich Internet application (RIA) design and development methodology that is database-based, SOA-enabled, and event-driven, using Oracle ADF, Oracle SOA Suite, Oracle complex event processing (CEP) and business activity monitoring (BAM), Oracle Web-Center Suite, and Oracle Application Integration Architecture (AIA) based on the Enterprise Grid architecture, which can be leveraged to build an RIA solution from the startup. Alternately, the same solution can be seamlessly generated using Oracle Application Express (APEX), which employs in-database design and code processing wherein SQL and PL/SQL dynamically interact and execute with JavaScript, PHP, Ajax, and even Groovy code to create a Web-enabled application solution that is robust in functionality and rich in a dynamic UI. Using Oracle JDeveloper enables building an accelerated solution suited for Java-based RIA (out of the database)—while still leveraging the power of the Oracle DB by enabling embedded logic stored in the DB. In either case, the resulting RIA solution can be exposed as a technology-and-language-agnostic Web Service callable via a Web browser.

21.   Design the embedded solution based on an SOA that allows it to be Software as a Service (SaaS) enabled as well as SaaS enabling. The former means that it can be deployed and run as it is in pure-hosted and Cloud-based platforms. The latter implies that the solution can be embeddable in other hosted, SaaS-based, or Cloud-based solutions. This kind of design goes a long way toward building a unified Web-based communication and collaboration platform that can deliver real-time, customized information in near real-time—as in archiving, instant messaging, e-mail messaging, digital signage and other next-generation collaboration strategies, like Mobility as a Service, which bring the desired

content closer to the customer/end users' interaction, just-in-time content generation and delivery, and "narrowcasting" or disseminating only the content that is reduced to the finest level of contextual granularity needed at any particular access point.

22.	Build interactive search capabilities on all kinds of data/content, using declarative, direct SQL-based full text– or regular expression–based searches that yield meaningful results and have the least response time.

23.	Design an end-to-end solution security framework that comprises:

- A centralized repository of all data and user activity, inside and beyond the enterprise, regardless of where and how it is stored, who is accessing it, and the manner in which it is being transmitted
- A centralized point-of-control that resides where the right business authority is (i.e., outside the realm of privileged and non-privileged IT users), implemented by a combination of role-based access control and context-based access control (which support dynamic enforcement of policies).
- Delegated authentication coupled with localized authorization (e.g., to enforce Segregation of Duties, or SoD)
- A pivotal differentiator in terms of how the solution can adequately segregate the protection of PII (Personally Identifiable Information) and other sensitive data of the business's internal employees, compared to that of the business's external customers or end clients.

The following list outlines the recommended best practices for a design and implementation framework of the same:

- Use query-based access control lists (ACLs) to ensure correctness of DB-access credentials. This must be augmented with context-based ACL for connection control, followed by virtual patching and standards-compliant strict protocol validation, as well as controlling authentication of queries outside of the normal usage independent of privileged user control. This can be done by:
  - Employing a security audit trail and restricting access to and control of the same by the DBA or other system admin users

- ■ Enforcing policies that are at a higher level than the privileged users' levels—for example, allowing the database administrator (DBA) to alter a particular DB table's structure without being able to view the data in that table and the like. The control of the same must reside outside of the DB environment. Note that the policies/roles governing such access control semantics can and must reside inside the Oracle database. Only the control of the same is managed from outside the DB Tier, for example, by using a specific admin console or Oracle Identity and Access Management tools, which can eliminate DBA activity
  - ■ Capturing the context surrounding the query executed, such as the client machine info, the client software, the day and time the query was executed, and the amount of sensitive data extracted, in addition to the user who executed the query and the number of records affected by the query
- ■ Protect PII and other sensitive data by using a structured approach that consists of:
  - ■ *Discovery and assessment*—Identifying the sensitive data and its classification, where this high-profile data is residing (in what databases, archives, etc.), and in what form (encrypted, unencrypted, masked, compressed, etc.)
  - ■ *Dynamic profiling*—Application interaction with data, user interaction with data via application, user interaction with data bypassing the application, capturing of data-in-transit bidirectionally to and from the database and the end-user presentation interface; this mandates tracking the user application profile in addition to the DB application profile
  - ■ *User activity tracking*—Monitoring user sessions to track user interaction with data and the application, and user session state reconciliation between applications
  - ■ *Correlated attack validations*—Analyzing the current threat-based data relative to other multiple database and Web applications
  - ■ *Virtual patching*—Running the threat-related data outside the Oracle DB, using a management server (MX); this aids in detecting vulnerabilities on end-device access points as well as in deriving a mitigation mechanism that can be incorporated

into the solution security framework in the form of alerts or event-based messaging notifications

- *Audit definition and control*—Oracle Audit Vault is a purpose-built audit solution that identifies and addresses threats and their mitigation, both proactively and reactively. The key best practices here are:
  - To do the audit of activity taking place external to the database, such as the audit of user activity between the database and the user, which is nothing but an audit trail of in-transit data flowing bi-directionally to and from the Oracle DB
  - To do an audit of all audits taking place in the solution-context space
  - To turn on auditing in production environments across the end-to-end solution space, and not just at the points of log-ins and failures

---

These measures are necessary, as vulnerability issues pertaining to the database protocol cannot be handled in the database server (such as direct network access to the database server, where there is no audit trail record and authentication checks are bypassed); additionally, they reveal data quality threads with evidential information tied to them that can be used for governance and compliance issues resolution.

10.3   Tuning SQL and PL/SQL Code for Optimality

In Chapter 8, the section on "Performance Tuning Framework" covered the best practices on how to approach SQL and/or PL/SQL tuning from a monitoring and tweaking perspective. This section highlights the necessary recommended standards and best practices to refactor SQL and/or PL/SQL code for efficient execution when embedded in a programming language or as a stored program call.

1. Use REF CURSORs when passing data between PL/SQL and embedded language environments. Passing a pointer to a result set is more effective than passing the entire row set, in this case. This preserves the underlying column collation, too. Declare cursor variables used to return result sets as weakly typed. This ensures that the definition of the cursor variable isn't constrained.

Use parameter passing by reference using NOCOPY when passing huge sets of data as parameters and boosts performance.

2.   Make use of dynamism in cursor variables by reusing the same cursor variable for opening multiple queries or assigning different queries to the same cursor variable depending on runtime conditions. Make use of cursor expressions to facilitate retrieval of multi-row data for which a join is too complex or will not suffice at all (such as with data combining two independent *n:n* relationships). This, however, comes at an execution cost involving additional logical I/O, use of recursion internally and avoidance of implicit array processing.

3.   Use embedded language–based stored procedures in the database for optimizing compute-intensive tasks that require database access and for extending database functionality not available in PL/SQL. The embedded language specific features, such as safer type system, automatic garbage collection, polymorphism, inheritance, multithreading, and the like, and Oracle's corresponding implementation of the same as DB-specific native driver API, ensure a high degree of compatibility between the two.

4.   Use fine-grained access control when accessing resources outside the database, such as operating system files from embedded language stored procedures.

5.   Use PL/SQL within HTML to seamlessly integrate an HTML-intensive application with the database. Using e-mail functionality from within PL/SQL eliminates the need to code external routines for e-mail, thus enabling tighter integration with the database and greater productivity for the application from a functionality perspective. One way to do this is to use the robust messaging mechanisms of the embedded programming language such as JMS, which is technology-agnostic, and code the desired e-mail functionality as a Java stored procedure in the DB. This can be used in any embedded language solution via a callable API.

6.   Make use of user-defined data types, subprograms, and user-defined exceptions. Use cursor-oriented records when a greater degree of flexibility is desired—for example, when you're choosing columns from multiple tables. Encapsulate collection-type definitions in a package when defining them in PL/SQL.

7.   Use associative arrays to transform database table data into PL/SQL structures, like lookup table caching. Populate the associative array using a loop when it's required to create the rows sequentially. Use character indexes for associative arrays when dealing with VARCHAR2 data. This improves performance by enabling fast lookup of individual array elements, eliminates the need to know the position of the individual element, and avoids looping through all array elements.

8.   Simulate multidimensional arrays using multiple associative arrays. This proves efficient while mapping $n{:}n$ arrays in embedded language code to PL/SQL and vice versa.

9.   Use nested tables and variable arrays for efficient in-database storage and manipulation of list-based data, which is typically in the form of arrays, including multidimensional arrays (via multilevel collections). Using nested tables and variable arrays to share result sets between subprograms that are solely PL/SQL based provides optimized data I/O when the result set returned is not conformable to data returned by a SELECT query. Using table functions enables one way of returning result sets in this manner. When you use table functions, pipeline them to incrementally return data for maximum efficiency—(near) real-time streaming of rows as the function keeps executing.

10. Use the SQL TABLE operator to retrieve the individual elements of a nested table. It's a recommended standard to include multi-level collection-type definitions of the PL/SQL type in a package so that they're available persistently across database sessions.

11. Use objects to model real-world entities in PL/SQL. The inherent advantages of object orientation help leverage objects in PL/SQL, such as richer encapsulation and binding of methods to data. Use GET and SET methods to retrieve and populate attributes of an object type. Use user-defined constructors to customize object initialization, enabling added flexibility, ease of use, and proper validation of attribute data. Use type hierarchies to model hierarchical relationships involving objects. Features such as super-class and sub-class definition, substitutability, and dynamic method dispatch accelerate the resulting model for efficiency and ease of use.

12.   Use object views to present an object relational view of relational table data. Using INSTEAD-OF triggers on these views enables behind-the-scenes DML operations based on the object views.

13.   An alternative method is to LINQ-enable pure embedded language code to implement some object-based features.

14.   Classify error messages into information, warning, and error messages, and handle each in a proper way. A reference imperative such a classification can be the severity level of the error in context. For a typical use case:

- Actual application/code failure messages resulting at runtime that mandate a handling mechanism by either propagating them to the calling environment or halting further processing can be classified as true errors.

- Specific alerts that caution an outlier mode of application behavior and can be ignored are classifiable in the warning messages category. Alert messages notifying that the runtime values are in close proximity to pre-set thresholds are a potential candidate to belong to this category. These messages can also be propagated to the calling environment, but don't mandate halting of further processing.

- Messages of type information simply convey general, hint, or successful status information, such as that pertaining to a particular input value. A good example is "Check this box to override the default selections" These can be handled as per application- and user-specific needs by outputting them in the manner desired without disturbing the application execution flow.

15.   Categorize errors in an application based on Oracle-centric and solution-centric indicators, by segregating them into predefined exceptions, non-predefined Oracle errors, user-defined exceptions, and user-defined PL/SQL (logical) error messages. For all of these types of errors, code reusable error-handling routines that separate error processing from business logic processing. Throw, trap, and handle customized error messages based on the related application-specific context. This also includes associating programmer-defined exceptions with these customized error messages that correspond to logical errors.

16.   Audit errors asynchronously by capturing detailed error information such as the error code, the error message text, the error line number where the error first occurred, and the error execution stack. Customize the error information using a combination of SQLERRM and DBMS_UTILITY.FORMAT_ERROR_STACK to get the complete error message text, or DBMS_UTILITY.FORMAT_ERROR_BACKTRACE to get the error line number, augmented by intelligent contextual parsing. Use EXCEPTION_INIT to associate a non-predefined Oracle error with a user-defined exception. Code an error-raising procedure that makes a call to RAISE_APPLICATION_ERROR within it for providing user-defined error messages in PL/SQL. To handle true error messages, this method can be used, as it not only raises the customized error and stops further execution, but it also returns the customized error number and error message as the SQLCODE and SQLERRM to the calling environment.

17.   Determine when to halt processing, ignore and continue program execution, or let the exception fall through after an exception occurs. For informative and warning messages, the messages can be ignored. In the case of high-severity error messages, the normal behavior should be to halt program execution at that point. However, a careful analysis can reveal when to continue after errors in certain exceptional cases. Avoid implicit fall through of exceptions by coding an explicit exception handler for each PL/SQL block or subprogram defined in the application. Define a WHEN OTHERS handler in each exception handling section. This traps any errors not handled explicitly or otherwise. In this case, trap the Oracle error raised using SQLCODE and SQLERRM.

18.   Define user-defined exceptions in a package for global access. Don't define duplicate user-defined exceptions while dealing with nested blocks. Handle all user-defined exceptions explicitly by coding an exception handler for each of them. Avoid associating more than one user-defined exception with the same error number. Always follow a naming pattern that is different from that of pre-defined exceptions for user-defined exceptions. Of critical importance are exceptions raised in declaration and exception-handling sections of a PL/SQL block. In the case of nested blocks, always include a WHEN OTHERS handler in the topmost level of every PL/SQL program.

19.   Use a customized error-reporting mechanism when defining errors from triggers. Use system-event and user-event trigger attributes to reference system events, object owner, or object name when a system-level trigger fires. These are available through the SYS.% attributes or by means of public synonyms named ORA_%. Make use of the new compound trigger introduced in Oracle 11g.

20.   A recommended standard is to analyze the database schema in context after logon using a user-event trigger to estimate statistics on the tables in the schema.

21.   Always use cursors for dealing with multi-row SELECTs. In this way, you can process the results of multi-row SELECTs, row by row, in a PL/SQL block. Always check for implicit cursor attributes with SQL% after performing a DML inside a PL/SQL block. Also, use the RETURNING clause to output information inserted or updated by the DML statement.

22.   Use a cursor FOR loop when processing all the rows in a cursor unconditionally and when there is no additional SQL processing involved inside the body of the loop. Also, use it to populate an associative array used for caching lookup values.

23.   Avoid SQL operations inside a PL/SQL loop. The only exception to this rule can be when using a cursor FOR loop, as outlined above. Use implicit cursors rather than explicit cursors. They are always faster, even when used with native compilation, than explicit cursors. A recommended best practice is to encapsulate a single-row SELECT...INTO as a packaged function to achieve reusability and greater performance, provided it is not used repeatedly in a loop.

24.   Use the SELECT FOR UPDATE cursor only when you want to update the table that is being selected from. In this case, specify the column names being updated. Doing so not only locks the rows after the cursor is opened and the result-set rows are identified for update, but it also eliminates a second fetch of the rows for doing the update and preserves the current row by the WHERE CURRENT OF clause. Don't commit or roll back inside the cursor loop while processing a SELECT FOR UPDATE cursor. Do so after the loop. Always access rows by ROWID rather than by primary key when you are using

SELECT...FOR UPDATE to retrieve, process, and then update the same row. This is faster than using primary key.

25.   Use array processing in PL/SQL only if using pure SQL is not viable. If PL/SQL is a viable option, array processing can be used to improve SQL (not bulk SQL) that is being used iteratively in a cursor loop. Using bulk binds improves performance with respect to overall PL/SQL parsing and execution; and context switching when processing sets of DML statements in PL/SQL such as multi-row inserts, updates, and deletes.

26.   Leverage the use of native dynamic SQL with bulk binding. Using bulk binding with dynamic SQL combines the performance advantage of using bulk binds to reduce context switching with the ability to execute quickly using native dynamic SQL statements, wherever appropriate. The word "leverage" implies that the disadvantages of using dynamic SQL should be kept in mind while choosing to use native dynamic SQL with bulk SQL. Use the RETURNING clause with bulk binds to output information from INSERT and UPDATE statements into collections.

27.   Use the SAVE EXCEPTIONS clause only when the driving collection is not sparse. As an alternative, use the VALUES OF clause. Always track exceptions in bulk DML, even when using INDICES OF and VALUES OF clauses.

28.   Do not use dynamic SQL when you can use static SQL. Dynamic SQL is costlier compared to static SQL in terms of parsing and execution and also has the disadvantages of loss of dependency checking and compile-time error checking. Always use invoker rights when using dynamic SQL and dynamic PL/SQL. When using native dynamic SQL, always define an exception-handling section by specifying it in an enclosing PL/SQL block.

29.   Use native dynamic SQL (NDS) over DBMS_SQL to perform dynamic SQL operations on the server-side. This improves performance because execution is faster. However, such use is restricted to the fact that the SQL statement is not being executed a large number of times, such as iteratively, in a loop. NDS proves very effective to mange dynamism involving CLOB-based data. Tough this can be done as of Oracle11g onwards.

30.   Use only weak REF CURSORs for processing multi-row queries using native dynamic SQL.

31.   Use bind variables when defining dynamic SQL statements only if their number is limited. Using bind variables for data values in native dynamic SQL makes the code execute faster and also makes the code easier to maintain. It's faster because the same SQL statement is executed with different values of the bind variables so that a single cursor is shareable by multiple SQL statements. Also, binding takes care of data-type conversion implicitly because native data types are involved. Only use bind variables for data values and not for values that hold metadata values such as table names, column names, and SQL statement clauses. DB object names can be validated using the built-in DBMS_ASSERT package prior to the final code run. This ensures that semantic integrity is not compromised for object names that involve dynamic binding. Use PL/SQL variables to hold metadata values. Using bind variables for specifying schema object names can result in errors that can result in misleading output.

32.   Use DBMS_SQL over native dynamic SQL when the same SQL statement is executed multiple times in the same session. Leverage the interoperability of native dynamic SQL and DBMS_SQL to increase flexibility of coding and achieve desired functionality. The inter-operability of NDS and DBMS_SQL is based on the type of binding and the degree of dynamism involved. As an example, DBMS_SQL can handle dynamic binding as well as dynamic queries for parsing and execution. Then the cursor handle can be converted to a REF cursor variable that enables cross-program result-set sharing. On the other hand, if the bind variables are known at compile time, but involves a SQL query with a dynamic column-list, converting the REF cursor to a DBMS_SQL cursor handle preserves its state, so that it can be reused to execute the same SQL statement any number of times. Method 4 Dynamic SQL. Also, as of Oracle11g, DBMS_SQL cursor handles come with implicit access and authorization rights. An attempt to execute an invalid cursor or by un-authorized user results in a failed attempt.

33.   Use dynamic PL/SQL to implement method 4 dynamic SQL, a situation of dynamic SQL in which the number of inputs and their types are unknown at compile time. This can be done using native dynamic SQL statements for dynamic PL/SQL. Using contexts to replace bind variables to achieve the "soft-parse" benefit

comes in handy in cases similar to those involving method 4 Dynamic SQL.

34. Using native dynamic SQL with objects gives the same performance benefits as that of using relational tables that execute code involving objects in the database efficiently.

35. Leverage the use of packages to globalize data and code and also to localize data and privatize code. This comes as an implication of modularity. Even in the case of a single program unit, if it performs huge tasks and is compute-intensive, or if it processes multiple SQL statements, it's good practice to place it in a package. Do not use a package for coding functions that are used in function-based indexes. However, function-based indexes render optimal calling of PL/SQL functions from SQL by eliminating re-execution of the function being called. Packages insulate code from other programs, provide a greater degree of modularity, and increase performance. Also, packages have the advantage that referencing programs need not be recompiled when the package body changes. Before Oracle11g, the use of packages enabled breaking of the dependency chain by avoiding cascading invalidations when there's a single invalid object in the chain. As of Oracle11g, PL/SQL implicitly enables fine-grained dependency control.

36. Use package variables to define PL/SQL global variables and always define GET and SET methods that use native dynamic SQL to retrieve and populate the same. Use a package initialization section to initialize any package variables needed for a session's duration.

37. Leverage the use of invoker and definer rights to take care of centralization/localization of code and data. Using invoker rights provides centralization of code and decentralization of data but comes with a disadvantage. Using invoker rights does not help in sharing the SQL involved, whereas in a definer rights scenario, the SQL can be shared. Always use invoker rights for coding generic routines and on object member methods. This provides a greater degree of flexibility to be used by a large number of users. Always implement customized access control tailored toward the specific application by using invoker rights in addition to the default authentication and authorization schemes provided by Oracle.

38.   Pin frequently used packages in memory to optimize performance of the shared pool. Overload similarly functioning subprograms that differ only in their parameter types or number of parameters.

39.   Use SQL and PL/SQL result-set caching by specifying the RESULT_CACHE hint for SQL and the RESULT_CACHE clause with functions (available as of Oracle 11g) to gain added performance for output-reusable functions and queries inside them. This way, the results of the previous execution are cached in the data buffer instead of the data block. Also, the cached data is available at the instance level and is auto-refreshed in case of underlying data changes. This also reduces the number of scalar (function) executions.

40.   Use native compilation of PL/SQL code when writing compute-intensive PL/SQL subprograms that perform database-independent tasks. In this case, native compilation results in faster execution of PL/SQL.

41.   Use the asynchronous COMMIT feature for transactions that are not recovery-based. When using autonomous transactions to partition transactions, avoid deadlocks with the main transaction for resources and locks. Code an explicit COMMIT or ROLLBACK in an autonomous transaction program to end it normally. Avoid abnormal jumps from the autonomous transaction to a ROLLBACK to a save point issued in the main transaction. In case of a package, each individual subprogram should be defined as autonomous. Autonomous transactions are a best-fit for use in functions callable from SQL such as auditing of SQL queries from PL/SQL.

10.4   Tuning Embedded Language Code for Optimality: Data Structures and Procedural Code

Chapters 3, 4, 6, 7, and 8 described the best practices and code accelerators pertaining to the design and usage of embedded language data structures and code—highlighting significant design patterns for optimal implementation of native embedded language data structures and data in heterogeneous formats such as objects, DataSets, arrays, and XML-typed hierarchies—and their relational mapping counterparts. This section lists the key differentiators in terms of recommended tuning standards that optimize the end-to-end solution for Web-transactional efficiency, scalability, and subsecond response times; and intersolution and intrasolution design optimization for data-based, service-oriented, and process-driven implementation that delivers business agility, resiliency, consistency, and continuity of the same.

1. Using the driver closest in nativity to the Oracle DB for the Data Access Layer enables the implementation of single sign-on (SSO) logic, so that it not only completes the authentication securely thereby closing the risk gap in terms of connectivity and privileged access control, but also enables optimized data access to and from the Oracle DB to the application solution. This is a key accelerator in boosting the performance of data-driven queries or requests by an order of *n* times in magnitude, where *n* can equal at least 2.

2. When using a .NET-based embedded programming language like C#, LINQ-enable the code for increased SQL-enabled data awareness. Complex processing of C# code for context-aware searching and filtering—as well as data rationalization via enumerations and structures—can be emulated using SQL-based data structures like SQL data, collections, XML, and DataSets – and using the same syntax.

3. Use Ajax functionality in existing ASP.NET-based Web applications to accelerate the solution UI by introducing self-service interaction and a highly personalized Web UI that also supports cross-browser–based access.

4. Design the solution for cross-platform portability by exposing it as a Web Service, by means of a callable API (in embedded code) AND as an executable that can be invoked via a Web browser. The Web Service provides portability of the solution in regard to its deployment and usability, regardless of the underlying application technology (i.e., .NET, J2EE, PHP/Perl/Groovy-based, PL/SQL-only, etc.), by employing a common callable interface. This portability is a direct benefit of making the database Tier independent of the solution architecture and can be used for external integration as well.

5. Design a SOA-based solution workflow, integration, and automation service that enables extensibility, customizability, and reusability of the same. The workflow is executed based on the triggering of (user-initiated/auto-generated) events. The key indicator here is to code this service using an embedded language that is same as that of the driving solution in context, i.e., the solution that will be implemented as the primary deployment solution.

6. Code both Data Services and Data Integration Services as part of heterogeneous data consolidation and presentation. Confine the data processing to in-memory computation by way of in-memory analytics and dynamic virtual data federation, or by using the in-memory database (IMDB) cache for persistent in-memory storage. This has at least three key design and performance benefits:

    ▪ The use of in-memory computation eliminates the need for additional metadata definitions to be stored persistently in the Oracle DB, as all the necessary metadata semantics are dynamically generated and encapsulated in the processing logic. This is especially a necessity for real-time analytical processing based on real-time data feeds.

    ▪ It provides ultra-fast access to high-volume SQL-based result sets, in addition to the SOA benefits of the Data Services and Data Integration Services.

    ▪ It provides direct access to such data by the solution application by passing the Oracle DB-based data warehouse or ODS.

7. Optimize the application performance by increasing the throughput of Web-based transactions. This can be done by adopting a transaction partitioning mechanism based on in-memory data replication distributed across multiple Web servers, by transparently deferring the actual committing of each transaction, in case of multiple concurrent transactions, and sending an instant response to the user requesting the transaction—without waiting for the two-phase commit synchronization to happen. However, the ACID properties of each transaction are preserved by means of a BASE mechanism coupled with RESTful session reconciliation.

10.5   Fine-Tuning Solution Methodology for Optimality

The primary goal of fine tuning the solution for optimality is to leverage the multiple benefits of integrated information, streamlined processes, and centralized management built into the solution to bring a unified view of the contextual business system of multiple domains.

> The solution must enable flexibility and scalability that aligns with the constant change in business operations—this is the bottom-line business imperative that must be the top-line IT imperative while architecting the design of the business-IT solution.

The following list outlines the recommended practices for best-fit pragmatics of the same:

1.   Apply the use of business activity, user activity, and interactivity between the Oracle database and the solution access interface, and enable continuous monitoring of Web transactions end to end, as they occur. Introducing performance metrics of URIs and URLs to SQL, the Oracle Weblogic Application Server, can be used as a monitoring agent for Internet activity, and at the same time can log the Web Server to/from Web browser activity. During this process, it can audit user-initiated transactions via the Web browser over a secure SSL connection by logging transaction-related statistics that pertain to the overall transaction execution summary, solution performance statistics that include the end-to-end transaction lifecycle metrics and their impact on the solution performance, and any business performance statistics like the resulting throughput, ability of each individual transaction to meet the desired business-centric process output, and the like. The same can be analyzed for editing or simulated in a playback manner for benchmarking or automated testing on related transaction sets. Automating this sequence of steps accelerates the monitoring process, the analyzed results of which can be used to optimize the transaction-processing capability by way of new/efficient integrated business rules—which serve as performance enhancers. The concerned business users are notified by auto-generated alerts when outliers are detected that impact the

business operation. Code dynamic visualization routines to generate visual graphics are based on the transaction summary and
the solution and business performance statistics are correlated
with the auto-notifications in real time, to IT as well as business
analysts/users.

2. Extend the Web-based search capabilities of the solution to
encompass contextual eDiscovery across all content/communica-
tion channels that comprise e-mail messaging–, instant messaging–, blog-, or Wiki-based content, including any archived
versions of the same. This can be implemented by a code design
based on search engine optimization techniques and powerful
Web-based filtering (e.g., one that is powered by Postini) in combination with Personal Search enabling functionality. The resulting code-modules can be componentized as reusable Personalized
Search Capsules and deployed as Web Services. The metadata
design and the metaprogramming algorithms can be stored as a
Personalized Search Model and as a centralized db-based or
XML-based file repository, and they enable SQL-based access to
the same using direct SQL or LINQ-enabled SQL API.

3. Align the solution programming interface design with that of the
solution-testing methodology, and arrive at a solution-testing
template that takes care of unit testing, integration testing, and
stress/regression testing not only in development and test environments but also in scenarios replicating "live" production environments—with regard to detection and troubleshooting for
better performance and reliability. The separation of the database
logic from the solution embedded logic (and the encapsulation of
the same in modular stored programs, along with Oracle DB-
compliant native language API calls for data processing) eases the
debugging and tuning process to a greater degree.

4. Implement auto-generated code testing routines that are customizable via parameterization or reference variables selected based
on the business process context. Deploy these as reusable Testing
Services tied to Testing Integration Services, enabling seamless
streamlining of the testing automation process.

5. Modernize the implemented solution or similar existing solutions by:

    ▪ Seamlessly integrating them with the current solution; this eliminates the need for introducing silos in the existing legacy system

    ▪ Preserving loss of functionality; the solution design must be business-centric and able to implement the right business processes and practices in place as context-centric services, thereby delivering a superior customer experience

    ▪ Increased flexibility for embedding/integrating custom interfaces and reports on demand

6. Classify customer-centric controls into need-to-have functionality vs. nice-to-have functionality—such as multiple sign-off levels, multilabel security, and the like. Include specific parameters focused on business issues, bind these business requirements to underlying technology implementable business rules, and prioritize the business processes; this determines the execution priority and preference in terms of business relevance. Log this ranked list as an Excel spreadsheet or electronic scorecard.

7. Implement real-time operational reporting, which eliminates the need to pull information from multiple systems to generate time-variant recurring reports. Real-time access to information, implemented via a multitude of mechanisms (as outlined in Chapter 6), enables timely and "current" data delivery to these reports, even in multiple formats including e-mail and "live Excel interoperability." This enhances the analysis of the information based on the reports for delivering the right information to the right user at the right time—as well as faster time-to-insight.

8. Raise the bar for a more pervasive solution in regard to its acceptability and adoptability. A customizable solution enables direct implementation of the same after the customization has been done, by way of click-once configurable deployment. The solution can be preconfigured based on a common group of settings that are business process–specific, without having to change the solution for each and every contextual customization. An SOA-oriented and no-silos-based solution architecture is the best fit design strategy for delivering such a solution; it has the flexibility for adaptable change, and a better, easier, and faster delivery of

the same. Additional business benefits include dynamic and enhanced configurability, dynamic provisioning of services via self-service interfaces, and/or dynamically manageable workflow logic built into the solution—providing A-A-A access to enterprise information that is centralized in terms of storage and management while being complete, consistent, and continuous in terms of business functionality.

9. Achieve a higher degree of optimization by delivering a solution with inherent collaboration capabilities that enable output shareability and expansion and execute multiple services in cohesion.

10. Design the solution for better visibility into the end-to-end business operations. Tracking and tracing—based on overall business metrics and real-time data feeds, individualized process analysis, and the correlation between the two—provides a single point of visibility across departments, applications, and all related business (access) touch points. The finer the visibility, the greater the business value of the solution.

11. Enable localization in terms of Governance, Risk, and Compliance (GRC) by location, and globalization in terms of handling cross-country currencies (wherever applicable).

12. Implement fine-grained data presentation and analysis:

- For aggregation by lines of business and by temporal and location-variant business attributes
- For proactive identification of value-added data that in turn helps in "mining" data relationships that provides deep-dive visibility for advanced analysis or improvements; this also helps in correlating projection-based trends with proposal-based forecasts—a true value addition to any business for operational efficiency
- For providing rapid business insight into all kinds of data—operational, historical, strategic, whatever the users need to see; however, it is a good practice to isolate old historical data that's least frequently used

13. Incorporate Web 2.0 functionality into the Web interface design; this not only enhances the look-and-feel for user interaction but also increases the efficiency of the UI by simplifying

and auto-generating advanced functionality specific to the interface design and online rendering.

14.   *Isolate the database Tier from the solution Tier.* Integrated in-memory data-set caching in the application layer (dynamically and on-demand) accelerates complex code execution involving high-volume data access/processing. The cache being persistent in-memory enables high-performance analysis (especially on real-time data) by dynamic generation of multiple views of information using the Web or Excel, without compromising solution performance.

10.6   Summary

This chapter described the pragmatics of recommended need-to-follow rules that can be adopted as best practice standards for embedded language solution coding and troubleshooting. Starting with coverage of a comprehensive list of best practices for Oracle11g-based embedded language programming, the subsequent sections dealt with recommended best practices for optimization of pure SQL and PL/SQL code, followed by the same for embedded languages focusing on the specifics involved. The final section covered the pragmatics of a best-practice methodology for fine-tuning and optimization of the end-to-end solution that encompassed design considerations for data structures, data, exceptions handling, application architecture and management, and end-to-end troubleshooting, comprising the monitoring, detection, and mitigation of solution loopholes and vulnerabilities, proactively and reactively.

ndex